T0329484

Ships and Shipwrecks
of the
Early Stuart Dynasty
1603–1647

SHIPS AND SHIPWRECKS OF THE EARLY STUART DYNASTY 1603–1647

by James D. Taylor Jr.

Algora Publishing
New York

Library of Congress Cataloging-in-Publication Data

Names: Taylor, James D., 1958- author.
Title: Ships and shipwrecks of the early Stuart Dynasty : a collection of
  logs, records and first-hand accounts of missing ships and lost
  treasures / by James D. Taylor Jr.
Description: New York : Algora Publishing, 2023. | Includes bibliographical
  references and index. | Summary: "Continuing this series, Mr. Taylor has
  painstakingly researched and collected information regarding shipwrecks
  from the early English Stuart era 1603-1647. This book will aid in the
  identification of wrecks, from the siege of Duncannon during the Irish
  confederate wars in 1645, to Hudson's Bay, to the coast of India"—
  Provided by publisher.
Identifiers: LCCN 2023017759 (print) | LCCN 2023017760 (ebook) | ISBN
  9781628945096 (trade paperback) | ISBN 9781628945102 (hardcover) | ISBN
  9781628945119 (pdf)
Subjects: LCSH: Shipwrecks—Great Britain—History—17th century. | Stuart,
  House of. | Underwater archaeology—Great Britain—Archival resources. |
  Great Britain—History, Naval—Stuarts, 1603-1714. | Great
  Britain—History—Stuarts, 1603-1714.
Classification: LCC G525 .T326 2023 (print) | LCC G525 (ebook) | DDC
  910.4/52094206—dc23/eng20230708
LC record available at https://lccn.loc.gov/2023017759
LC ebook record available at https://lccn.loc.gov/2023017760

Printed in the United States

Dedicated to:
Dr. Charlene H. Berry, DD, MA
Madonna University

Her spiritual and scholastic inspirations and friendship
are sorely missed.

"A ship is always referred to as 'she'
because it costs so much to keep one in paint and powder."

— Chester W. Nimitz (1885–1966),
Society of Sponsors of the United States Navy, Washington, D.C., February 13, 1940. AP
dispatch, *The New York Times*, February 15, 1940, p. 39.

TABLE OF CONTENTS

Part 3. The Wrecks.   131

PREFACE

The evolving and improving methods used by relic and treasure hunters include sonar and proton precession survey magnetometers to explore and map a section under water. LiDAR is a recent technology that is revealing many new locations for archaeologists to explore on land. Those tools have produced incredible results filling museums with artifacts for future generations to learn and enjoy, but even with those tools, it is like searching for the proverbial needle in an extremely large haystack hundreds of square miles wide. Even using a 'magnet' to locate the needle is very time and cost consuming.

The study of archaeology is not just knowing how to use various hand tools, and then picking an arbitrary place to push a shovel into ground hoping to come up with something, but knowing where to dig enhanced with years of field research experience and education to be able to identify something if found. Those high-tech tools are augmented by old-fashioned, time-consuming, and tedious archival exploration of hundreds of volumes of documents contained within a narrow window of time in English history seeking information of maritime historical significance. Furthermore, these searches often occur in dark and cool basement archives often wearing masks and cotton gloves. Those thousands of hours of research time sometimes yield an occasional reward which becomes part of this book. Slowly those incidents multiply to form the book I present to you.

I would like to believe that all my publications have helped researchers to better understand their subjects. We live in an age of instant gratification and unfortunately, not enough people are willing to devote large portions of their life to conduct extensive research. My closest friend Dr. Charlene Berry of Madonna University once called it the "mis-information age" in the early 1990's.

A single source of information regarding English Stuart era (1603 to 1647) ships and shipwrecks was non-existent prior to this book, and it is a sincere desire to provide a reference source and or inspiration for those with the sophisticated search tools to uncover information for a revision to maritime history.

The core purpose of this book is to supply enough information to help locate or identify a wreck, some of which have great significant historical value such as the *Duncannon* frigate wreck. This frigate was involved in the siege of Duncannon during the Irish confederate wars in 1645. This ship lies perhaps within the first mile of the Blackwater River and could be a historical wreck site for the country of Ireland. If the Duncannon wreck is located, honor the men that lost their lives on this ship for their country and treat it as a war memorial.

The secondary function is to share the facts that ships such as the *St. Anthony* and the *Royal Merchant* may still contain unrecovered Spanish gold and silver bullion and reales, jewels, and other items of great value such as, "one crest on dagger with a gold handle, one fair lance part plated with gold" and to present enough recorded information located in numerous archives to determine a probable wreck site.

Many of these facts have been distorted or are missing on information websites. A great example to share is from a popular website of information that the *Sea Adventure* had wrecked on the Bermudas in 1609 and the few survivors formed and colonized the Bermudas as a British colony. Great story. This misinformation is based upon a solitary letter dated 20 May 1610 describing the plantation of Virginia from the *Calendar of State Papers, Colonial Series, East Indies, China and Japan, 1513-1616, p. 66-67*, "after the *Sea Adventure* was wrecked and with them 100 persons barely provided." From that sentence, a long tale was spun of the formation of the English colony on the Bermudas. The citations for that story were nonexistent. Well, I am happy to report that the *Sea Adventure* can be tracked until well after 1616, of which time I discontinued my search.

If the wording of the original documents is ambiguous, then I attempt to determine if those ships wrecked, blew up, burned, leaked beyond repair, or otherwise sank and were no longer in service for the royal navy or the East India Company. If in doubt, I would explain my reasoning.

Prepare your ships to sail. Set your rigging to explore the locations of lost, unidentified and unknown shipwrecks and the events that led up to their loss during the early Stuart period of English history. Your chart is the information contained in this book. Calibrate your compass to locate lost shipments of gold and silver in various forms such as Spanish pieces of eight and or bullion and bars, sheets of copper, brass and iron cannons by the hundreds, hand tools, gun powder and ammunition, weapons of war, wheat, wine, and spices, and jewelry. All these goods are among the cargoes carried by ships ranging in size from 50 to 1000 tons, some of them war ships, which never arrived in port.

Despite having reviewed hundreds of electronic and hardcover manuscript collections, traveling to view rare and wonderful manuscripts that have not been digitized, I greatly doubt I have reviewed everything out there.

Besides, I love revisions from learning or recovering lost information. The following is an example of the rare hand-illuminated manuscripts I reviewed while accumulating material for this volume.

Crane, Ralph. Title page, *A Brief Abstract, Exposition and Demonstration of all Terms, Parts and Things Belonging to a Ship; and the Practice of Navigation.* 1626.

The word "treasure" has a different meaning to different people. Some of these wrecks contain treasures that could not be recovered by the means available at the time and eventually were forgotten. History moved on and those manuscript collections were reviewed by fewer people, buried in archives, or — as will be shared further — disappeared when hundreds of years of information were purposely destroyed.

Some define treasure as knowledge ensuring facts are presented to future generations and that is the star I steer my ship by.

Image by Chinese artist Zhang Bing Rui Xiang

INTRODUCTION

The science of navigation was in its infancy and detailed accurate navigational charts that we take for granted now, did not exist during the reigns of James I or Charles I. The passage by sea to India and parts of Asia was not discovered until the late fifteenth century and attempts to establish strong trade had failed until Queen Elizabeth I established a charter on 31 December 1600 that formed the London East India Company. Through several years of trial and error, they established a limited trade in parts of India and Persia, making small settlements or houses of trade called factories for the residence of their factors and servants that grew in size. Furthermore, they opened and established shipping routes many of which are followed today.

The records of the East India Company's "governments in India are probably the best historical materials in the world," said James Grant Duff in his History of the Mahrattas (ed. 1826, vol. ii, p. 185). From the earliest days of the company, it was a rule that the commander and other principal officers should keep a full account of the voyage, to be turned in upon their return. From about the beginning of the eighteenth century, these were supplemented by an official log to be kept in a special form book supplied by the company. The East India Company maintained excellent records and their libraries grew quickly and required additional storage accommodations.

During the seventeenth and eighteenth centuries, those records began to suffer from neglect or deliberate destruction. In April 1682, court minutes mention, "old books and papers which are in a confused manner laid in the upper garret of the (East India) House."

Furthermore, it was reported in 1717 that one of the Surat Journals had been cut out of its covers and stolen and "great quantities of the company's packets and other papers were thrown on heaps in the back warehouse." A committee was formed to select a safe location for their storage, but there appears to be no results recorded. However, in 1720, the court again attempted to solve their storage problems "to consider what was to be done with great numbers of papers, packets, and old books removed and carried into the warehouse on the other side of the garden, where they lie in utmost confusion, and it is feared many are destroyed."

Several decades passed while the company continued to amass large quantities of logs and volumes and attempts were made to address the issue several times. On 26 March 1771, the Committee of Correspondence reported:

The Committee having considered of the present confused and disorderly state of the repository for the books, records, and accounts from the several presidencies and factories in the East Indies, consisting of many thousand volumes, which are annually increasing, and that, in order to remedy the inconveniences, difficulties, and loss of time at present experienced in collecting and arranging the books, to which frequent recourse is necessary to be had, the committee consider it a matter of essential consequence that a capable and experienced officer be appointed to have the care and custody of the said books, records, and papers, to arrange, number, and register them in proper catalogues; also to keep an account of the deliveries thereof to any person or persons, so that the same may be preserved from being lost or injured. And Mr. William Barnett being recommended as a proper person for this employ, the committee offer it to the court as their opinion that he be appointed register and keeper of the Indian books, records, accounts, and other papers deposited in the room usually called the book office, under such regulations, instructions, and directions as he shall from time to time receive from this committee, at the salary of £100 a year, to commence from this day. *A Guide to the India office Records, 1600-1858.*

In March 1818, the existence of a vast accumulation of books from the East India Company was brought to the notice of the court of directors. On 18 March, orders were given that within "the captain's journals and the company's logbook, the chief and second mates' journals were to be destroyed for all the voyages before 1800. The boatswains' books and surveyors' books were also to be destroyed and future destructions were to be carried out at intervals of ten years." Furthermore, in 1860 there was a general destruction of journals and other official logs by the hundreds, "All log books dating further back than 1855 have been burnt at Calcutta." That is a great loss to maritime history.

It was the duty of the East India Company librarian that the revised catalogue of original correspondence was compiled (about 1827-31). It is not known when the function of the librarian ceased, but apparently all active work with the records came to an end at the retirement in February 1835, of Peter Pratt, the clerk specially engaged in that duty. Early records share the death of Sir Charles Wilkins in May 1836, and the appointment of his successor Professor Wilson, but no mention was made of any duties in connection with the records.

As regards to the documents themselves, since there is no trace that they were transferred to the book office, it may be presumed that they remained in the librarian's custody until 1858. Furthermore, in December 1858, authority was granted to sell about 21 tons of tradesmen's bills, safe books, catalogues, appearance books, etc. as wastepaper. In June of 1859, approximately two tons of documents were disposed of in the same manner. In February 1860, a proposal was made to dispose of over 300 tons of additional documents and a committee was appointed for the task. Series of important records were to be discarded and the minutes of the India Board were to be destroyed also, but that proposal was dropped.

"The present surviving index is mainly a summary of the India Office publications which were only printed for official use and not generally available. Its scope, however, is in one way more restricted, since the press lists include records of later than 1858. For the same purpose a considerable amount of explanatory matter has been inserted, giving information regarding the contents of the various series; while, especially in the case of the consultations of the Indian Governments, the genesis of each section is briefly recorded. In cases in which any series, or portion of a series, has been printed or calendared, a note has been made. As the particulars given have been purposely condensed as far as possible, the handbook does not entirely obviate the necessity of referring to the press lists when using the records. For instance, if it is desired to consult the Court Minutes or the Despatches or the Consultations for any particular date, it will still be necessary to go to the relevant press list, in order to specify the volume required. Otherwise, if the year only is given, the Record Department may (in the case of Consultations) be put to the trouble of producing a dozen volumes when only one is really wanted. In order to facilitate the task of looking up the press lists, references have been inserted in the handbook whenever there is likely to be a difficulty in identifying the series by means of the index." *A Guide to the India office Records, 1600-1858.*

I will always ponder the quantity of fascinating and informative log books describing where a ship perished with or without treasure, purposely destroyed over several centuries. Though many of the useful documents had been destroyed, they were sometimes copied, though often enough incomplete, and included in various collections such as the Calendar of State Papers. Though I must credit modern digital storage and the ease at which all the many volumes of Calendar of State Papers residing in numerous collections can be reviewed, it may surprise the reader to understand how many volumes have not been digitized yet, which required the physical review of dozens of delicate volumes. One such review of hard cover volumes after 13 hours in a library at Wayne State University, the last two hours I was distracted by a dirty bearded face peeking around the various dimly lit stacks late at night. Fortunately, I was in a corner behind a very large round table with a small wall of reviewed volumes of books which offered protection if required. Though it was a matter of concern, it was also very humorous.

Though chiefly concerned with the documents in the Public Record Office itself, these calendars included both the court minutes and the original correspondence series of the India office. They came to an end upon the appearance of a fifth volume in 1892.

Compounding the loss of information was the Great Fire of 1666 that devastated about 436 acres of London.

PART I. THE SHIPS.

Part One of this book will be different from the *Ships and Shipwrecks of the Late Tudor Dynasty* because of the greater quantities of individual ship records from the Royal Navy and mostly the East India Company, making it not practical to attempt to encompass them in a single volume as there would be thousands of entries and hundreds of additional pages.

In the early days of the East India Company, they bought, built, or repurposed vessels required for importing/exporting anything that would fit in a ship. In 1639 they experimented with hiring ships, and after the discontinuance of the company's dockyard at Blackwall in 1652, freighting became the general practice, though in the early part of the nineteenth century several of the vessels they employed were described as their own ships. Furthermore, the company also employed crews and ships for the purpose of defense and establishing further routes.

For the purpose of this book, two categories of ships in service from 1603 to 1649 are merchant ships and those that served the crown; bearing in mind that sometimes merchant ships were asked to defend the crown as well.

The ship a mariner served on was not only his home, but his life and many fought for their lives in perils from battles or storms. A mariner received skills passed down through many generations of sea faring old salts to be refined by years or decades at sea. These sailors often worked in freezing blowing cold winds in wet and dangerous conditions during typhoons or storms. Even worse; no wind. Days to several weeks could consume vital rations without possibility of resupply coupled with the sheer boredom from inactivity praying for wind, posed a real threat.

These unbathed, sometimes underfed, and clothed, thirsty sailors would continue on in the hopes that a treasure lurked over the horizon allowing a man to retire comfortably early.

Common illnesses that we take for granted in present times, could be fatal to a mariner who was thousands of miles away from medical care hoping to receive treatment in forms we now regard as barbaric.

Imagine a 1600 ton three-masted enemy ship with 50 to 100 heavy iron and brass guns on one, two or even three-gun decks, bearing down on you. Meanwhile, you only weigh maybe 100 tons, and your cargo is Spanish gold and silver pieces of eight and bullion and other precious commodities that you stole from an enemy ship. There are many hazards of life at sea during this era. Queen Elizabeth I addressed the increasing threats of piracy by granting permission to captains to protect their cargo by whatever means possible. Of course, some took that as a license to steal with the crown's blessing and of course the crown received a percentage of 'prizes' taken at sea well beyond her reign.

The following is a brief description of the ship types generally referred to in these accounts and events. These are not intended to be all inclusive descriptions but helpful references. Many ships are described by weight. Ships often fell into classifications of rate. A few modern historians indicate this is a recent endeavor. Yet, here we have *Steel's Original and Correct List of the Royal Navy* description of classifications from 1782, a not-so-modern description.

1st rate: 100 guns and upward. 750 to 850 men.
2nd rate: 90 to 98 guns. 700 to 750 men.
3rd rate: 64 to 80 guns. 580 to 650 men.
4th rate: 50 to 60 guns. 350 to 450 men.
5th rate: 30 to 44 guns. 220 to 250 men.
6th rate: 20 to 28 guns. 160 to 200 men.

"All ships were sheathed with copper plate. Sloops, bombs, fireships, armed ships, and store-ships are commanded by masters and commanders. Cutters, schooners, brigs, armed vessels, armed transport, armed store ships and surveying sloops are commanded by lieutenants."

Barque or sometimes Bark.

General term for a small ship prior to the 1700s. It was later modified to be slightly more specific for a ship with three masts with squared rigged sails on the first two masts. Described as a fast ship with shallow draft.

Caravel.

This ship's design is often attributed to the Portuguese and is seen during the time of this book. It was constructed using the carvel method and was reliable for oceanic exploration voyages of long duration.

Carrack.

This ship is often attributed to being developed in Portugal in the 1400's and is slightly larger than the caravel. One example is the *Santa Maria* used by Columbus. Sometimes with six sails that constituted the typical design. Carracks were the largest type of ship prior to the galleon, sometimes with a weight of 1000 tons. 3 masts with square sails and very high fore and aft-castles. These often-carried multiple decks of brass and iron ordnance. These were often used as ships of war and for long deep-sea voyages.

Crayer.

Often described as a vessel of 30 to 50 tons and was used mainly in the English Channel.

Galliot.

Sometimes referred to as a half galley in the 1500's, it was a small, long, sleek ship, with 2 masts, about 2 rows of 8 oars, and a flush main deck. It acquired sails into the 1600's and continued to use oars if there was no wind. Sometimes carried smaller ordnance. This ship is perhaps best known and seen in the Mediterranean.

Galleon.

These ships often transported cargo but were well defended with one or two decks of heavy iron ordnance. King Phillip of Spain used these ships in his famous attack on England.

Galley.

Galleys have a long history for use in trade and warfare. It afforded oars as a second means of propulsion in the event of no winds and was some-times used in the seas of Northern Europe, but its low freeboard and lack of stability in rough seas sometimes placed it in great peril. This ship is seen more around Italy.

Hoy.

This ship's origins are 1400's Flanders with a single mast and usually of about 30 to 80 tons. This lighter vessel was primarily used along coasts or shallower water short voyages. Evolutions of this ship occurred later, and it disappeared in the 1800s.

Hulk.

This vessel has an early history. They were flat-bottomed boats distinguished by not having a stem or stern posts or deep keel. They varied in size also and included several English ships such as the *Jesus* and the *Mary Rose*.

Picard.

This ship has its origins into the early 1300's as a single masted ship of about 25 to 40 tons. This ship often saw service as support for large fishing fleets or transporting cargo from large, anchored ships into port. This ship was widely used around England, Ireland, and Scotland.

Pink.

There are two classifications of this ship. The name is attributed to the Italian pinco (small). A small, flat-bottomed ship with a narrow stern primarily used in the Mediterranean for cargo. In the Atlantic region, the name describes a small ship with the name attributed to a Dutch word pincke.

Pinnace.

These were often used as merchant transport and even small war ships. Primarily built by the Dutch they had a hull that resembled a small 'race built' galleon that were generally square rigged on three masts.

Ship of the Line Man-of-War.

Often regarded as the 'heavy guns' during the 1500-1700's when they began resembling galleons but were able to carry more ordnance of about 40 to 100 iron and brass cannons. These were designed to be large enough to be effective in battle-line tactics and maneuvers, ergo, the name. These ships at the time of this book belonged to the three main sea powers: England, France, and Spain.

During the Reign of James I

The only naval expedition of consequence undertaken during the reign of King James I was the attempt on Algiers between 1620 and 1621 with the intent to end Muslim piracy. His reign was peaceful, and he is well recorded in history of not having a warlike disposition. The state of his navy he inherited from Queen Elizabeth I was strong, and King James I did not allow it to depreciate as can be seen from records that he spent about £50,000 annually in maintaining the navy including £36,000 spent in maintaining timber and the royal forests for good wood to build ships with.

Records share that the king often took delight in visiting the dockyards during the building of a ship and one visit of many is recorded that the king and the Prince of Wales were present at the launching of two large East India ships at Deptford in 1610. The largest ship that came from the English docks was built by King James I in 1610 called the *Prince Royal* at 1400 tons and carried 64 pieces of ordnance.

"This year (1610) the king built a most goodly ship for war. (Her keel was laid in October 1608 and launched 25 September 1610) The keel whereof was 114 feet long and the crossbeam was 44 feet in length. She will carry 64 pieces of great ordinance and is of the burden of 1400 tons. This royal ship is double built and most sumptuously adorned, within and without, with all manner of curious carving, painting, and rich guiding, being in all respects the greatest and goodliest ship that even was built in England: and this glorious ship the king gave unto his son Henry Prince of Wales. The 24 September, the king, queen, prince of Wales, duke of York and the lady Elizabeth, with many great lords, went unto Woolrich to see it launched; but because of the narrowness of the dock, it could not then be launched; whereupon the prince came the next morning by three o'clock, and then, at the launching thereof, the prince named it after his own dignity, and called it Prince." *Memoirs of the Rise and Progress of the Royal Navy*, p. 46-47.

A valuable source of information was reviewed about the life of Mr. Phineas Pett, written by himself, sharing his time as an apprentice ship-wright in Deptford yard and later appointed master shipwright of Wool-wich yard in November 1605. Furthermore, he shared his relation to the *Prince Royal* and other ships including the following:

The *Answer*. 'In the summer of 1603, I began to new build her (*Answer*) at Chatham; launched her 17 May 1604.'

The *Red Lion*. 'On 7 June 1609, she was launched at Deptford, being newly built: the king and prince were present.'

The *Phoenix*. 'In June 1612, I began to make ready by the prince's command, the frame of a new ship at Chatham, for a pinnace to the great ship *Prince*, in which his highness did propose to solace himself sometimes in the narrow seas, and therefore she was appointed to be fitted with a very roomy cabin, and all other accommodations for the purpose. Her burthen was 250 tons. She was launched 27 February 1613.'

The *Defiance*. 'On 13 June 1612, I received orders to take charge of the rebuilding of this ship, then in the dry dock at Woolwich; old Mr.

Baker having charge of rebuilding.'

The *Mer Honeur*. '... at the same time in the same dock. The 14 February 1613, I began to victual all the shipwrights and workmen employed on the two ships abovementioned, Mr. Baker being dead: both ships were launched in December 1613.'

Mercury and the *Spy*. 'In June 1620, I was commanded to do in hand with building this pinnace, for the expedition against the Algiers Pirates, which I contracted for with certain merchants of the city. 300 tons and launched 16 October 1620.'

Memoirs of the Rise and Progress of the Royal Navy, p. 48-49.

During the reign of King James I, fourteen ships were built besides three to five that were rebuilt and considered additions to the navy at the time. Not surprisingly, the accounts of the navy at the death of James varied considerably with the number of ships from 50 to 62 and their tonnage from 20,000 to 23,000 tons.

The King's Ships and Pinnaces in the first year of the reign of James I, 1604.

The list originates from *Pepys's Miscellanies, V.2, p. 129.*

Ship Names	Burthen-Tons	Mariners	Gunners	Soldiers	Total Crew
Elizabeth Jonas	900	340	40	120	500
Triumph	1000	340	40	120	500
Bear	900	340	40	120	500
Victory	700	230	30	90	350
Honour	800	268	32	100	400
Ark	800	268	32	100	400
Due Repulse	700	230	30	90	350
Garland	700	190	30	80	300
Warspight	600	190	30	80	300
Mary Rose	600	150	30	70	250
Bonadventure	600	150	30	70	250

Assurance	600	150	30	70	250
Lion	500	150	30	70	250
Defiance	500	150	30	70	250
Rainbow	500	150	30	70	250
Nonsuch	500	150	30	70	250
Vanguard	500	150	30	70	250
Dreadnought	400	130	20	50	200
Swiftsure	400	130	20	50	200
Antelope	350	114	16	30	160
Adventure	250	88	12	20	120
Crane	200	76	12	12	100
Quittance	200	76	12	12	100
Answer	200	76	12	12	100
Advantage	200	76	12	12	100
Tramontane	140	52	8	10	70
Charles	70	32	6	7	45
Moon	60	30	5	5	40
Advice	50	30	5	5	40
Spy	50	30	5	5	40
Merlin	50	30	5	5	40
Lion's Whelp	90	50	6	4	60
La Superlativa	Galley	84	8	243 Rowers	335
La Advantagia	Galley	84	8	233 Rowers	325
La Volatillia	Galley	84	8	233 Rowers	325
La Gallarita	Galley	84	8	233 Rowers	325
Mercury-Galleon	80	34	6	100 Rowers	140
George-Carvel	100	10	-	-	10
Primrose-Hoy	80	2	-	-	2
A French Frigate	15	14	2	-	16
Distain	-	3	-	-	3

Memoirs of the Rise and Progress of the Royal Navy, 38-40.

The King's Ships and Pinnaces in December 1607

Ship Names	Tonnage	Men
Elizabeth	900	500
Triumph	1000	500
Bear	900	500
Victory	900	500
Honour	800	400
Ark	800	400
Repulse	700	350
Garland	700	300
Warspight	600	300
Mary Rose	600	300
Assurance	600	250
Bonadventure	600	250
Lion	500	250
Nonsuch	500	250
Defiance	500	250
Vanguard	500	250
Rainbow	500	250
Dreadnought	400	200
Swiftsure	400	200
Antelope	350	160
Adventure	250	120
Crane	200	100
Quittance	200	100
Answer	200	100
Advantage	200	100
Tramontane	140	70
Lion's Whelp	90	60
Charles	70	45
Moon	60	45
Advice	50	40
Spy	50	40

Merlin	50	40
Superlativa	100	335
Advantagia	100	223
Volatilla	100	223
Galarita	100	223

Memoirs of the Rise and Progress of the Royal Navy, 41-43.

Accounts vary as to the state of the navy at the time of the death of King James I. Vast inconsistencies include quantities of 50 to 62 ships. A report of the commissioners determined that as of 1618, there were 39 ships.

The following list labels these ships as 'may be serviceable'.

Ship Names	Tonnage
Prince Royal	1200
White Bear	900
More Honour	800
Ann Royal	800
Due Repulse	700
Defiance	700
Warspight	600
Assurance	600
Vantguard	600
Red Lion	500
Nonsuch	500
Rainbow	500
Dreadnought	400
Speedwell	400
Antelope	350
Adventure	250
Crane	200
Answer	200

Memoirs of the Rise and Progress of the Royal Navy, 50.
The following ships are labeled 'May be made serviceable.'

Ship Names	Tonnage
Phoenix	150
Lion's Whelp	90
Moon	100
Seven Stars	100
Desire	50
George, hoy	100
Primrose	80
Eagle Lighter	200

Memoirs of the Rise and Progress of the Royal Navy, 51.

The following ships are labeled 'Decayed and unserviceable.'

Ship Names	Tonnage
Elizabeth Jonas	500
Triumph	1000
Garland	700
Mary Rose	600
Quittance	200
Tramontane	160
Disdain	30
Ketch	10
Superlative	100
Advantagia	100
Vollatilla	100
Gallerita	100

Memoirs of the Rise and Progress of the Royal Navy, 51-52.

During the Reign of Charles I

The reign of Charles I began with great difficulties and ship building supplies were sparingly voted on by parliament, even when the nation was at war with Spain. In 1625, the king visited Plymouth to inspect naval preparations with additional visits to Deptford and Woolwich yards during his reign.

King Charles was obliged to resort to levying ship money through taxation, which had once been imposed by Queen Elizabeth, and when Charles took further steps, violent discontents resulted.

In 1624, the commission inventoried the ordnance of 33 ships and vessels.

Ship names	Burthen Tons	Pieces of Ordnance	Cannon Petro	Demi-Cannons	Culverines	Demi-Culverines	Sakers	Minions	Faulcons	Port-pieces	Fowlers
Prince	1200	55	2	6	12	18	13			4	
Bear	900	51	2	6	12	18	9			4	
More Honour	800	44	2	6	12	12	8			4	
Ann	800	44	2	5	12	13	8			4	
* Repulse	700	40	2	2	14	12	4			2	
* Defiance	700	40	2	2	12	12	4		2		
* Triumph	921	42	2	2	16	12	4		2		
* St. George	880	42	2	2	16	12	4		2		
* St. Andrew	880	42	2	2	16	12	4		2		
* Swiftsure	876	42	2	2	16	12	4		2		
* Victory	870	42	2	2	16	12	4		2		
* Reformation	750	42	2	2	16	12	4		2		
Warspight	650	38	2	4	13	13	4		2		
* Vanguard	651	40	2		14	12	4		2		
* Rainbow	650	40	2		14	12	4		2		4
Red Lion	650	38	2		14	12	4		2		4
Assurance	600	38	2		10	12	10				4
Nonsuch	600	38	2		12	12	6		2		4
Bonadventure	674	34			4	14	10	2			4
Garland	680	32			4	12	10	2			4
Entrance	580	32			4	12	10	2			4
Convertine	500	34				18	10	2			4
Dreadnought	450	32				16	10	2			4

Antelope	450	34			4	14	10	2			4
Adventure	350	26				12	6	4			4
Mary Rose	388	26				8	10	4			4
Phoenix	250	20				12	4	2			4
Crane	250										
Answer	250										
Moon	140										
Seven Stars	140	14				2	6	6			
Charles	140	14				2	6	4			
Desire	80	6							2	4	

*Notes that the particulars of the ordnance do not correspond with the total.

Memoirs of the Rise and Progress of the Royal Navy, 54-56.

An Inventory of the King's Ships of 1633.

Ship Name	Keel Length In Feet	Tons	Crew Size	Guns
Prince Royal	115	1187	500	55
Mer Honour	112	828	400	40
Ann Royal	107	776	400	44
Triumph	110	792	350	44
St. George	110	783	300	44
St. Andrew	110	764	300	42
Dieu Repulse	108	876	300	40
Defiance	104	751	280	38
Vanguard	112	746	280	40
Swiftsure	106	731	300	44
Rainbow	112	742	270	40
Reformation	106	721	280	40
Victory	106	702	300	40
Warspight	97	810	250	36
Charles	105	793	300	44

H. Mari	106	875	300	42
James	110	767	300	48
Unicorn	107	512	250	49
Leopard	103	698	250	36
Red Lion	103	619	250	40
Nonsuch	88	610	250	38
Assurance	104	621	250	34
Covertine	96	567	250	34
Bonadventure	96	552	200	32
Garland	96	557	200	34
Dreadnought	92	539	200	30
Happy Entrance	96	528	200	30
St. Dennis	104	512	200	38
Antelope	92	321	180	38
Mary Rose	83	287	120	26
Adventure	88	512	120	24
Swallow	103	186	250	36
First Whelp	62	186	70	14
Second Whelp	62	186	70	14
Third Whelp	62	186	70	14
Forth Whelp	62	186	70	14
Fifth Whelp	62	186	70	14
Sixth Whelp	62	186	70	14
Seventh Whelp	62	186	70	14
Eighth Whelp	62	186	70	14
Ninth Whelp	62	186	70	14
Tenth Whelp	62	186	70	14
Providence	58	89	30	8

Expedition	58	89	30	8
Henrietta	52	68	25	6
Madrid	52	6	25	6
Roebuck	58	80	30	8
Greyhound	58	80	30	8
Swan-frigate	40	60	10	3
Nicodemus-frigate	40	60	10	3

Memoirs of the Rise and Progress of the Royal Navy, 58-61.

The manuscript written by Mr. Pett mentions the following ships.

Unicorn. 'In February 1634, the *Unicorn* built at Woolwich, by Mr. Boat, was launched, his majesty was present, as he was likewise the next day at Deptford, at the launching of the *James*.'

Robuck and *Greyhound.* 'In January 1636, we were ordered to build two small pinnaces out of waste timber from the new ship. They were named the *Greyhound* and *Roebuck* when launched, which was soon after the order had been given.'

The following was the only account of the navy I was able to locate when the rebellion broke out in 1641.

Rate or Class	Number of Ships	Tons
First	5	5306
Second	12	8771
Third	8	4897
Fourth	6	2206
Fifth	2	600
Sixth	9	631
Total	42	22411

In 1642, the management of the navy was taken out of the hands of the king. King Charles I was put to death on 30 January 1649. There are no known accounts of the navy at that time.

Inventories of East India Company ships

Inventory of 1617–1621 (2 columns)

Advice	James Royal
Andrew	Lion
Anne Royal	Lioness
Ascension	Little James
Attendance	London
Bear	Mayflower
Bee	Merchant Royal
Blessing	Moon
Bull	New Year's Gift
Centaur	Osiander
Charles	Owl
Claw	Palsgrave
Clove	Peppercorn
Defense	Primrose
Diamond	Reformation
Discovery	Robert
Dragon	Roebuck
Dragon's Claw	Rose
Eagle	Ruby
Elizabeth	Samaritan
Endeavour	Sampson
Exchange	Solomon
Expedition	Speedwell
Fortune	Star
Francis	Sun
Gift	Supply
Globe	Swan
Godspeed	Thomas
Greyhound	Thomasin

Hart	Trades Increase
Hector	Trial
Hope	Unicorn
Hopewell	Unity
Hound	

CSP-C, EI, C&J, v.3, 1617-1621, p. 530, index.

Inventory of 1622-1624

Abigail	Bull
Abbe Royal	Charles
Attendance	Clove
Bear	Defence
Bee	Discovery
Blessing	Dolphin
Dragon	Richard
Eagle	Roebuck
Elizabeth	Rose
Exchange Royal	Ruby
Expedition	Sampson
Fortune	Scout
Gamaliell (sold)	Solomon
Globe	Spy
Hart	Star
Hope	Sun. Lost Nov. 1618.
Hound	
James Royal	Supply
Jonas	Swallow
Lesser James	Swan
Lion	Trial

London	Unicorn. Lost 1620.
Moon	
Palsgrave	Unity
Peppercorn	Whale
Primrose (sold)	White Bear
Reformation	William

CSP-C, EI, C&J, 1622-1624, p. 530-531, index.

Of all the East India Company inventory lists I reviewed; this appears to be the most comprehensive.

Comprehensive East India Company inventory

Ship Name	Birth	Death	Comments	Tonnage
Advice	1615			
Anna	1699-1701			
Anne Royal	1617	1620	Wrecked near Gravesend	900
Antelope	1699		Captain H. Hammond.	
Ascension	1600	1608	Forth E.I.C Voyage wrecked.	260
Attendant	1614			
Bear	1618	1620	Burnt by the Dutch.	
Bear's Whelp	1596		Sent to China, never returned.	
Bee	1617		Pinnace	150
Belfast	1699		Captain John Hudson	
Benjamin				
Blessing	1616			
Blessing	1629			
Bull	1616		Captain Robert Adams	400
Carolina	1682		Captain John Harding	
Chambers	1695		Captain T. Smith	

Chandos				
Charles	1618		Journal of Henry Crosby	
Charles	1629		Journal of Nicholas Priu	
Charles II	1695		Captain John Dorrill	
Christopher	1616			
Claw	1620			
Clove	1611		Captain Saris. Eighth E.I.C	
Clove	1616		Journal of John Borden	
Coaster	1633		John Muckrell's Journal	
Concord	1614			
Concord	1659		Captain Roger Kilvert	
Consent	1607		In third E.I.C. Voyage	115
Consent	1609		To be sold	
Darling	1610		In the Sixth E.I.C. voyage	90
Defence	1614		Journal of John Moden	
Defence	1616			
Defence	1686		Captain W. Heath	
Diamond	1618		Built at Deptford	
Discovery	1616		Journal of John Vian	
Dolphin	1621		Journal Richard Swanley	
Dragon	1600		Lancaster's ship. First E.I.C. voyage.	600
Red Dragon	1604		Sir H. Middleton's ship. Second E.I.C.	
Eagle	1620			
Eagle	1644		Captain Thomas Stevens.	
Edward Bonaventure			Lancaster's ship on the first voyage.	
Elizabeth	1618			978
Exchange	1620		Journal of Richard Swanley	
Expedition	1609		Captain David Middleton	
Expedition	1618		Voyage from Surat to Jask	
Falcon	1644			
Fleet Frigate	1698		Captain John Merry	

Flying Eagle	1678		Voyage from Bantam to China	
Fortune	1621		Robert Burgess, master	
Globe	1610		Captain Hippon. Seventh E.I.C. voyage.	
God Speed	1620		Junk (type of ship)	50
Great Thames	1624		Journal of Richard Monck	
Guest	1600		Abandoned at sea	
Hampshire	1699			
Hart	1620		In Shilling's fleet	
Hector	1600	1614	Made many E.I.C. voyages. Burnt by Dutch.	
Hinde	1644		Voyage from Surat to Macao.	
Hope	1618		Journal of E. Dodsworth	
Hopewell	1627		Journal of Peter Andrewes	
Hopewell	1644		Journal of William Broadbent	
Hoseander	1612		Tenth E.I.C voyage. Journal of Ralph Crosse.	
Hound	1618		Taken by the Dutch in 1619	
James	1611		Ninth E.I.C voyage. Captain E. Marlowe.	
James Royal	1616		Rowland Coytmore master	
John and Rachel	1688		Captain R. Cox. Journal of Nathaniel Ball. Relieving homeward bounders.	
Jonas	1621		Journal of Richard Swanley	
Josiah	1698-1700		Captain Stratton	
Julia	1699		Charles Coatsworth. Voyage to Borneo.	
Kempthrone	1690			
King William				
Lannarett	1614		Consort to the Falcon	
Lesser James	1621		John Wood master.	

Lion	1614		The ship in which Sir J. Roe went to India.	
London	1620		Captain Shilling. Journal of Archibald Jemmison.	
	1639		Journal of James Birkedall	
	1689–1701		Captain George Matthews	
Macclesfield	1699		Journal of Robert Douglas	
Madras	1682		Captain Benjamin Prickman. Journal of Zachary Toucy.	
Mary	1627		Journal of Peter Andrews	
Massingberd	1683		Captain Joseph Haddock	
Merchant Royal			In Lancaster's first voyage. See Bear.	
Merchant's Hope	1613		Nicholas Emsworth	
Moon	1618		Journal of Richard Bragge	
Nassau	1693		Captain John Lloyd	
Neptune	1699		Journal of John Lesley.	
New Year's Gift	1614		Captain Downton. Returned 1616.	800
	1617		In Captain Pringle's fleet	
Palsgrave	1618		Captain Charles Clevenger	1083
	1621		Sailed from Firando, to cruise off Manilla	
	1632		Richard Forder's Journal	
Penelope			Lancaster's first voyage	
Peppercorn	1610		Captain Downton. Sixth E.I.C. voyage	
	1614		Captain Walter Peyton	
	1621		At Firando	
President	1679		Captain Jonathan Hide	
Reformation	1629			

Relief			Name given to Sir H. Middletons pinnace in the sixth voyage.	
Richard	1621		Small vessel employed to explore the Cape.	20
Roebuck	1620		Captain Richard Swan. In Captain Shilling's fleet.	
Rose	1626		To Persia	
Royal James	1624		Captain John Weddell. Journal of Robert Fox.	
Ruby	1618			
Russell	1695		Frigate	
Samaritan	1614		Consort of the Thomas	
Samuel			A victualler for the sixth voyage.	
Sampson	1619		Captain Jourdain. Taken by the Dutch.	
Scout	1624		A small pinnace.	
Sea Adventure	1617		Captain Adam's junk. Journal of Edward Sayer.	
Solomon			In the tenth E.I.C. voyage.	
Spie	1624		A small pinnace.	
Speedwell	1614			
Starre	1622			
Sun	1617	1619	Wrecked	
Supply				
Susan	1600		In Lancaster's first E.I.C. voyage.	
Swan	1616		Captain Nathaniel Courtorp.	
Thomas	1611		In Captain Saris's fleet	
	1614		Journal of John Milward	
Thomasine	1614		Consort of the Thomas	
Tiger	1604		Sir Edward Michelborne and John Davis.	

Trade's Increase	1610		Sir H. Middleeon. Sixth E.I.C. voyage. Burnt by the Dutch	1000
Triplecaine	1675		Journal of John Stead.	
Thrumball	1699-1702			
Unicorn	1617	1620	Wrecked.	
Union	1608		Fourth E.I.C. voyage.	
Unity	1619			
Whale	1621			
William	1616			
William and Ralph			Name changed to Starre.	

The Voyages of Sir James Lancaster, Kt. to the East Indies. p. 295-301.

PART 2. THE LOGS.

The life of a mariner was full of peril and even daily routines possessed many hazards especially the farther north from the equator the ship was. Climbing the sometimes-wet freezing cold rigging to the yards with cold stiff hands in a rough sea with high winds to knock the inch thick coating of ice off the rigging and sails were a man could be blown to his death whether he landed on deck or in the ocean. These ships could not quickly turn around to rescue their crewmate, and the cold sea would kill the man before the ship arrived back. I witnessed this same type of incident during my time in the United States Navy. Those duties were dangerous no matter what point in time you examine.

Sanitation, hygiene, and medical practices were very different from modern standards. Sleeping quarters were wherever a man could hang his hammock, usually below decks during bad weather or above when weather allowed it. Without a decent sleep or rest off watch or work, the sailor could not think clearly while on watch duty, endangering not only himself but his ship and mates if he fell asleep on iceberg watch and collided with an iceberg. An additional hazard to those at sea was scurvy. Fresh vegetables, fruit and meats had to consumed before they spoiled, and that made the time until re-supply perilous, with the threat of a deficiency of vitamin C and other nutrients.

Boredom while not on watch, at workstations or on drills, was another hazard and some men carved wood figurines or Scrimshaw art to pass time, but the lack of wind could strand a ship for days, weeks or longer while the crew pondered their own mortality and why they joined the navy. Firsthand accounts were recorded in early maritime logs and journals of the extreme conditions' humans were sometimes forced to endure hoping to return home and many non-religious men prayed for their own safety. Two examples from the rare surviving logs and journals within this part.

"On the thirtieth, the captain made the surgeon cut his hair short, and take off his beard, for icicles hung from both, and gave him intolerable pain."

"The last article of food which they had consumed was a leather belt, belonging to one of them, which they had equally divided into shares, and wholly eaten up."

The perils of life at sea were sometimes offset by rare rewards. The capture of a Spanish ship in the channel to find thousands of gold and silver pieces of eight, bars of bullion, jewels and spices in addition to valuable pieces of ordnance that gave the ship an advantage over others. These prizes were often divided into portions for the crew and the amount they received depended on their time in service and rank; a windfall which could set a man and his family up for life.

The stories in this part not only share first-hand accounts of the hardships encountered by early mariners as they established trade routes into the Indies, but of brutal sea battles or stranded in the Arctic by thick sheets of ice exerting so much pressure on the hull, men described it as sounding like a slow and painful death, and of their survival in extreme sub-freezing temperatures with only what clothes they had on.

These stories are not fictional nor made up. They are from the surviving daily logs or journals of early mariners that escaped destruction and do not always describe the joyful completion of a long journey, the launching of a new ship or of the discovery through the Northwest Passage, but of those first-hand accounts of early mariners who could not navigate with maps or charts (none available) as they attempted to push farther into unknown territories hoping to find a faster passage to the Indies or China.

Treasure has many definitions, but the rare logs and journals shared in this part are often never reprinted or quoted from and are most certainly treasures themselves for recording the events and lives of early sailors in perilous survival conditions and their willingness to do anything including cannibalism, to survive.

Captain Thomas James.

The following is the narrative of Captain Thomas James while he was in search of a north-west passage during the reign of Charles I, 1631:

It was one of the earlier attempts to explain the mystery which Parry and Franklin have at last elucidated. The place where Captain

James's vessel was frozen up is in the southern end of Hudson's Bay. He was a bold and intrepid navigator, though he does not seem to have had much nautical experience. The expenses of his outfit were borne by a body of merchants, and James went under the patronage of Sir Thomas Roe. He chose one ship rather than two, and of no more than seventy tons. A good ship-boat and long-boat completed his equipage. He found that at ordinary allowance he could victual twenty-two men for eighteen months with this tonnage. This number was double what was needful to navigate the ship, which had been built as strong as possible. The victualling department was well served, and the crew were picked men, unmarried, sober, and active. He would not suffer any to join him who had been in the Polar Seas before. He provided himself with all journals and works which might help him, and with staves, quadrants, compasses, and semi-circles, made by the best workmen. Everything being put on board, upon the second of May 1631, Captain James repaired to his ship at Bristol, with a divine who preached them a sermon, and on the third of the same month they set sail for Milford.

They did not leave Milford until the seventeenth. On the fourth of June they saw Greenland, and got among the ice. There they were beset, and one of their boats crushed, which they afterwards repaired. On the sixth they beat fearfully amongst huge masses of ice, and saw their blue angles projecting under their keel, fathoms below. At length, after much beating and tossing about, they got through them. Having passed Cape Farewell, they encountered a heavy sea, and saw ice-mountains higher than their masthead. In the night of the seventeenth of June, they imagined they heard the break of the sea upon the shore, but it really broke upon an island of ice that lay aground. The noise was described as singularly hollow and frightful, like the deep roar of a cataract. It was so foggy they could not see beyond the ship.

When day broke they discovered the Island of Resolution. The night had been so cold, that their sails and rigging were frozen. The fogs continued to envelop them, and the ice gathered round the ship. A strong tide ran into the strait. The fog spoiled their compasses, making them so heavy that they would not traverse (probably the card was exposed to the air, for Captain James recommends that they should be covered with Muscovy glass, or something that would keep out the moisture). They were now a second time hemmed in with ice, though they could find no bottom with two hundred and thirty fathoms of line. The wind set upon the shore, and the ship, as well as the floating ice around her, was driven towards it. The motion of the sea was new and strange. While they were thus situated, they were hurried among frigid masses, some of which were aground in forty fathoms of water. Pieces projected from these masses so far over the vessel that they feared they would fall upon the deck and crush them. In this perilous situation, they contrived, by means of ropes and grapnels, to attach a couple of large pieces of ice to their sides, of such a depth under water, that in case of their approaching near the shore, the ice might get aground first.

The floating ice, however, meeting and rubbing against the pieces which were attached to the sides of their ship, tore them away, together with the ropes and grapples. These they contrived to save by means of their boats. They were still driving towards the shore, in such shallow water, that they could see the points of the rocks under their vessel at one time, while at another they were borne out into deep water again. At last they were constrained to let go an anchor, with only fifteen feet of water between their keel and the rocks, A piece of ice helped to bring them up, and they were at last able to warp out into three fathoms of water, under shelter of a piece of ice that had run aground, which served to break off the drift ice during the ebb tide, though at the flood they were very much distressed to keep clear of it.

At full tide, too, they found the mass that sheltered them afloat, and at length it drifted away from them, leaning the vessel exposed until ebb, when they regained its friendly shelter. All night they were employed in fastening their hawsers and cables high on the rocks, that the ice might float past under them. At length it began to blow and snow hard, and the ice was driven in again towards the shore. The flukes of their anchors were broken, and they were obliged to toil hard to repair the injury they had sustained. At the next ebb the loose ice drove the ship upon a sharp rock, and as the tide fell, she heeled over so that they could not stand in her, though they made cables fast to her mast, and strained them tight with their tackle to prevent it.

All now seemed to be lost, and the crew getting upon a piece of ice, fell on their knees, praying God to be merciful to them. It was just an hour to the time of low water, and a foot and half of ebb was wanted to the level it had fallen the preceding tide. The ship lay so far over, that part of the forecastle was in the water; and at one time the cables gave way so, that she sunk half a foot lower at a slip. All at once they perceived the flood tide, and then the ship rose. As soon as the vessel was afloat, the crew labored to move her further out, but the ice, which came driving in, put them to great distress. They were obliged to content themselves with getting as many pieces as they could between them and the shore.

One piece, of three hundred paces in circumference, came upon their quarter, but luckily took the ground before it could touch them. In a short time they were so hemmed in, that the ice might be walked over to a great distance. The next day the tide ebbed two feet lower than before had it occurred while they were on the rock, their wreck would have been certain. The next ebb tide, the ice, stopped by the large piece which was on shore, gathered close around them; so that, with axes and iron bars, they were obliged to break away the rough angles and to make way for it to drift by them. Their labor was not in vain; and they got so much of the ice between them and the rocks, that they remained for some time in tolerable security, though at low water the pieces on shore breaking asunder made a fearful thundering noise. The same day, Captain James went on the land, and they built up a large heap of stones, put a cross upon it, and, called the place the "Harbor of God's Providence."

On the twenty-third of June, Captain James went on shore upon the eastern side where the ship lay, in hopes of finding some spot in which she might be safer than in her present position, and he succeeded in discovering a place among the rocks, which he thought might answer. Here he heard a terrible noise which arose from a large mass of ice breaking up. He feared that the vessel might have been ruined by it, and hastened therefore to the ship, but found all safe. He then sent his boat to sound the place he had seen; finally they unmoored and warped the ship away from the icebergs, of which they had scarcely got clear when the ice broke up. They were fortunate enough to get their vessel safely into the cove which they had found, and making fast to the rocks, remained in comparative safety.

On shore all was rocky and barren. Neither tree, herb, nor grass, grew there. The traces of foxes were discovered, but those of no other animals. This cove was in latitude 61° 24'. A gale of wind springing up on the twenty-fourth, they set sail from the cove, which they named Price's Cove, and steered between great pieces of ice which were aground in forty fathoms of water, and twice as high out of it as their topmast head. By noon they were again caught in the ice, which grated on the side of the vessel with so much violence, that they feared it would tear away the planks. Thus they were driven about from day to day, until the twenty-sixth. Not an acre of sea could be seen from the mast head. The weather was calm with sunshine, and bottom was found at one hundred and forty fathoms. The nights were very cold, and the rigging froze. The ponds of water upon the ice were frozen half an inch thick.

Until the fifth of July, they sailed continually through the ice, the weather sometimes foggy and oftentimes fine. They were in latitude 63° 15', in the strait between the Island of Resolution and Digges Island. On the sixteenth they found it impossible to shape their course to the north-west, which was the great object of their voyage; and they then steered west-south-west, for Mansfield Island, the ice still besetting the ship and striking violent blows. They were now obliged to go upon half allowance of bread, and two of the crew complained of being ill. On the evening of that day, they came to an anchor close to Mansfield Island, and some of them went ashore, but they had difficulty to recover their boat again, on their return, the weather had become so thick.

The twenty-seventh they had clear weather, but on the twenty-eighth and ninth they were again enclosed by the ice, so that with all their sails set they did not move. They now left the ship with her sails set, and got upon the ice to recreate themselves. One piece was a thousand paces long. For the first time the crew began to murmur, thinking it impossible to get clear. Some conjectured the bay was covered over in a similar manner, and that it was doubtful if any land could be reached to winter upon. The nights were long, and so cold that they could not sail, and by day it was the same. Captain James encouraged the crew in the best way he was able, and they drank his Majesty's health upon the ice, not a soul being left on board, though all sail was set. But while endeavoring to cheer their spirits, Captain James felt that their murmuring was not without reason.

It was but too probable they might be frozen up on the ocean, and in fear of it he ordered a fire to be made on board but once a day, lest in such a case the fuel should fall short. On the thirtieth they made some way through the ice, by breaking the angles of the shoals, and heaving the ship forward by main force. On the sixth of August they succeeded in getting into the open sea, tolerably free of ice. They now stood to the north-west, wishing to get as high to the northward as possible, and on the eleventh saw land in latitude 59° 40'. The space they had crossed was from Digges Island to the western shore, a bay about one hundred and sixty leagues wide. On the thirteenth of August, during foggy weather, they saw breakers ahead. They were then in nine, or ten fathoms of water, but on luffing to clear them, they suddenly struck on the rocks, and were in great consternation, the ship having several sails set. They had scarcely taken them in, when two or three heavy seas lifted them over the ledge into three fathoms and a half of water. They now let go their anchor, and tried the pumps, but found the ship made no water, although she struck so violently three times, that they feared the mast would be carried away, and that the hull must have bulged.

They now hoisted out a boat to find a channel by which they might free themselves, but there arose such a fog, that all sight of the vessel was lost: the wind subsided; by hint of firing the artillery, they recovered the vessel, and brought word they had found a passage where there was two fathoms and a half of water, and that it soon became deeper. They were surrounded where they lay with rocks and breakers, and gladly weighed anchor. They sailed over two rocky ledges, on which there were only fourteen fathoms of water; it then deepened to three, four, and fourteen, and again shoaled. They came to an anchor that night, and the next day prepared everything on board to meet the exigencies of their situation. On the seventeenth they stood to the southward, and at noon were six or seven leagues on the southern side of Port Nelson. On the twentieth they saw land in latitude 57°, and named it 'The New Principality of South Wales.'

This is the territory on the south-western side of Hudson's Bay, where York Factory is at present situated, and terminates on the south shore of James's Bay, opposite East Main. In the evening they came to an anchor, and rode all night, and the next day and night, owing to a contrary wind. The ship labored much. At nine p. m. it began to blow hard, and the vessel drove. They manned the capstan to heave in the cable, fearing they had lost their anchor. The latter now hooked the ground again, and the sea chopping, threw the men from the capstan. A small rope got foul of the cable, and about the leg of the master, who cleared himself only after a severe bruising. Two mates were hurt. One man barely escaped with life, and another was struck down by a blow on the breast. All were sorely bruised, but the unfortunate gunner's leg was caught between the cable and the capstan, his foot torn off, the flesh stripped from his leg, and the bone crushed to pieces. He lay crying in anguish, until the crew had recovered themselves, and were able to clear him. Eight men were hurt at this most critical moment, and while they were conveying the gunner below to the surgeon, the ship drifted into shoal water. A second time the anchor hooked fast, and they rode out the night safely. The gunner's leg was taken off near the knee, and the wounds of all the men hurt were dressed. In this miserable plight, the crew comforted themselves as well as they could. On the twenty-second, they found themselves in a little bay, out of which they immediately stood, and on the twenty-seventh came to high land.

They anchored and sent a boat to the shore, well manned and armed. When the boat came back, the crew reported that they had seen a great deal of drift wood on the shore, and some trees, also tracks of various animals. On the twenty-ninth, they saw the vessel commanded by Captain Fox, which had been sent out to seek the north-west passage. Fox and some others from his ship went on board, and were entertained by Captain James, as well as he was able. They took their leave, and were seen no more. The weather, though but the end of August, now became very cold; they were still coasting along the land, when the surgeon announced that several of the crew was tainted with scurvy.

September the third, they saw a headland, which they named Cape Henrietta Maria, in latitude 55° 5'. On the morning of the fourth they saw land, and it soon began to blow very hard from the south-east, with lightning, snow, and rain, such as none of them had ever before seen equaled. They shipped several very heavy seas, one of which they feared would cause them to founder, and they had great difficulty to keep things fast in the hold.

On the fifth the wind shifted, but did not abate in violence; then it went back to its old quarter of the north-west, and blew with unabated fury. The vessel labored fearfully; they were in an unknown sea, and the distress of all on board was pitiable. At night the storm broke up, and they had a little rest.

On the seventh they saw an island, named it Lord Weston's Island, and anchored at night among rocks and breakers, in a most dangerous spot, but fortunately the weather was calm. The next day Captain James went on shore. There he could not find either sorrel, scurvy-grass, or any kind of herb that would refresh the sick. They were now in latitude 52° 45'. (*Southern Hudson Bay, now about Akimiski Island.*)

On the twelfth it blew hard again, and the ship began to drive. They hove in the anchor, and sailed under courses, when soon after, by some blunder, the ship ran upon the rocks. The shock roused Captain James in his cabin, who sprang upon deck, thinking all was lost. They struck their sails, tore down the stern to bring the cable through the cabin to the capstan, laying out an anchor to heave astern. All the water was staved in the hold, and pumped out, and the coals thrown overboard, the ship still beating hard, and some of the sheathing of her bottom swimming by them. The cable broke with the purchase, and they then put out another, though from the water they had staved in the hold, they could not tell whether the ship leaked or not. It seemed to be taken for granted that she did; and the carpenter's tools, a barrel of bread, one of powder, six muskets, some match, a tinder box, fish-hooks, lines, pitch, and oakum, were put into the boat, and taken on shore in the miserable hope of prolonging life for a few days more.

The vessel beat for five hours, and did not strike less than a hundred times, the crew thinking each blow must be the last; yet they did not perceive that she made any water, and at length she beat clear over the rocks. The pumps were now tried, and she proved leaky. They got farther from the shore, and came to an anchor, but it began to blow fresh again, when, had they been still on the rocks, they must inevitably have perished.

On the thirteenth they were completely beleaguered with rocks in the midst of fog. Captain James resolved to go down to the bottom of Hudson's Bay, and see if he could discover a passage into the 'river of Canada,' and, failing of that, to winter on the main land, which was better than to perish among rocks and shoals. On the fourteenth they saw land, which scarcely cheered them with a glimpse than it came on to blow a storm again, and they gave themselves up once more for lost. Again it cleared, and land appeared once more, for which they bore up, and rode safely in a good anchorage all night a thing necessary to give them rest from their incessant toils. They lost one of their boats before they could make the anchorage, and that which they had left was much damaged.

On the nineteenth they anchored under another island, and the carpenter repaired their only boat. Captain James went on shore, but found neither herb, flesh, nor fowl, and returned 'comfortless' on board. The wind still continuing northerly, so that they could not get round into the bay, they began to deliberate on the best course to be pursued. Some were for going to Port Nelson, where there was a safe cove for the ship, but Captain James thought it a very dangerous spot on account of the ice. It was then so cold that the rigging froze every night, and in the morning they had to clear the deck of snow half a foot deep. To shape their course towards a colder climate did not seem advisable. It was resolved, therefore, to steer to the southward in search of some place of security for the ship. Miserably tossed about until the twenty-second, they were rejoiced to see another island, which they made, and went on shore to look for some creek to lay up the vessel. This was now become necessary, as she leaked much, and the crew were sick, dispirited, and exhausted from incessant labor. They had great difficulty in getting to their boat again, being obliged to wade in the sea, while it froze and snowed bitterly, and not without peril they regained their ship. The island they named Sir Thomas Roe's Island; it lay in latitude 52° 10'.

On the twenty-fifth, the weather being stormy with snow and hail, they were encompassed with shoals and obliged to anchor; and in much the same state, expecting every day to terminate their miseries, the time passed until the first of October. They were still in the midst of rocks and shoals, from which it seemed as if they would never be disentangled. They got out their boat to find a channel, and after unparalleled hazards, they at length freed them-selves.

On the second they landed upon an island, which they called the Earl of Derby's Island. Traces of savages were seen upon it; it was well wooded; from the high ground nothing but rocks and shoals could be seen to the southward, worse even than those they had already passed. It was now the setting in of winter in a frigid climate, and the prospects of the crew were full of gloom. Captain James attempted in vain to find a creek or river to bring the vessel into, that she might lie in some sort of security; he regained his ship with great difficulty. The weather continued severe and stormy till the sixth, when they stood in nearer to the shore, and came to an anchor.

On the seventh, it snowed all day, blowing a storm, and they were obliged to clear the deck with shovels. It froze so hard that the bow of the ship and her figure-head were cased in it, and the cable became as large round, from accumulated ice, as a man's body, so that they were forced to hew it away. The sun shone clear, yet they were obliged to tear the topsails out of the tops, they being one entire lump of ice, nor had the sun the least power in thawing them. The bows of their boat were covered with ice half a foot thick, which they were obliged to beat off; and when they attempted to reach the land, they could not get through the water nearest the shore, it was so thick with the snow which had fallen on the sands at low water. With four cars they found it difficult to land at all. They now cut a large quantity of wood, and took it on board, fearing that in a short time they would be unable to perform such a necessary duty. On board the ship everything froze even in the hold, and by the side of the fire. The sails were now found to be useless; and this circumstance, which clearly showed that the vessel could not be navigated any longer during the cold season, convinced them that they must winter where they had now anchored. Wood for three months consumption had been got on board, and it seems to have been still doubted what course to take, when the sick men implored that some hut or hovel might be built for them on the shore, where they would find a better shelter, and recover more rapidly, than in the vessel. This request was complied with. The carpenter and assistants were landed, and went to work immediately.

Captain James and others set out into the woods to see if he could find any trace of savages, in order that they might be on their guard against them, but they found none. The snow now lay half way up the leg in depth, and they returned to where their companions were at work upon their house in a most comfortless plight. In the mean while the topsails were taken down and thawed before a large fire, and then stowed away. The next day they took down the mainsail, thawed it, and took it ashore to cover their house, which was accomplished the same evening. Six of the crew, who were employed in erecting it, slept that night within its shelter, having two dogs with them, and also firearms. The next night the hut was ready to receive its inmates.

On the fifteenth of October, a party that had gone out to hunt returned with a lean deer which they had brought twelve miles, and reported they had seen others. This party consisted of the six men who erected the house. They had wandered above twenty miles, and had slept the night of the fourteenth in the woods. They did not recover the suffering from the cold for several days. They met no wild beasts, nor did they see any harbor for the ship. Notwithstanding their sufferings, six others set out on the seventeenth to explore the island. They encountered more misery than the preceding party. They returned much disabled with the cold, having lost the gunner's mate, who to save distance had attempted to cross a pond about a quarter of a mile over. The ice gave way near the center, and closed upon him, so that he was never seen again.

Up to the last day of October the cold was very severe, and the month ended with a snow-storm. On the first of November they surveyed their provisions, which they found as much in quantity as they could expect, owing to careful management and saving. A similar survey Captain James made every month. On the third the boat could not get ashore through the congealed water, but on the fourth they succeeded in getting it to the land, but were only able to do so afterwards once in two or three days.

On the ninth they carried a barrel of beer ashore to the men in the hut, where in one night it froze through. When thawed in a kettle this beer did not taste well, and they were obliged to break the ice ponds to obtain water to drink, but it was bad in smell; and at last they were forced to sink a well near the house, in which the water was found good; they thought it had the taste of milk. The carpenter now set about making a small boat, which might be carried by hand over the ice. The latitude of the place was found to be 52°. Traps were set to catch foxes.

On the twelfth their house took fire, but it was fortunately extinguished before any serious mischief had occurred. They were forced to keep up a large fire day and night, but afterwards a watch was continually kept over it, for if their house and clothing had been lost, there was no chance of their surviving the rigor of the season. Captain James slept on shore till the seventeenth of November, during which period their sufferings continued to increase, and it was constantly snowing and freezing. The ship appeared like a lump of ice; the snow around her was frozen, and shoreward it was firm ice. Captain James now went on board, where the long night was spent by him in bitter and anxious thoughts on their situation, for in the day there seemed no hope of saving the vessel. Indeed he began to think there was little hope for their lives, and that nature could not endure the miserable state in which they were much longer. The gunner, whose leg had been taken off in consequence of the accident at the capstan, was now grown very weak. He saw he had but a short time to live, and begged that he might be allowed to drink unmixed sack, most probably, to lessen his misery. Captain James granted his request.

On the morning of the twenty-second, death put an end to his bitter sufferings. A close boarded cabin had been allotted him in the gun-room, and as many clothes as were needful, together with a pan of coals and a large fire. Notwithstanding this, the plaster froze at his wounded stump, and his bottle of wine at his head. His companions committed him to the sea a considerable distance from the vessel.

On the twenty-third the ice began to increase. The snow lay in flakes in the water as it fell, and a good deal of ice drifted by the ship, which fortunately escaped without receiving any fresh injury. In the evening, after the watch was set, a very large piece of ice came down, at least a quarter of a mile broad, followed by four other pieces, each of equal size to the first. They now feared the ship would be forced upon the rocks by the pressure. The anchor and cable bore the stress of these floating masses, sometimes even stopping them, without breaking. On board they fired off their muskets as signals of distress to those in the house, but in vain, for they could not afford them assistance. The ice, at length, drifted past without doing any material injury.

The next day a piece came foul of the cable, and the ship drove. Captain James now determined to run the ship aground; neither anchors nor cables could hold her where she lay. The weather was fine and the sun shone warm; the wind blew upon the shore. The ship was brought into twelve feet water, and preparations were made to run her on the shore when it became necessary. They were in hopes some rocks which were near would keep off the floating ice. They then lay a mile from the dry land. In the night, however, the ice driving down upon them, the anchors came home, and the ship drove two cables length. The wind fortunately blew upon the shore, and the ship running aground stopped the ice, which, notwithstanding, did no fresh injury.

The following day the wind again changed, and brought down much ice upon them. At flood tide they toiled hard, drawing home their anchors by main strength, and endeavoring once more to run the ship aground. Still she drove to the eastward, and they had great fears she would drift on the rocks. The weather for two days had been fine warm sunshine, or they could not have borne the exposure. The wind now coming round to the south, the topsails were brought up from below, where they had been stowed away, and being hoisted, the ship was forced ashore when she had drifted within a short distance of the rocks; they then broke a channel through the ice, and put out an anchor towards the shore in five feet water, to keep the ship firm. They feared being driven out to sea and starved, as they supposed was the fate of Sir Hugh Willoughby, the recollection of whom added greatly to their depression at such a moment.

About nine o'clock the same night, the wind blew a storm from the northwest, which sent away all the ice. A rolling sea came in with a surf, and the ship was still aground. She soon began to roll and then to beat. The crew stood, some to the capstan and some to the pumps, expecting every blow would break her up. They hove with all their might to keep her bottom to the ground, till, from the wind making a high flood tide, they were doubtful if they should ever be able to get her afloat again, even if she were able to swim. About two in the morning she seemed to settle from the tide falling. The crew, exhausted by toil, now endeavored to restore themselves by sleep, with the miserable expectation of having to renew their labor again the next tide. In the morning, however, they found the ship remain stationary, and thus they had an interval of rest. They went to prayers, and the captain held a consultation with his officers, and proposed that as they were in the utmost peril, all the provisions should be taken ashore, and that when the wind came from the north they should draw the ship further off the shore, and sink her. By this means there was a better chance of preserving her. They all agreed to it and communicated the scheme to the crew. They then got ashore their provisions with a great deal of labor, owing to the frozen snow and water.

On the twenty-seventh, the bay in which they lay became again full of ice, which they hoped would freeze, and thus prevent the necessity of sinking the vessel. In the meantime the carpenter prepared a place towards the keel to sink the ship at a moment's notice. On the twenty-ninth it blew hard; and expecting it might shift to the northward, the cooper was ordered into the hold to stave the casks, or get up such as were empty, to coil the cables on the lower tier, and get all ready. It soon began to blow a storm from the north-west. The ship was already bedded two feet in the sand, and yet she rolled so that they could scarcely keep their feet.

The captain now let in the water, but she would not sink as fast as they hoped and expected, but continued to beat in such a manner that they thought no ship could have borne it without going to pieces. At length the lower tier rose and beat about the inside of the vessel, knocking the bulkheads of the bread and powder rooms to pieces, the chests and casks rolling about wildly; and the water dashing and flying in such a manner from side to side, that they expected to see the ship's frame break up every moment. The rudder was soon gone; the sea at last came to the upper deck, and the vessel settled down. Unfortunately, they had none of them preserved their clothes, nor the surgeon his medicine chest. A part of the crew was already on shore looking upon these operations, almost dead with cold and misery, and pitying the sufferings of those on board. Night closed the miserable scene. Those in the ship got into the boat, expressing their attachment to their commander, as loth to part from him, but he informed them he should accompany them to the land. There were seventeen in the boat, all fearful that they had but exchanged one misery for another. The ebb tide had set in, and the water was so thick with snow, that they feared they should not be able to make head against it, but, being carried out to sea, perish miserably there. With much labor, double manning four oars, they got to the land and hauled up their boat.

They now greeted their comrades on shore, who scarcely knew them by their voices or appearance, they were frozen in the face, hair, and dress. The party now went along the beach towards the house, where a good fire was made. They thawed themselves, and took for refreshment bread and water, being all they had to comfort them. Their conversation turned principally on the fate of their ship. The carpenter thought she had foundered, and would never again be serviceable. He contended she had been so shook and beaten, that her beams must have opened, and that as there was no creek or cove near, where she could be laid up, he could devise no mode of repairing her. Moreover, the rudder was gone, and he had no iron to hang another. Some said she had been hove so high on the sand that she was already docked three feet in it, and could not be got off, others that the ice would destroy her, that her anchors which were under the ice would be broken by it, and there would be none on board for use if they were able to get her off.

Captain James bade them be of good heart and trust in God; that if they were to end their days there, they were as near Heaven in that spot as in England; that they were by no means past hope they might, as others had done, build a boat, and recover their friends again; that nothing was too hard for courageous minds, which they had so far shown, and he doubted would not fail to show again. They all protested they would do their utmost, and obey the captain even to their deaths. To the carpenter, in return for his willingness and spirit, Captain James promised a fixed reward, and also that he would not forget those who distinguished themselves if he got to England. It was then resolved to build a new boat frame with the wood which they might obtain on the island; and if the ship should not be found serviceable in the spring, to plank the boat with her timbers. Matters thus decided, they all huddled round their fire, and went to sleep. On the thirtieth, the captain made the surgeon cut his hair short, and take off his beard, for icicles hung from both, and gave him intolerable pain. The crew followed the example. They now prepared themselves for their future labors. They were anxious to get some clothes and provisions, for when the tide fell, there remained of course but little water in the vessel.

The master was appointed with those under him to go on board and get the things out of the hold, the coxswain, and others to bring them ashore, while the captain and the rest were to carry them nearly half a mile to where they proposed building a storehouse. The heavier things were to remain upon the beach. The party succeeded in getting on board, and made a fire there as a signal. They also got some things out of the hold upon the deck, but as night came on speedily they dared not venture to come on shore, but were nearly starved to death with cold on board, being obliged to remain all night in the ship. The next day it was so cold that they walked on the ice to the ship, where the boat had gone the day before, and carried back in bundles a good quantity of food, and much of their bedding and clothes, which they dug out of ice within the vessel. The next day the weather fell mild again, and some of the crew venturing on the ice fell through, and were with difficulty recovered. No visit could, therefore, be made to the vessel, and they began building their storehouse.

The third of December, numerous large pieces of ice were stopped by the ship as they floated by, but they afforded no passage across. The boat reached the vessel, and was loaded; but as it then drew four feet of water, it could not come within a good distance of the shore, and the men were obliged to wade through the freezing water to carry the things upon their backs, a sight extremely painful, from the misery they endured. The boat at length got frozen in the tackles; she could not be lifted upon deck from the weight of ice about and within her, and it was left.

On the tenth the carpenter found timber to make a keel and stern for the new boat. The crew were principally employed in getting the provisions on shore until the thirteenth, when they dug their boat out of the ice with great toil, and then got her upon it. In this service many had their noses, cheeks, and fingers frozen as white as paper. The cold increased, and on the nineteenth they could get nothing more out, leaving five barrels of beef and pork, all their beer, and other things, frozen up in the hold. The twenty-first was so cold that none of them could venture out of the house. They attempted on the twenty-third to drag their boat ashore, by running her over the oars; but by ten o'clock in the morning the fog came on so thick that it was dark as night; and though they made haste to the shore they discovered it with difficulty, losing each other in the gloom. At last they all met in their house dreadfully frozen. Upon some the cold raised blisters, which they imagined arose from coming too quick to the fire out of the freezing atmosphere. Their well too was frozen up, so that they could get no water. Melted snow they found unwholesome, and fancied that it made them short-breathed. Wine, vinegar, oil, and everything liquid, were frozen hard as wood, and were cut with a hatchet. Their house was iced over on the inside, and things froze within a yard of the fire. Yet the latitude differed but little from that of London, a proof that two centuries ago the American continent had the same severity of winter temperature that at present distinguishes it so much from the "Old World."

They were fortunate enough to find a spring under the snow, about three-quarters of a mile from their house, which did not freeze so hard but that by breaking the ice water could be obtained. They had great difficulty and toil in getting a stock of wood for their fuel at this time, owing to the depth of the snow through which they were obliged to carry it. Their bedding and provisions being now all arranged, they determined to keep Christmas day as joyfully as possible in their circumstances, and also St. John's Day. They named the wood in which they were wintering, "Winter's Forest." The house which they constructed was placed in the warmest situation they could find, yet as near to the ship as possible. It lay among a tuft of thick trees, under a southern bank, a short distance from the shore. They could not dig to sink this house in the ground, which had else made it warmer, for they found water within two feet of the surface. The soil was a fine white sand, so they could not construct a mud wall if the frost had allowed. Stones there were none, nor had they boards. They therefore marked out a spot twenty feet square, being the size their main canvass would conveniently cover. Then they drove strong stakes into the ground; these they wattled with boughs, beating them down very close to the height of six feet. The gable ends were ten feet high, and left open at the top corners for the smoke to pass out, and the light to come in. At both ends three rows of thick bushy trees were placed on end quite close. Then trees cut as far as possible from the house, in lengths of two yards, were piled up to the thickness of six feet at the sides, and ten at the ends. A very small low door was left to creep in at, and a porch was erected before it, made of piles of wood, that the wind might not blow in. A rough tree was placed lengthwise over all, upon which rafters rested, and then the main course upon them, which reached the ground on both sides. Within, other sails were made fast to the walls; and on three sides, stakes driven into the ground formed a double tier of bedstead frames, the lowest being a foot from the ground. These were first filled with boughs, then some spare sails were laid upon them, and then each man's bedding and clothes. The hearth for the fire was made in the center, and some boards were placed round it to stand upon, and keep the cold from their feet. Some made their waste clothes serve for canopies and curtains, and others the small sails. The second house was erected about twenty feet distant from the first, somewhat smaller, made also of wattling, and covered with the fore course. It had no piles on the south side, but the wall consisted of the chests of the crew piled up, the heat reflected from the fire upon them and back again, made it warmer than the other house. Here the victuals were dressed, and the common sailors generally remained during the day.

A third house, made of a rough tree, rafters resting against it from the ground, and covered with a new set of sails, was built at some distance, for fear of fire. On the inside, upon small trees covered with boughs, the stock of bread and fish was laid about two feet from the ground, to preserve it more carefully. The other stores lay about less regularly. The two inhabited houses long before Christmas were covered with snow, which nearly reached the roof from the ground. The storehouse was buried in it. This made both houses warmer. They could not go out unless they made paths in the snow, middle deep in some places, treading down the snow after shoveling a good quantity aside: by this means it made a hard walk for such of the sick as could venture forth on a fine day. These walks they extended by degrees farther and farther.

They succeeded on the twenty-seventh of December in getting their boat on shore, and they brought up their provision from the beach to the storehouse, but not without excessive labor and suffering, having to make a path with shovels through the deep snow from the seaside to the hut. In this hut they saw the close of the year 1631.

The first of January set in extremely cold. By an observation of the latitude, the weather being clear sunshine, it was found, no doubt owing to refraction, to be 51° 52'. Every day in this month the cold was extreme. On the twenty-first they remarked that the sun appeared to rise of an oval figure along the horizon. It was twice as long as it was broad, but as it got higher it assumed its usual circular form. On the thirtieth and thirty-first, early in the night, there appeared more stars in the heavens than they had ever seen by two-thirds at least. The lightish nebulous appearance in Cancer was full of stars. The "via lacteal" consisted of nothing but small stars, while the Pleiades were clouded with them. When the moon got up, about ten o'clock, they were not to be seen in greater numbers than usual. The wind had been northerly, and the cold was extreme, yet at intervals they worked upon their boat and fetched wood. The sea was frozen over as far as the eye could see early in the month. It was remarked that the men found it less painful to wade through the water in December than in June, when the sea bore floating ice, notwithstanding the severer degree of cold. The ground was now frozen to the depth of ten feet.

In February the cold continued as severe as in the preceding month. The unfortunate seamen now began to complain of sore mouths; their teeth became loose, their gums swollen, and the black flesh which increased upon them was obliged to be cut away daily. The pain was so great they could not eat their ordinary food. Some had pains in their heads and breasts, others in their backs, others swellings of the legs, and aching pains in the knees and thighs. Two-thirds were soon under the surgeon's care, and yet in this deplorable state they were forced to go daily to fetch wood, though most of them had no shoes to wear. Their store shoes were all sunk in the ship, and those they had, upon coming to the fire out of the snow, were burned. They bound cloths about their feet, and labored by that means to perform their duties. They seem to have been an excellent set of men, cheerful in privation, and obedient in suffering.

The carpenter next fell ill to the dismay of all, for his skill was a main prop to their hope of seeing England again. Neither clock nor watch, though kept in a chest of clothes by the fire, would go. The cold in any open spot, such as that upon the ice in the way to the ship, was sometimes not endurable at all; no clothes were proof against it, no exercise resisted it. The hair on their eyelids was frozen, so that they could not see if they attempted to brave it at those periods. The cold in the woods was not so severe, though it would bite any joint or exposed part of the body. The inside of the house was now hung with icicles. The clothes on the beds sparkled with hoar frost though near the fire. The cook's tubs, which stood not a yard from the fire, and in which melted snow water was poured in the day, were frozen to the bottom if he slept but one watch at night.

On the first of March they kept holiday, it being St. David's day. On the fifteenth, one of the men, thinking he had seen a deer, set out with others in the pursuit, but they returned in the evening so disabled with the cold, that it was a fortnight before they recovered their former state of health. Blisters of the size of walnuts came upon their legs and feet. On the twenty-sixth, three others set out on the same errand, and returned still worse, and more disabled. That evening the moon was observed to rise of a very long oval in the horizon, as the sun had done once before. The carpenter, who was so weak as to be led to his work, had contrived by the end of the month to set up seventeen ground timbers, and thirty-four straddles of the projected boat. These timbers were not obtained without vast toil and labor. Three men were sent with a mold of the crooked piece of timber required. They were forced to wade and scramble through the snow in the terrible cold of the climate. When they saw a tree likely to do, they were first obliged to clear away the snow round it, and then try the mold. If it did not do after all, they were obliged to go in search of another that did. When they found one fitting, they were obliged to thaw it with a fire, or they could not cut it, and it was then to be got home a mile through the snow.

Under the circumstances in respect to cold, scanty food, and the ill health of the greater part of the crew, such labor must have been almost beyond human strength. They were obliged to search out dry trees for fuel and fell them; for green wood made a smoke so thick that it could not be borne, and the men would rather have perished of the cold than sat by it. The trees too which they procured so abounded in turpentine, that they were blackened all over. Their clothes were scorched, and hung in pieces. Their fuel was still to be brought home through the snow, and all that was selected for the carpenter's use it was necessary to thaw. The healthy had to wait upon the sick, of whom by Easter day there were five unable to do anything, and one of these was unfortunately the carpenter. The boatswain was very weak, and only five retained enough appetite and strength to devour their daily allowance of food. In fact, though they kept Easter day, which was that year the first of April, with religious solemnity, and talked around their fire of their situation, it seemed they were never in a more fearful state, nor hope more distant.

The weather was still intolerably cold, not the slightest mitigation of its intensity had taken place. The boat was not half finished, and the carpenter was growing worse. The ship appeared to be full of solid ice, which they imagined must have opened all her seams, especially after the blows she had received. As the result of a good deal of discussion, it was agreed, notwithstanding their miserable and helpless plight, that the first moment the warm weather would allow of it, they should endeavor to clear the hold and ascertain her state, that they might afterwards be enabled to take some other step in the event of her proving inefficient. They took the first opportunity, therefore, of mustering such tools as might be useful for that object, more particularly to dig the ice out of the hold. They had but two iron bars and two damaged shovels, yet they planned to throw it out over the larboard bow, to serve as a defense against the floating ice when breaking up, fearing else it might tear the ship to pieces.

On the sixth of April the snow fell deeper than ever it had done before. All their paths to the wood were filled up; its nature was moister than that which had fallen earlier in the season, which was dry as dust, and drove before the wind like fine sand. The weather did not alter until the fifteenth. It was observed by Captain James, that in the clear fine weather he could not see a little island about four leagues off, but if it was misty, he saw it from the lowest ground; this he ascribed to refraction. On the sixteenth, they had a day of comfortable sunshine, and began to clear the snow off the deck of the ship. They made a fire in the cabin, (which it appears the water had not reached,) to dry and warm it. On the seventeenth, they dug down through the ice to get out an anchor which had been in shoal water, and succeeded in taking it up and putting it on board. The next day they tried to dig down to the place near where they thought their rudder might be. They came to the water, but could not meet with what they sought: they judged that, if the ice broke up, there would be no chance of its recovery, as it would be driven to sea with the ice.

On the nineteenth, they continued to mine in the ice, and the master and two men, who had supped on shore, requested that they might be allowed to sleep in the ship's cabin, by which they would escape hearing the groans and sufferings of the sick during the night, who were now enduring intolerable anguish. They labored so hard on board, that by the twenty-first they reached a cask, and could perceive there was water in the hold, which they knew could not arise from thaw, as it then froze hard both day and night in the ship as well as on land. Two days afterwards they were able to get at some beer, which proved good, except tasting a little of bilge water. It greatly refreshed them all, particularly the sick. They now thought the water they had found had stood in the ship all the winter, and that the holes they had cut to sink the ship were frozen up. The following day they found, ongoing to work, that the water had risen above the ice. It had blown hard during the night, and in the morning blew off the land, which led them to hope that the water would fall to its lowest point at ebb tide. They began outside to cut through the ice down to the lowest hole they had made in the ship's bottom. For this purpose they toiled all night, and found the place unfrozen; the water within having fallen to a level with the hole, and without, a foot below it. They secured in their caps, as if in England, trying every mode to keep up their spirits. How dependent the bodily health is upon the spirits in similar circumstances they well knew.

That they escaped with life as they had done from the scurvy, must be ascribed to their bodily exertions. Their diet, especially what they called their porridge, was the very food to promote that disease. It was made of the broth in which their salt beef was boiled. The cook boiled the next night's supper the day before, in a kettle of water, with a quart of oatmeal. The meat in an hour was taken out, and the broth boiled to half the quantity: this must have made it salter and more injurious. They called it porridge, eating it with bread as hot as they could bear. They then took salt fish for the solid part of their meal. Pork and pease made their Sunday's dinner, and the beef, before mentioned, their supper, so that at night they had always something warm, which they felt a great comfort. As might be expected, however, soon after Christmas they were attacked with scurvy. When their mouths became sore, they could eat neither beef, fish, nor even porridge. They were obliged to pound bread or oatmeal in a mortar until it was fine, and eat it fried with oil, or pease boiled to a soft paste. They caught a few foxes in the winter, which they boiled for the sick. Some of the crew were so ill they could not move in their beds, and it was necessary to attend them like infants. Others were crippled by the attacks of the disorder, and all were more or less affected.

The surgeon every morning cut away the dead flesh from their gums, during which they themselves bathed their extremities and legs in a decoction of any herb or leaf they could procure, boiled over the fire. This softened the diseased parts, and though, when they got up, scarcely able to stand, they could then go out and move about. At night it was necessary to bathe their limbs again, and dress their mouths. Such was the state of acute misery they encountered; and, what is more extraordinary, the greater part of them survived. The captain had providently kept untouched a ton of Alicante wine, wisely judging that, in the spring, they would stand in most need of it. Of this mingled with water, although it had been frozen, and was weak, they made a tolerable beverage. The sick had a pint of the pure wine, daily, and also a dram of brandy every morning. No wiser disposal of what little they had at their command could be adopted.

On Mayday they went again to the ship to throw out ice. The next day the snow fell, and it was so cold they were obliged to keep within their house, this unexpected bad weather affected the sick so much, that they grew worse; they could not be taken out of bed without fainting, and animation was often with difficulty restored to them. On the third, those who were able went again upon the ice to the ship. The snow on the land had begun to melt, and was plashy. On the fourth, the captain and surgeon went out, to see if they could shoot wild fowl for the sick, geese and crows beginning to appear; but they were too wild to be approached. On the sixth, the master's chief mate died, and they buried him upon the top of a sandhill, which they called Brandon Hill; his name was John Warden. It now froze again of a thickness sufficient to bear a man's weight.

On the ninth, they had worked so hard in their ship, that they got up five barrels of beef and pork, which they had been compelled to leave on board, and four butts of beer, and one of cyder, which they found to be very good. A day or two after they met with their store shoes, soaked in sea water, but they contrived to dry and use them. They struck down their cables into the hold, and prepared to sink the ship again, if it should be needful when the ice broke up. They could not find that she leaked, though the carpenter still contended that she must do so, from the shocks which she had received. The rudder, however, was still wanting. They were as much as ever the prey of apprehensions by no means calculated to aid their hope of ultimate deliverance.

On Sunday the thirteenth, the weather was tolerably warm, though it froze at night; patches of bare land now began to appear. The next day they commenced putting together the rigging, which had received much damage. They prepared to float the vessel on casks, by passing cables under her, if it should be requisite. A party was sent to kill wild fowl for the sick, who were obliged to manufacture their own shot. They sowed a little spot of ground with pease, hoping to have something green for the sick in a short time. On the eighteenth, to the despondency of all, William Cole, the carpenter, died; he was greatly beloved. Three others of the crew lay expecting death every hour. The carpenter they buried near the master's mate, all who were able to attend following him to his last resting place with heavy hearts. The poor carpenter, despite his illness, had labored until he had got the boat ready for bolting and tree nailing, and the survivors hoped to render her serviceable, if the ship should fail. Her size was twenty-seven feet in length, by ten, and her burthen twelve or fourteen tons. The same evening the body of the gunner, committed to the deep so long before, and at such a distance from the ship in deep water, was found under the gun-room ports, and dug out of the ice, as free from decay as when first committed to the ocean; but the flesh was loose upon the bones. They carried the body and interred it by the carpenter and his comrade. A mournful and depressing scene terminated another week of suffering and privation.

The snow was now rapidly disappearing. There was a high tree, which they called their "watch-tree," growing upon a lofty part of the island. Upon this they climbed, but could not yet see water. Whit Sunday, the twentieth, they kept with due solemnity, and made a meal of wild-fowl. On the twenty-second, they pumped their ship dry. The days became so warm now, that they could scarcely hear the sultriness. Hot glooms came over, but in the nights it froze, so that the alternation was painful, and the sick seemed worse.

On the twenty-fourth, the ice broke all along the bay with a fearful noise, and began to move by the ship, on which they determined to sink her again. They were fortunate enough to recover their rudder and get it on board. The ice now began to drift in heaps along the shore, and on the rocks. The sight was a joyful one to them, and they returned thanks to God for it. They kept the twenty-ninth, the birth day of Prince Charles, (afterwards Charles II) and named the island "Charlton Island," and on the thirtieth, were able to communicate with the ship by means of their boat. The last of May they found some vetches growing, which they picked and boiled for the sick. They got all their rigging ready, dried their fish in the sun, and packed it anew. Except the captain and master, not one of them could eat the salt provisions. It was remarkable that, up to this time, not one of them had been troubled with colds or similar complaints.

June now commenced with snow of four days duration, and the pools out, and the vessels of water in the house, were frozen over. Their clothes, which they had washed and hung up to dry, remained frozen all day long. On the fifth, it blew hard, yet they got up an anchor and cable which had lain in the ice all the winter, and were uninjured. They attempted to hang the rudder; and some of them, venturing into the water to assist, could not endure the cold many minutes without fainting. By the eighth, at night, the ship had again been pumped dry, and at high water was afloat in the dock she had made for herself in the sand. They next proceeded to lighten her, and heave overboard her ballast. The sick, who had been fed on vetches, began to mend so much, that those who could not sit up for two or three months before, were able to move about the house.

Thrice a day greens were gathered, washed, and boiled, and eaten with thawed oil and vinegar; many of them ate nothing else. Herbs were also bruised and mixed with their drink, or eaten raw upon bread. On the eleventh, they succeeded in hanging their rudder. The sea was still frozen as far as could be seen from the watch-tree. The latitude of the island was again observed, and found to be 52° 3′: it is probable that the imperfection of the instruments used in those days may account for the difference in their observations. On the sixteenth, the weather was hot, and the crew went into the ponds to cool themselves, but found them very cold. Flies now appeared of various kinds, with such an abundance of fierce and blood-thirsty mosquitoes, that they were more tormented by them than by the cold weather. Ants in abundance and frogs were observed, but the latter looked so like toads, the seamen were afraid to eat them. No bears, foxes, or fowls were yet seen. On the sixteenth, the wind blew from the north, and they expected a high tide. That day they hove the ship into deeper water, and returned thanks to heaven for their success.

The next day they stowed a good deal of ballast, and on the nineteenth saw open water from their watch-tree, for the first time, by which they expected the breaking up of the ice to take place soon. They now perceived rocks and stones all around them, so that, had the ship not grounded exactly where she did, she must have been destroyed. They toyed their vessel out, and moored where they had anchored the year before. They got their stores on board, though they were obliged to wade to their boat from the shore with them, a tedious and painful operation for men in such a state of suffering. Captain James now made a cross of a high tree, against which he fixed the portraits of the king and queen, carefully wrapped in lead, taking care to add to the usual titles, that his sovereign was king of Newfoundland and of "these territories," and to the south as far as New Albion, and northward to eighty leagues. The captain also enclosed or fastened some other things to the cross, and then, on Midsummer day, they raised it on the top of the hill where they had buried their comrades, taking possession of the territories for his

Majesty's disposal, as a return for the inhospitable, though fortunate shelter it had afforded the survivors a melancholy ceremony as connected with the recollection of the poor sufferers, who now lay unconscious under their feet.

On the twenty-fifth, they proceeded with the rigging of the vessel, while the captain took a musket and one of his company, and proceeded to the watch-tree, intending to make a fire and see if it would be answered by any savage inhabitants of the island, wishing in the event of finding any, to have an interview with them, and if possible obtain intelligence of the geography of the country. In making the fire to the windward of some trees, they caught. The weather had been hot and dry, and the tree in which the captain was, got inflamed at the bottom so quickly, that he was obliged to leap down and run towards the shore, escaping with great difficulty. The dry moss on the surface of the ground burnt like flax. The fire ran along the earth in the manner of a train of gunpowder. The musket and lance carried by Captain James were both burned, and he and his companion were happy to escape with their lives. It continued to increase, and burned furiously, until they could see no limit to its ravages. The powder and stores were immediately got on board, while a sentinel was kept on the hills to watch the progress of the blaze. They took their new sails to the sea side, to secure them. The wind now shifted to the north, and the man set to keep watch over the progress of the fire came running as fast as he could to his companions, crying that the fire was coming hard at his heels.

There was need of no other excitement to urge them to hurry the remainder of their things to the sea. The fire came on with a terrible rattling noise down to their house a full mile in width, but fortunately they had just placed the last of their stores in security, when it seized their house, and in a minute destroyed it. The appearance of the flame was so terrible, that the dogs ran into the sea, and got on the rocks howling. The following night they all slept again on board their ship. Until the twenty-ninth, they were employed in getting the last of their stores on board, and taking in wood and water. They were obliged to take in drift wood, for their tools were now past use. The frame of their boat they cut up, and took on board also. They then built tombs of stones over their dead comrades, carrying about two tons for each tomb, and filling up the middle with sand—a pious but useless employment, yet speaking the honest warmth of their feelings.

By the thirtieth they had rigged and put their ship in order, intending to sail the next day but one, and to spend the first of July, which was Sunday, on shore, to take leave of the Island. The days were intolerably hot, while at night it frequently froze. The mosquitoes were so intolerable, that they were obliged to tear up an old ensign, and make bags of it to put their heads in. On the first of July they adorned their ship in the best way they were able, though no eyes but their own could witness it.

A short account of all the events of the voyage to that day was written, with the future intentions of Captain James as to his course and prosecution of discovery, with a request that any who might find it would preserve it, that thus their toils, sufferings, and endeavors, might be made manifest at home, if they should subsequently perish. They then with their arms, drum, colors, cook and apparatus, went on shore, and marched up to the cross near which they had buried their dead. There they read morning prayers, and then walked up and down until dinner. They found the fire had swept full sixteen miles, the whole breadth of the island, but to the cross or near the dead it did not come, because the spot had no herbage, being a mere sand-hill. They then gathered herbs to boil with their meat, read evening prayers, and when the sun had set, went up to take the last view of the tombs of their companions; on which occasion Captain James composed the following lines, reclining at the time, he tells us, upon the tombs themselves. They are very creditable to his talents, and to the feeling which prompted them. He need not have imagined they would provoke derision, though he hints as much as that he feared they would.

> I were unkind unless that I did shed,
>
> Before I part, some tears upon our dead;
>
> And when my eyes be dry,
>
> I will not cease,
>
> In heart to pray their bones may rest in peace.
>
> Their better parts, good souls, I know were given,
>
> With an intent they should return to Heaven.
>
> Their lives they spent to the last drop of blood,
>
> Seeking God's glory and their country's good,
>
> And as a valiant soldier rather dies,

Than yield his courage to his enemies,

And stops their way with his hew'd flesh, when death,

Hath quite deprived him of his strength and breath,

So have they spent themselves, and here they lie,

A famous mark of our discovery.

We that survive, perchance may end our days,

In some employment meriting no praise.

They have outlived this fear, and their brave ends,

Will ever be an honor to their friends.

Why drop you so, mine eyes? nay, rather pour

My sad departure in a solemn shower.

The winter's cold that lately froze our blood,

Now were it so extreme, might do this good,

As make these tears bright pearls, which I would lay,

Tomb'd safely with you, till doom's fatal day:

That in this solitary place, where none,

Will ever come to breathe a sigh or groan,

Some remnants might be extant, of the true,

And faithful love I ever tender'd you.

Oh, rest in peace, dear friends, and let it be,

No pride to say the sometime part of me.

What pain and anguish doth afflict the head,

The heart and stomach when the limbs are dead!

So grieved, I kiss your graves, and vow to die,

A foster-father to your memory!

There is something singular and touching in a sailor, at such a time, and in such a climate, feeling. the inspiration of the Muse; surely in the connexon of poetry with the human heart there is much that is past all comprehension. They embarked and landed no more on the scene of so much peril, privation, and suffering.

On the second of July they sailed, and touching at another place to take in more wood, anchored until the following day between Charlton Island and an island they had named after Sir Thomas

Carew the year before. They saw much ice about them, as well as rocks and shoals, and continually, until the twenty-second, were in peril from floating ice. The fogs were so thick they could not see out of the ship, and the blows she received often made them go below to see if she leaked. Beating about from one iceberg to another, sometimes enclosed by ice, then struck violently in the bottom by pieces which were detached from the masses under water, and rose to the surface, at length the crew murmured at their toils and sufferings being renewed. They called those who lay buried on the island "happy," saying they would give a thousand pounds to be lying by them. They saw the cape they had named Henrietta Maria: they anchored and erected a cross upon it, with the King's arms. They observed also some deer, but their dogs could not overtake them; they caught a few geese, and, repairing on board, left their dogs behind them as useless.

Their course was as perilous as ever among floating ice. They were driven back beyond the cape again on the thirtieth. The ship had become leaky, and it was necessary to use the pumps. They now gave up going to the northward or eastward. The nights were beginning to grow long, and the sea between the pieces of ice was observed to be frozen. Their perils continued to be very great until the second of August, on which day they were obliged in a fog to make fast to a piece of ice in order to obtain sleep and refreshment.

On the seventh they had a fine day, and on the eighth found themselves in latitude 55° 34'. The ice now again threatened their destruction. They were afraid lest the main body should come upon them and force them on shore. The next day they left the ship without pumping, to examine places which they might again open if it became requisite to sink her. They were now in as much danger as they had ever been, and the bottom where they sailed was rocky. They were unexpectedly extricated from this difficulty by the moving of the ice. Thus they continued to encounter dangers every moment, from fogs and ice, until the sixteenth, when it blew a storm which broke the ice in pieces. They let the ship drive, and on the seventeenth, they got clear, after six weeks hazard day and night.

The year seems to have been one of remarkable severity, and the ice more than usually strong. In July and August, they took blocks of it two feet square, and put them into the sun's full rays in the boat upon deck, where there was also a strong reflection besides the warmth of the ship, and yet it took eight or ten days to melt them. The heat of the sun in those regions is often 90° of Fahrenheit during the short summer. Captain James had never heard of any navigator being so pestered with ice as he was. They were, on the twenty-second of August, in latitude 58° 20', and two days afterwards in 63° 30'.

A storm then came on, and continued during the twenty-fifth, so that they could neither eat nor sleep for twenty-four hours. The weather was cold, when suddenly the sea became smooth. The day after they fell in with ice again, and nearly struck against it. From the top-mast head ice only was visible around them, with a smooth channel of sea between the fields. They were now all desponding. A consultation of the officers was held, and the result was that the shattered state of the crew's health and of the ship, made it necessary to get home as fast as possible. They were then not far from Nottingham Island, in latitude 65° 30'. The weather was very cold.

It was the third of September before they saw the south end of the Island of Resolution. The men could hardly take in the topsails, and they sailed once more among icebergs higher than the mast-head. On the eighth of the month, they took leave of the ice, but it was the twenty-second of October before they reached Bristol, to the last continually crossed by tempests and adverse gales. On examining the ship in which they had been thus preserved to see their native land again, it was found little short of a miracle that they were saved. Her cutwater and stern were torn or beaten away, together with fourteen feet of her keel, as well as a good deal of her sheathing; her bows broken, many timbers shivered within, and under the starboard bend a sharp rock had cut through the sheathing, plank, and an inch and a half into the ribs. Few crews ever encountered greater perils or survived hardships more severe than Captain James and his men. *Constable's Miscellany, or Original and Selected Publications. V.78, 133-181.*

Four Englishmen wreck survivors.

A supplement to this narrative may be found in the relation of John Cornelius of Muniken, who sailed to Spitzbergen (Spitsbergen) on the whale fishery in a galliot from the Texel on 6 May 1646. His deliverance of four Englishmen, "whose sufferings were still greater than those of Captain Albert Raevn, and his twenty seamen," is related as follows:

> Cornelius reached Spitzbergen on the third of June, intending to anchor in a bay of that island, but was prevented by vast fields of ice floating near the land, and was obliged, in consequence, to keep out at sea. He cruised up and down, among the ice shoals, for some time, until he was able to get into the bay and anchor. Seeing two whales further out at sea, he sent his sloop in pursuit of them. While the people of the sloop were watching the motions of the whales, with the view of capturing them, they fell in with a vast ice field, on which, at a great distance, they discovered something white. They took it at first sight for a bear, the arctic animal of that name being white. One of the crew, named Elliot Johnson, who was standing in the sloop with a harpoon to strike the whales, thought by the motion of the object that it could not be a bear, and persuaded the crew to row in that direction. They agreed to do so, and when they got nearer perceived it was a man holding up a piece of rope belonging to the sail of a ship, apparently as a signal of distress.

> They pulled hard towards him, and on coming up found to their great wonder four living men, and one dead body, all Englishmen, and all upon the ice field. They fell upon their knees, and expressed their thankfulness for their deliverance the moment the Dutchmen came up. They were taken into the boat, and carried on board the galliot in the bay. Their story was a dreadful one. These sailors belonged to a vessel which had been lost, and were part of forty-two who had reached the ice in the boat, and also saved some provisions and tools. The commander who was with them, perceiving it impossible for men to live long in such a situation, determined to go on shore, with seventeen of the crew, in the boat, and if possible, endeavor to send aid to them from thence. He set sail, but the weather became bad, it blew very hard, and as no tidings were heard of him anymore, by the people on the ice, they concluded that the boat and her crew had perished.

> Twenty-four had been left on the ice. Their provisions now grew scanty, and being all of them nearly starving, and expecting death

every moment, they dispersed themselves being in hopes to reach other ice shoals, and by chance drift upon the shore, or get taken off by some vessel. What became of the men who left them afterwards they could not tell. Those who were found on the ice field or shoal, cut a great hole in the ice like a cave, and round the entrance placed the pieces they had cut out to form the concavity, as a fence to keep off the wind and spray of the sea. In this cold and dismal excavation, they had lived fourteen days from the time they lost their ship. Four were all that now remained out of forty-two. They who had quitted them could be no better situated, for what hope could be indulged of prolonging life in wandering from one piece of ice to another, and every moment drifting further and further from land, as must have been the case at that season of the year, the ice having broken up for the summer. The seamen saved, it may be judged, were at the last extremity. They were found huddled together on the field emaciated by frost and hunger.

The last article of food which they had consumed was a leather belt, belonging to one of them, which they had equally divided into shares, and wholly eaten up. They were carefully attended by the surgeon of the Dutch ship, notwithstanding which three out of the four died within a few days after they were taken on board. Thus, only one escaped out of the ship's crew, and he sailing to Holland, with the Dutchmen, arrived at Delft, in 1646, and from thence reached England.

Constable's Miscellany or Original and Selected publications, V.78, 197-199.

Shipwreck of the *Dr. Johnson*, 1648.

The narrator of the following shipwreck, as well as the sufferer, was Dr. William Johnson, a chaplain to King Charles II. He embarked from Harwich in the ship William and John, under the command of Daniel Morgan on 29 September 1648. The ship belonged to merchants of Ipswich. The writer does not say where the William and John was bound, but it seems probable that it was to some part of Norway, as that was the destination of the vessel in company, which took them up from the boat.

This narrative is in Dr. Johnson's own words:

"We embarked at Harwich on Michaelmas-day, the twenty-ninth of September, 1648. A dull kind of sadness oppressed my spirits, so that I could not look cheerfully on my friends, at parting, but

I took leave of them as if I had been going out of the world. This seemed unaccountable to me, for I went on a good message—the cause of religion. I had embarked in a stout ship, with a fair wind and a skillful pilot, so that I could not suspect danger. Yet no sooner was I at sea, than I suffered the extreme of shipwreck, the pain of sickness was so great and grievous, combining all human evils, as it seemed, together, that to have been drowned would have been no punishment. One afternoon, about four o'clock, the master of the ship came into our cabin with more than ordinary haste; though he concealed from me the cause, I saw plainly fear and amazement on his countenance. I asked him whether all was well; to which he, like a tender hearted man loth to tell his friend he was near his end, answered "all is well."

His clothes I saw him shift and hasten out again with great speed; I then rose from my bed, and crawling upon deck, beheld a melancholy spectacle; the ship having sprung a leak, was ready to sink. How every man's face was changed with terror! We could hardly know each other! One was at prayers, another wringing his hands, and a third shedding tears; but, after this fit they fell to work, though, as happens in such extremities, all were busy doing nothing. They began with one thing, then went to another, but perfected nothing to accomplish their safety. The master's mate, and a man who had been down to search out the leak, returned with sad countenances, and pale with fear. In faltering accents, they signified that the leak was incurable, that it could not be stopped, and that the water was rushing in so fast, we must instantly perish. They said nothing, however, that we did not read in their visages, where our fate was pictured.

There was no time for consultation; the long boat was hoisted out, and guns discharged as a signal of distress to Bartholomew Cook, the master of a ship in company, only a little ahead. Trusting to relief, we leapt into the boat; but unfortunately, I fell short, and with difficulty got out of the sea; no sooner had I secured myself, than a mariner leapt from the ship upon me, and crushed me down with his weight. This I did not regret, as I should willingly have borne them all to have saved their lives. There was only one person remaining on board, who made such grievous lamentations, that although the ship's sails now lay on the water, and her sinking would have drawn down the boat along with her, we approached and took him in.

We now rowed clear of the ship, when not seeing Bartholomew Cook come to our relief, we began to talk reproachfully of him, as if he were negligent of our welfare; unhappily this honest master drank a deeper draught of affliction, for in that hour he and all his men had perished. Our hopes of safety were small. We were in the North Seas, which are seldom smooth, and at this time a storm raised the waves into mountains. How could we hope to escape in a small and open shallop, when a large ship had not been able to resist them? We were many leagues from shore, wanting a compass and provisions, and night was approaching, nothing was in the boat except a small kettle, which was employed in baling out the water, and three bags of pieces of eight, to the value of 300 Pounds Sterling. Money was then truly proved to be only a burthen of no worth. We betook ourselves to prayers, our complaints were louder than our invocations; but God had compassion upon us, and we descried a vessel making towards the boat.

Unfortunately having only two oars, we could make little effect on the boat, and the sea ran high; we sat with our backs to receive it, but it broke so much over us, that we had difficulty in clearing it out with the kettle. Notwithstanding all our endeavors, we could not reach the ship. She got before the wind, and drove much faster than our little vessel could follow. Thus, having death before our eyes, and at the same time the possibility of relief, increased our distress. A dark night came on, which made us more desperate to reach the ship. The master of her hung out a light, and redoubling our energy, we began to get nearer. Lest he should think we were lost, as the darkness precluded him from seeing us, and therefore make sail, we gave a loud shout whenever we rose on the top of a wave. At length by God's assistance, we drew very near the vessel, and not to endanger our safety from too much haste, resolved to go up the side regularly, and in the same order in which we sat. However, we had no sooner arrived, than all strove to run up at once, and the seamen being more dexterous in the art of climbing, accomplished it in a moment, leaving me alone in the boat. I was now in the greatest danger, for besides a natural weakness in my hands, they were so benumbed with cold and wet, that I was incapable of climbing a rope, though my existence depended upon it.

Nevertheless, I held fast by one which they threw out, with both my hands, to prevent the boat from staving off; and, while doing so, the boat struck three times against the ship's side, owing to the heavy sea, and as often the shock threw me down to the bottom, which was half full of water. Fortunately, the boat did not give way, and two seamen at length came down to assist me up the ship's side, which the weight of my clothes, and weakness, had prevented; a rope with a noose was handed down by one of them, who directed me to put it about my middle; but he began to pull when I had got it over one shoulder, and nearly drew me overboard. Having secured myself, and the boat casting off, I was drawn through the sea, where I had the narrowest escape; for the seamen having neglected to tie the rope, as he afterwards told me in England, it was prevented from slipping, by a knot, which was by chance at, the end, otherwise I must have gone down; I may truly say there was not an inch between me and death. The next pull stunned me against the side of the ship.

When I came to myself the following morning, I found the master's own cabin had been devoted to my service. Though severely bruised, I rose from my bed to make inquiries concerning my fellow sufferers, and found them, contrary to my expectation, overcome with sorrow. Their looks were dejected, and every man brooding over his misfortunes. The truth is, that, having saved their lives, they now had leisure to think of the loss of their goods, though it bore differently on different individuals. For my own part, the losses I then suffered, involved me in debt, from which I have not yet extricated myself. But what grieved me most, was the being deprived of my library, and all my sermons, as also my notes and observations, during my travels abroad, the fruits of many years labor and study. But I was impious to grieve for such losses, when God had so miraculously preserved our lives.

Next day, which was Tuesday, the wind was fair for Norway, whither our ship, which was a how zoner, was bound. About twelve o'clock we came in sight of the coast, rugged and full of rocks; and as we could not reach it during daylight, we designed to stand off and on till morning. We then sat down to a repast. Some of us had taken no sustenance since being at sea, and I myself, having ate nothing for five days, now made a hearty meal.

About ten at night, when we had set our watch and prayed, and then laid ourselves down to rest, the ship, in full sail, struck on a rock with a shock so great that it awakened the soundest sleeper. Though I was ignorant of what had happened, the mariners better aware of the danger, loudly cried, "Mercy! Mercy! Mercy!" I hastened out of my cabin, and, coming on deck, met the master of our own vessel, who while tears streamed down his cheeks, desired me to pray for them, for we should certainly perish. I could not believe the truth of what he said; so falling on my knees, like a condemned person awaiting the stroke of the executioner, I began to pray. But, after having prayed some time, under perfect resignation to death, I wondered that the waves did not overwhelm us. It had pleased God that the ship ran herself so fast between two ledges of rock with her bow over another, that she stood fixed as firm as the rock itself. I immediately rose and pulled off my coat, designing to throw myself into the sea and swim ashore; but the height of the waves breaking against the rocks, deterred me. The stern of the vessel was soon beat in by the sea, which compelled us to retreat towards the bow, when Mathew Bird, the same seaman who had formerly drawn me on board, leapt ashore with a rope in his hand, and held it so securely, one end being tied to the mast, that another seaman got down by it.

In this manner the whole of our company, and some of the Danes who were eight-and-twenty in number, reached the rock in safety. All this time I was ignorant of the means used for our deliverance; but perceiving the people crowd towards the head of the ship, I also repaired thither, and discovered what had taken place. A Dane was then endeavoring to slide down the rope and carry a small leather trunk along with him; but he presently removed his trunk, and desired me to descend. I repaid his kindness by requesting him to do so first, not so much out of compliment, but that I might know how to slide down, as I had seen none go before me. However, I got on the rope, from which I was almost beat by the waves, and came safely to the side of the rock, whence I crawled on hands and feet to the rest who were ashore, I was the last who accomplished this manner of escaping. The ship at this moment began to give way, which the master, who was still on board, perceiving, earnestly implored us to assist him with our utmost endeavors; but she broke up and immediately went down.

Thus was that good man, and four of the mariners drowned. I observed the master, who had a light in his hand, fall into the sea. It was the saddest sight I ever beheld, to see him, who had saved our lives, lose his own. I cannot even now look back upon it without regret. Perhaps, had he not delayed on our account, he might have reached the haven in safety.

We knew not where the rock which had received us was situated; some of the people, before my arrival, had ascertained it to be an island, but uninhabited. We waited the rising of the sun, in hopes of discovering land in the neighborhood. It was a long and melancholy night, for stones make but a hard pillow, besides having thrown off my coat when intending to swim, I was thinly clad. Wandering up and down the rock, I often fell owing to its slipperiness: and wanting shoes, my feet were cut with the sharp stones. This being winter time, the cold I was extremely piercing. At length we found a hole in the rock, which sheltered us from the wind, and then morning broke. During the twilight we flattered ourselves that every black cloud was land; but when the sun rose, we saw nothing except a glimpse of the coast of Norway at a distance. When I viewed the sea and the place, the sight of so many hundred rocks environing us, struck me with amazement.

It was only from God's providence that we had not gone among the breakers during the night, and under full sail, instead of running between the two ledges, which proved an asylum. Had we touched in any other part, we must have instantly perished. Our sole hope of relief was the approach of some ship, from which we might be seen; but of this I thought there was little prospect; for should one accidentally come by day, she would be deterred by the surrounding dangers, from giving us succor: and if she came in the night, she would certainly be wrecked, like our own vessel. Having seen nothing in the course of the whole day, we began to despair; and wanting sustenance to support us, and hardly having clothes to keep us warm, we crept into a hole of the rock, and there rested during the second night.

Next morning, we arose before the sun, and some of our company, searching with their arms in the sea, drew out small muscles, which they ate heartily; and one of the boys brought me a leaf of scurvy grass: but I began to be sick with a feverish complaint, and became so parched with thirst, that I would have given all I had for a draught of fresh water. Trusting that the water which stood in holes would be freshest in the highest part of the rock, I sought for it, but it proved salt: I drank it, however, until my thirst was quenched, though vomiting followed, which I am persuaded preserved my life.

Between ten and eleven we saw a ship in full sail standing towards us, which lifted up our hearts with joy. She came nearer and nearer, and we all ascended to the top of the rock, and waved our hats to show ourselves to the men on board. But they neither approached nor sent their boat to learn our condition, for what reason we knew not. The captain was a Dane, of the same country with our former kind master. As the ship receded our hearts began to fail, and our countenances changed to their former paleness. We conceived ourselves utterly abandoned. We could not suppose, even should another ship by chance come in sight, that the mariners would venture their own lives to save ours; therefore we betook ourselves to our old devotions, and as long as I was able to speak, I prayed with the company. After some exhortation to my fellow sufferers, I lay down on the rock, thinking I should rise no more in this world; but I overheard one of the seamen, he who had first leaped on the rock, say, "Let us make a raft and venture to sea, I had rather be drowned than lie here and be starved. The rest coincided with him, and though the design was full of danger, everything conspired to favor it; the water had at this time fallen, and left the bottom of the ship on the rock, the anchors, mast, and sails, lying also there, like linen on a hedge. The seamen soon broke up the mast, and untwisted a cable for small cords. Next they tied four or five boards to the broken mast, got up the mizen-top-mast, and made a slight stern; then having cut out a small sail, two Danes and two Englishmen embarked on the raft.

A moderate breeze carried the adventurers safely through the breakers, and towards that part, where, according to our supposition, the coast lay. We followed them as far as our eyes could reach, with great anxiety, for the hope of our deliverance rested on their safety; but we did not long remain in suspense, for before night their security was announced by several yawls rowing towards us. They brought provisions likewise, which we little regarded, from our eagerness to get on shore. The rock where we were now situated, was called Arnscare; and by God's goodness, having embarked we reached an island in Norway, named Waller Island by its inhabitants. This island is so inconsiderable, that Ortelius overlooks it in his maps, but, although unworthy to be remembered by him, it ought not to be forgotten by us. There was but one house where we landed, belonging to the parson, an honest Lutheran, whose family consisted of many individuals, all of whom showed us no little kindness. They spoke the Norse language, which I think, resembles the Dutch, for those of us who spoke Dutch, could partly understand them, and make ourselves understood.

When we made a shift to explain our misfortunes to the people of the house, the relation drew tears from their eyes; and whatever provisions they had being now set before us, the seamen soon repaired their long fasting. The ordinary bread of the inhabitants was rye pancakes, and they had beer which was very strong. This reminded me of the English proverb, "A cup of good beer is meat, drink, and clothing; and surely these people thought so, for though at such a cold season, while they had neither stockings nor shoes, they kept themselves warm with beer." Next morning we began to examine each other's finances, to discover what money had been saved from the shipwreck. Suspecting concealment in one of our number, we searched him, and found no less than four-and-twenty pieces of eight, which he undoubtedly stole from our bags in the boat, after our first shipwreck; when every moment we looked for destruction. It was well for us he had done so, for in the second all our money was lost. We remained in the island until Sunday, and in the morning heard our landlord preach, after which he gave us a meal, full of variety in one dish, as beef, mutton, lard, goat, and roots, mixed together, according to the custom here.

We then parted with the good old priest, having returned him many thanks, accompanied with a little money; and travelled to Fredericstadt, a city in Norway on the coast. There we were kindly entertained by the burgomaster, whose chief discourse was in praise of the late Archbishop of Canterbury, though I wonder how he came to know him. Truly we were much indebted to this person, for he not only commanded several persons of the city to entertain us civilly, but gave us some provision at his own charge. Everywhere we experienced great civility, and the people ran after us in the streets to bestow, what we needed, without asking.

Having left Fredericstadt, we repaired to Oster Sound, three or four miles distant, where shipping lay, and laid in as much provision as our stock could afford, into one bound for England. We embarked in the evening. In the morning before making sail, a ship from Lynn, in Norfolk, coming in, was wrecked on the rocks near the harbor. We had not been at sea above two or three hours, when great alarm arose from the ship very nearly striking on a half sunken rock, unseen until almost touching it. But about noon we cleared all the rocks on the Norwegian coast.

A fair wind brought us in view of the English coast, near Winterton, after four or five days sail. There we saw the remains of a shipwreck, and the country people enriching themselves with the spoils. At length having reached Yarmouth Roads we came to an anchor. It began to blow hard, and the ship in driving, nearly ran afoul of a Scotchman. But we brought up again and rode securely through the night. On a signal next morning for a pilot, four men came off from Yarmouth. They demanded no less than thirty shillings to carry me, a single person, on shore, while our whole stock was only two pieces of eight; and although I did long for land, I could not purchase it at such a rate, therefore they were content to take less. But no sooner had I got into the boat, than they rowed up and down to weigh anchors, for the storm during the preceding night, had occasioned many ships to part with their cables.

Nevertheless, they were unsuccessful, and then made for the shore. The landing place was so bad, that four other men awaiting the arrival of the boat, ran up to their middle in the sea, and dragged it on the beach. I thence got into the town of Yarmouth, with a company of people at my heels, wondering at my sad and ragged condition. The host of an inn, with a sign, the arms of Yarmouth, treated me with uncommon kindness, and I hope God will reward him for it." *Constable's Miscellany or Original and Selected publications,* V.78, 200-213.

Wreck of the *Ascension*.

Captain Alexander Shapleigh's account of his voyage to India, and of the loss of the Ascension.

The *Ascension* and *Union* had a quick passage from England to Saldanha Bay. After leaving that bay the *Ascension* lost sight of the *Union* and the pinnace. Having failed to obtain a supply of water at Comoro, Captain Sharpeigh touched at the Island of Pemba, the natives of which place treacherously attacked his men who were engaged in filling the water-casks. On the day after this attack, he put to sea; during the night the *Ascension* touched the ground, but fortunately floated off without sustaining any damage. Next day three small native ships were captured, and some thirty men of their crews were brought on board the ship. These men were seemingly unarmed, but suddenly they with their knives attacked the *Ascension's* crew, for which they were either put to the sword or thrown overboard.

A further supply of fresh water was obtained at some islands in latitude four degrees ten minutes south. Off the Island of Socotra the *Ascension* fell in with a Guzerat ship; in company with this vessel Captain Sharpeigh proceeded to Aden. At that city he was at first kindly entertained by the governor, who, however refused him permission to return to the ship. Finally, Captain Sharpeigh "by a slight", got on board, first having promised to pay customs not only for the goods on shore, but also for those in the ship. This governor insisted on sending Jourdain and Glascock to the Bashaw, from whom they failed in obtaining any redress, and he told them that in future he would not allow any persons to remain in those parts, unless they had the grand Turk's command to him to do so.

From Aden Captain Sharpeigh went to Mocha, where Jourdain and Glascock rejoined him. From Mocha he returned to Socotra, where the *Ascension* lost all her anchors save one. While off that island the pinnace had again parted company from the *Ascension*, being driven out to sea by adverse winds. Having on the 20th of August 1609, sailed from Socotra, the *Ascension* next anchored in a bay some thirty leagues south of Diwe. At that place no pilot could be obtained to carry the ship to Surat. On again setting sail the master shaped his course in accordance with the information which he had obtained at Mocha, from the pilot of a great ship of Surat, and also by a "Plot or draught of the Bay of Cambay", which this same pilot had given him. With frequent use of the lead the *Ascension* ran into 10, 9, 8, and, suddenly, 4 fathoms of water.

The master attempted to carry her across the shoal, but she struck astern, which, though no great blow, carried away the rudder. As she floated off her anchor was let go, which held her for some time; but during the following evening it gave way, when she struck frequently with great force, and began to leak to such an extent that in two hours all hopes of saving her were lost. At midnight, the ship's hold being then full of water, the crew, to the number of 78 persons, left her in two boats, and the wind being fair the next day they fell in with the land. At first, they supposed it was the bar of Surat, but it proved to be that of "Gadavee". There Captain Sharpeigh learned that the pinnace, having entered the river, had been seized by the Portugal's, who "had no other thing save stones for their purchase", for the crew had, in anticipation of an attack, removed all the goods, and thrown the ordnance overboard. "Some 40 miles up the river is the town of Gadavie, where we landed, and were courteously entertained by the governor, and the next day sent us away, fearing the Portugal's to come and take us from time." A journey of two days carried the company to Suratt, where they found W. Finch and three other Englishmen.

They were not allowed to enter the city, but remained in a neighboring village during some fourteen days, after which time the party, except some of their number who had by stealth entered the city, set out for "this place". After travelling for 18 days Captain Sharpeigh and his company reached the city of "Baramportt", where he was attacked by a fever. While he was ill most of the men left him, some for Surat, others for "this place". Upon recovery he set out from Baramportt, having previously obtained a pass from "Caun Cauntt", the king's general in those parts.

On the second day of the journey a cabinet containing the king's letters and some money was stolen: in hopes of recovering this cabinet Captain Sharpeigh returned to Baramportt, but failed to recover it. The general, who was much grieved at his misfortune, gave him a letter to the king, in which mention was made of the loss of the king's letters. With this letter Captain Sharpeigh again started, and arrived in safety at "this place", "where the king at present is not, but within these 20 days will be here, until when I know not how he will takes this loss of ye letters." Captain Hawkins was, by all accounts, in great favor with the king and nobles; the former had granted him the pay of 400 horse (with a promise to increase it to that of 1000), and the privilege of free trade. Should the company determine to trade in the Red Sea, it would, be well to "procure the great Turks Comte and copy of our privileges, or else there will be no trading hither. Ye port must be Mocha, for Aden is a town of Garisone." The commodities of the country are not fit for England; but Indian goods were the same as at Aleppo and Alexandria, only better and cheaper. There must be two factors, one with the Bashaw at Cenaw, the other at Mocha.

Ships for the Red Sea must be at the Cape in March or April, as then the wind is fair for the voyage to Socotra and Mocha. Ships trading in the East must carry out with them pinnaces of force to enable them to embark their cargoes "despite of the Portugal's who ordinarily in the summer lie at the bar, with 40 or 50 frigates, that no boat can go in or out without their license".

Captain Sharpeigh concluded by hoping that judgment on any charges brought against him would be suspended until he returned to England. If again employed he would serve faithfully. There must be greater care for the future in selecting the crews of ships, both of men skilled in mariners' art, and of men of general good conduct.

The Voyages of Sir James Lancaster, Kt. To the East Indies. 1877. 126-130.

Memoirs of Sir Robert Mansel.

Following is a log record of an English officer's encounter with six Spanish gallies in 1602 and of his fight for survival and the ships that he sank with approximate locations. The transcription had to be cleaned up to ease readability.

> This celebrated officer, descended from an ancient and noble family, was the third son of Sir Edward Mansel, knight, by his wife, the lady Jane daughter to Henry, earl of Worcester. He entered early into the sea-service under the patronage of the illustrious lord Howard of Effingham, high-admiral of England. During the expedition to Cadiz, his gallantry attracted the notice of the earl of Essex, who rewarded him with knighthood; and, thence forward considered him as a favorite, appointing him previous to his departure, on the island voyage to the command of the *Mary-Honora*. On his return, he adhered to his former patron the earl of Nottingham, and was frequently employed at sea during the reign of Elizabeth, but more particularly, curtly, for the defense of the coast, a service in which his prudence and intrepidity attracted the admiration of his fellow subjects, and the censure of his enemies.
>
> When, in the year one thousand six hundred and two, he attacked six of the Spanish gallies on their passage to Flanders, sunk three, and dispersed the rest, the Dutch and after them, the French historians misrepresented his behavior. Sir Robert, eager to vindicate his injured honor, drew up a full relation of his conduct, and addressed it to the lord high admiral. Following the example of a naval writer we here present an extract, from what he deems a curious, and authentic paper, to the reader.

On the twenty third of September, being in the *Hope*, and having in my company the *Advantage* only of the queen's ships, which captain Jones commanded, and two Dutch men of war, I rode more than half channel over, towards the coast of France, upon a north-west, and south-east line, myself being nearest that coast, captain Jones next to me, and the Dutch men of war a sea board, and to the westward of him. The small force, at that time present, and with me, remaining thus disposed for the intercepting of the Gallies, having dismissed the Dutch men of war that served under me, upon their own entreaty, to revictual, and trim, and having employed the rest of the queen's ships, upon so especial services, I descried, from my top-mast-heads, six low sails, which some made for gallies, 66 whilst others affirmed them to be small barks that had struck their top-fails, and were bound from Dieppe, towards the Downs. To which opinion, although I inclined most, yet I directed the master to weigh, and stand with them, that I might learn some news of the gallies, which, by your lordship's advertisement sent me, I knew had either passed me that night, or were near at hand, unless the sea had swallowed them up in the storms which had raged three days before.

Having set myself under sail, the weather grew thick, which obliged me to lay some two points from the wind, towards the English coast, left the continuance of that dark weather might give them power to run out ahead of me. About eleven o'clock, the weather cleared, when I discovered them plainly to be the Spanish gallies so long time expected, at which time, with the rest, I plied to receive them, by crossing their fore foot, as they stood along the channel, which they endeavored, until they perceived that by the continuance of that course, they could not escape the power of my ordnance. All this time, these two Ay-boats were between them, and me; and as the slaves report that swam ashore at Dover, they determined, with three gallies, to have boarded each of those ships; and could have executed that resolution, but for the fear of her majesty's great galleon, (as they termed the *Hope*,) whose force that they shunned in that kind, considering the disadvantage that twice six of the best gallies that ever I saw, have by fighting against as one ship of her force, I do as much commend, as otherwise, I do detest their shameful working, in that, full of cowardliness and weakness, they rowed back to the westward and spent the day by running away in hopes that the darkness of the night would give them liberty sufficient to sun the only ship they feared; or that was indeed in the sea, all that time, to give them the cause of fear, I mean between them and Dunkirk, or Newport.

This error only of theirs bred their confusion, as you may perceive by the sequel. For they no sooner began that course of rowing back again, but I instantly made signs for captain Jones in the *Advantage*, belonging to the queen, to come to me, whom I presently directed to repair to Calais Road, and thence to send the alarm unto the army of the States, assembled before Sluys, and to advise such men of war as kept on the coast of Flanders, upon any other occasion to stand off to sea to meet with the gallies in the night, which should be chased by me with my lights in my top-mast-heads and a continual discharging of my ordnance. Captain Jones having shaped his course according to my directions, I gave orders for hoisting, and trimming of my sails, by the wind, to keep sight of the gallies; and the two fly-boats, being still a weather of me, did the like.

Which chance we held, until sun-setting, observing this course following all the day. They being a weather of me, kept their continual boards, that the gallies were always between them and myself being to leeward made such short turns, as I kept all the afternoon in a manner even in the very eye of their course, between them, and the place of their design, ever discharging my best ordnance to warn the *Answer* belonging to her majesty, that said, by my directions, at the Downs, upon important service, as your lordship knows; and the Flemings that were there, having left the sea, upon unknown grounds to me, yet sent from Portsmouth, by the most provident direction of her sacred majesty, to await the coming of the gallies, upon advertisements that her highness received of their being set sail, who else had received no understanding of the gallies, neither came they within shot of them until after night howsoever the reputation of the service is wholly challenged by them..

Having given your lordship an account how this day was thus spent by me, from eight o'clock until the evening and with these only helps, I beseech your lordship to be pleased to understand that with the setting of the sun, I could both discern the ships last mentioned under sail at the Downs, and the gallies to have set their sails, directing their course close aboard of our shore, each of them being out of sight of the other; and my Dutch consorts, by this time to have been left by the gallies to a stern chance. When I perceived them to hold that course which would bring them within shot of the *Answer*, and the rest that were in the Downs, I held a clean contrary course from them, towards the coast of France, to confirm the secure passage they thought to find on our coast, which I continued, until the report of their battery gave me assurance of the gallies being engaged with them. How the battery began, who began it, how it was continued, how ended, and to whom the reputation of the service is due, I leave to be considered by your lordship, by the perusal of the true discourse s following.

The *Answer*, belonging to the queen, which captain Broadgate commanded, as she rid more southerly at the Downs than the *Flemings*, so came the first to the gallies and bestowed twenty-eight pieces of ordnance in them, before the *Flemings* came in, who, at length seconded him with very many shot.

During this battery of ours upon the gallies, which I so term, because they never exchanged one shot at the very first report of the *Answer's* ordnance, I directed the master of my ship to bear up with the south end of the Godwin, with which directions, I delivered my reasons publicly, as I stood on the poop of my ship, namely, that if I stood discreetly in the gallies, before I could recover the place, would either be driven ashore, or sunk, and so there would prove no need of my force; or else by their nimble sailing, they would escape their ships of whom (once getting ahead,) they could receive no impediment; for, there was no one ship, but the *Advantage*, in the sea, that could hinder them from recovering any port in Flanders, or the east-countries, (Sluys only excepted,) unless I stayed them at that Sandhead. Having recovered as near that place as I desired, I stayed at least a quarter of an hour before I could either see the galley, hear, or see any of those ships, 6 their lights, or the report of their ordnance which made me and all my company hold opinion that they had outsailed the *Answer*, and the rest of the lemmings, and shunned light of me, by going a seaboard of my ship, which I so verily believed as I once directly determined to sail for Sluys, with hope only that the preparation which I knew the States had there, would be able to prevent their entrance into that place.

Whilst I remained thus doubtful, or rather hopeless to hinder their recovery of Dunkirk, or Newport, in case they had been a seaboard 6 of me, some of my company decried a single galley plying from the shore, to get ahead of my ship. When she approached within culver-shot, I discharged about thirty pieces of ordnance of my lower and upper tier at her alone; myself, with 56 many others in my ship, saw when her mainyard was shot asunder, heard the report of many shot that hit her hull, heard many of their most pitiful outcries which when I perceived to continue, and instead of making way from me, I forbore shooting and commanded one that spoke the Portuguese language to tell them that I was contented to receive them to mercy; which I would accordingly have performed, had not the other five gallies offered to stand ahead of me, at that very instant, and thereby would have left me, as they had both the first two Dutch ships, and afterwards the *Answer* with the rest of the Flemings, had I omitted any small time of executing the advantage I had of their being on my broadside which as appears, was so effectually employed, (howsoever the night wherein this service was performed, might hinder the particular mention of their hurts,) as none can deny, but that God pleased thereby only to work their confusion.

For, since that time none hath said nor can speak of any one shot made towards them; yet four of them are sunk and wrecked, the fifth past doing the enemy service, and the sixth they are forced to new build at Dunkirk, where (if I be not much deceived,) she will prove more chargeable than profitable if the default rest not in ourselves. The disagreement between the Dutch captains themselves, touching the stemming and linking of the gallies, (whereof one challenged before your lordship, and in many other public places, to have stemmed and sunk two himself,) and the printed pamphlet containing the stemming and sinking of three gallies, gives the reputation thereof to three several captains amongst whom no mention is made of the first; and whereas there are but two in all sunk, I leave to be reconciled amongst themselves and to your lordship, whether that the same of right appertained not to her majesty's ship the *Hope*, in respect of the allegations before mentioned, every particular whereof being to be proved by the oaths of my whole company and maintained with the hazard of my life, with that which followed.

First, as the shooting of the single galley's mainyard; my bestowing above thirty pieces of ordnance, upon that one galley, within less than culver-shot. Secondly, that they in the galley made many lamentable outcries, for my receiving them to mercy. Thirdly, that I would accordingly have received them, but for giving them over to encounter with the other five gallies, which else had left me to a stern-chance. To these reasons, I add the assertion of the vice admiral himself who told me (whatsoever he spoke in other places) that one of the gallies, which he stemmed, had her mainyard shot asunder before his coming on board of her; by whomsoever she was then stemmed, your lordship may judge who ruined her considering she made no resistance by his own report, but by crying to him for mercy. Touching the other galley stemmed and sunk, I have already proved how she (as all the rest) had got ahead of the *Answer*, of the queen's, not named, and the rest of the States men of war with her who challenge the whole credit of this service.

They (as all other seamen cannot deny but that the gallies will put sail all ships, in such a loom gale of wind, and smooth sea as we had that night. The gallies then being quicker of sail than they, how could they, by any means possible, fetch them up, but by some impediment? Impediment they received none, but by my ordnance, which amounted to fifty great shot at those five which came last from the shore, when all the ships were above a mile astern. Some, notwithstanding, out of their detracting dispositions, may perchance, say that the two which were wrecked at Newport, would have perished by storm, although they had not been battered: whereto, although I have speedily answered, first, in showing that they might have recovered any of the places thereabouts before eight o'clock that night, for but for me and then the second time before the morning, had they not been encountered by me alone at the South Sand-Head; yet for further proof that they miscarried by our battery only, I say that if one of the gallies which received least damage by our ordnance, did outlive Friday's storm, continuing until Saturday noon being driven amongst the 6 islands of Zealand to recover Calais, then surely those two (unless they had been exceedingly, torn,) would have made shift to have recovered the ports of Newport, Graveling, or Dunkirk; especially since from of the place where I battered them, they might have been at the remotest of those places, about four hours before any storm began.

But such seemed as their haste to save their lives, as their thought ran of a shore, and not of a harbor. Now that I have delivered unto your lordship the whole and true discourse of this business, I shall forbear to trouble your patience with any farther relation of that night and next day's spending my time (although the same, in her chance, had like to have cost her majesty her ship and the lives of as many as were in her) and conclude with the admiration of their not holding her majesty's ship, nor I, (her unworthiest servant,) and then, and yet by her highnesses grace, and your lordship's favor, admiral of the forces in that place, am not once mentioned especially since the six gallies might safely have arrived before seven o'clock that night at any of the ports of Flanders to the Westward of Ostend. And that the Dutch ships had not come from an anchor in the Downs but for the signs (Signals) they received from me. Then that the force of her majesty's ship, wherein I was, enforced them to keep close aboard the English shore, whereby those ships in the Downs had power given them to come to fight, which fight was begun by the *Answer*, belonging to the Queen.

And lastly, since the gallies escaped their battery and had gotten ahead of those ships above a mile at least and never received any impediment after, but only by me who lingered them (as you have heard,) until the coming up of those ships that challenge to stem them; which being granted, I cannot see how any other credit can be rightly given them (for that stem, I mean,) than to a lackey for pillaging of that dead body which his master had slain. *Biographia Nautica, of Memoirs of Those Illustrious Seamen.* p. 271-280.

The *Exchange*

"The famous and wonderful recovery of the Exchange of Bristol, from the Turkish pirates of Argier," printed in London 1622.

In the year 1621 the first of November there was one John Rawlins born in Rochester, and dwelling 23 years in Plymouth, employed to the strait of Gibraltar by M. Richard and Steven Treuiles, merchants of Plymouth, and freighted in a bark called the *Nicholas* of Plymouth, of the burthen of 40 ton, which had also in her company another ship of Plymouth called the *George Bonaventure* of 70 ton burthen, thereabout; which by reason of her greatness beyond the other, I will name the Admiral; and John Rawlins bark shall if you please be the vice admiral. These two according to the time of year, had a fair passage, and by the 18 of the same month came to a place at the entering of the straits named Trafalgar: but the next morning, being in sight of Gibraltar at the very mouth of the straits, the watch decried 5 sail of ships, who as it seemed used all the means they could to come near us, and we as we had cause, use the same means to go as far from them: yet did their admiral take in both his top sails, that either we might not suspect them or that his own company might come up the closer together.

At last perceiving us Christians, they tell from devices to apparent discovery of hostility, and making out against us we again suspecting them pirates, took our course to escape from them, and made all the sails we possibly could for Terriff, or Gibraltar but all we could do, could not prevent their approach. For suddenly one of them came right over against us to wind ward, and so fell upon our quarter another came upon our luff, and so threatened us there, and at last all five chased us, making great speed to surprise us.

Their admiral was called Callsater, having upon her main topsail, two top gallant sails, one above another. But whereas we thought them all five be Turkish ships of war, we afterwards understood that two of them were their prizes, the one a small ship of London, the other of the west country that came out of the Quactath laden with fig's and other merchandise, but now subject to the fortune of the sea and the captivity of pirates. But to our business. Three of these ships got much upon us, and so much that ere half the day was spent, the admiral who was the best sailor, fetch up the *George Bonaventure*, and made booty of it. The vice-admiral again being nearest unto the lesser bark, whereof Rawlins was master, showed him the force of a stronger army, and by his Turkish name called Villa-Rise commanded him in like sort to strike his sails, and submit to his mercy, which not to be gained nor prevented, was quickly done and so Rawlins with his bark was as quickly taken, although the rear admiral being the worst sailor of the three, called Riggiprise, came not in, till all was done.

The same day before night, the admiral either loath to pester himself with too much company, or ignorant of the commodity was to be made by the sale of English prisoners, or daring not to trust them in his company for fear of mutinies and exciting others to rebellion; set 12 persons who were in the *George Bonaventure* on the land, and diverse other English whom he had taken before, to try their fortunes in an unknown country. But Villa-Rise, the vice-admiral that had taken John Rawlins, would not so dispense with his men, but commanded him and five more of his company to be brought aboard his ship leaving in his bark three men and his boy, with thirteen Turks and Moors, who were equally efficient to over master the other, and direct the bark to harbor: Thus they sailed directly from Argiers but the night following, followed them with great tempest and foul weather which ended not without come effect of a storm: for they lost the sight of Rawling's bark, called the

Nicholas and is a manner lost themselves, though they seemed safe a shipboard, by fearful conjecturing what should become of us at last by the 22 of the same month, they or we, chose you whether (for I would not be mistaken in altering the persons, by either naming the first or the third, or the third for the fifth, but only make the discourse equal, by setting down the business honestly and truly, as it chanced) arrived at Argier and came in safety within the Mould, but found not our other bark there; nay though we earnestly inquired after the same, yet heard we nothing to our satisfaction but much matter was ministered to our discomfort and amazement.

For although the captain and our over-seers, were loath we should have any conference with our countrymen; yet did we adventure to inform ourselves of the present affaires both of the town and the shipping: so that finding many English at work in other ships, they spared not to tell us the danger we were in, and the mischief's we must needs incur, as being sure if we were not used like slaves, to be sold as slaves for there had been 500 brought into the market for the same purpose, and above a 100 handsome youths compelled to turn Turks, or made subject to more wilder prostitution and all English yet like good Christians they bade us be of good cheer, and comfort ourselves in this, the God's trials were gentle purgation's, and there crosses were but to cleanse the cross from the gold, and bring us out of the fire again more clear and lovely. Yet I must needs confess that they afforded us reason for this cruelty as if they determined to be revenged of our last attempt to fire their ships in the Mould, and therefore protested to spare none, whom they could surprise, and take alive but either to sell them for money, or torment them to serve their own turns. Now their customs and usages in both these was in this manner.

First, concerning the first. The Baham had the over-seeing of all prisoners, who were presented unto him at their first coming into the harbor, and so chose one out of every eight for a present or see to himself: the rest were rated by the captains, and so sent to the marker to be sold; where at if either there were repining, or any drawing back, then certain Moors and officers attended either to beat you forward, or thrust you into the sides with goads and this was the manner of the selling of slaves.

Secondly, concerning their enforcing them, either to turn Turk; or to attend their filthiness and impieties, although it would make a

Christians heart bleed to hear of the same, yet must the truth nor be hid, nor the terror left untold. They commonly lay them on their naked backs, or bellies, beating them so long, till they bleed at the nose and mouth, and if yet they continue constant, then they strike the teeth out of their heads, pinch them by their tongue and use many other sorts of tortures to convert them nay many times they lay them their whole length in the ground like a grave and cover them with boards, threatening to starve them, if they will not turn, and so many even for fear of torment and death, make their tongues betray their hearts to a most fearful wickedness and so are circumcised with new names, and brought to confess a new religion. Others, again, I must confess, who never knew any God, but their own sensual lusts and pleasures though at any religion would serve their turns, and to for preferment or wealth very voluntarily renounced their faith, and became renegades in despite of any counsel which seemed to interpret them and this was the first news we encountered with at our coming first to Argier.

The 26 of the same month, John Rawlins his bark with his other three men and a boy, came fast into the Mould, and so were put all together to be carried before the Bashaw, but that they took the owners servant, and Rawlins boy, and by force and torture compelled them to turn Turks: then were they in all English, besides John Rawlins, of whom the Bashaw took one, and sent the rest to their captains, who set a valuation upon them, and so the soldiers hurried us like dogs into the market, where as men fell hackneys in England, we were tossed up and down to see who would give most for us; and although we had heavy hearts, and looked with sad countenances yet many came to behold us, sometimes times taking us by the hand; sometime turning us roundabout, sometimes feeling our brawns, and naked arms, and to beholding our prices written in our breasts; they bargained for us accordingly, and at last we were all sold, and the soldiers returned with the money to their captains.

John Rawling was the last, who was sold by reason of his lame hand, and bought by the captain that took him, even that dog Fila Rife, who better informing himself of his skill fit to be a pilot, and his experience to be an overkeep bought him and his carpenter at very easy rates. For as we afterwards understood by diversee English renegades, he paid for Rawlins but 150 doublets, which make of English money seven-pound ten shilling. Thus, was he and his carpenter with diverse other slaves sent into his ship to work, and employed about such affairs as belonged to the well rigging and preparing the same. But the villainous Turks perceiving his lame hand, and that he could not perform so much as other slaves, quickly complained to their patron, who as quickly apprehended the inconvenience; whereupon he sent for him the next day, and told him he was so serviceable for his present purpose, and therefore unless he could procure fifteen pound of the English there, for his ransom, he would send him up into the country, where he should never see Christendom again, and endure the extremity of a miserable banishment.

But see how God worketh all for the best for his servants, and confounded the presumption of Tyrants, frustrating their purposes, to make his wonders known to the sons of men, and receives his people, when they least think of succored resentment. While John Rawlins was thus terrified with the dogged answer of Villa Rise, the *Exchange* of Bristow, a ship formerly surprised by the pirates, lay all unrigged in the harbor, till at last one John Goodate an English Turk, with his confederates, understanding she was a good sailor, and might be made a proper man of war, bought her from the Turks that took her and prepared her for their own purpose now the captain that set them on work, was also an English renegade, by the name of Rammetham Rise, but by his Christen name Henry Chandler, who resolved to make Goodale master over her and because they were both English Turks, having the command notwithstanding of many Turks and Moors, they concluded to have all English slaves to go in her, and for their gunners English and Dutch Renegades, and so they agreed with the patrons of nine English, and one French slave for their ransoms, who were presently employed to rig and furnish the ship for a man of war and while they were thus busied; two of John Rawlins men who were taken with him, were also taken up to serve in this man of war, their names James Roe, and John Davies, the one dwelling in Plymouth, and the other in Foy, where the commander of this ship was also born by which occasion they came acquainted, so that both the captain, and the master promised them good usage upon the good service they should perform in the voyage, and withal demanded of him, if he knew of any Englishman to be bought, that could serve them as a pilot, both to direct them out of harbor, and conduct them in their voyage. For in truth neither was the captain a mariner, nor any Turk in her of sufficiency to dispose of her through the straits in security, nor oppose any enemy, that should hold it out bravely against them, Davies quickly replied, that as far as he understood, Vile Rise would sell John Rawlins his master, and commander of the Bark which was taken. A man every way sufficient for sea affaires, being of great resolution and good experience and for all he had a lame hand, yet had he a sound heart and noble courage for any attempt or adventure.

When the captain understood thus much, he employed Davies to search for Rawlins, who at last lighting upon him, asked him if the Turk would sell him: Rawlins suddenly answered, that by reason of his lame hand he was willing to part with him, but because he had disbursed money for him, he would gain something by him, and so prized me at three hundred doublets, which amounted to fifteen pound English: which I must procure or incur for endurances. When Davies had certified thus much, the Turks a shipboard conferred about the matter, and the master whose Christen name was John Goodale joined with two Turks, who were consorted with him, and disbursed 100 doublets a piece, and so bought him of Villa Rise, sending him into the said ship, called the *Exchange* of Bristol as well to supervise what had been done, as to order what was left undone, but especially to fit the sails, and to accommodate the ship, all which Rawlins was very careful and indulgent in, not yet thinking of any peculiar plot of deliverance, more than a general desire to be freed from this Turkish slavery, and inhumane abuses.

By the seventh of January the ship was prepared with 12 good cast pieces, and all manner of munitions and provision, which belonged to such a purpose, and the same day hailed out of the Mould of Argier, with this company and in this manner. There were in her 63 Turks and Moors, 9 English slaves, and one French: four Hollanders, that were free men, to whom the Turks promised one prize or other, and so to return to Holland, or if they were disposed to go back again for Argier, they should have great reward and no enforcement offered, but continue as they would both their religion and their customs: and for their gunners they had two of our soldiers, one English and one Dutch Renegado; and thus much for the company. For the manner of setting out, it was as usual as in other ships, but that the Turks delighted in the often bravery of their streamers, banners, and top-sails: the ship being a handsome ship, and well built for any purpose: the slaves and English were employed under hatches about the ordnance and other works of order and accommodating themselves: all which John Rawlins marked, as supposing it an intolerable slavery to take such pains, and be subject to such dangers and still to enrich other men, and maintain their voluptuous filthiness and lives, returning themselves as slaves and living worse than their dogs amongst them.

Whereupon after he had conceited upon the indignity, and reproach of their baseness and the glory of an exploit, that could deliver himself and the rest, from this slavish captivity, being very busy among the English in pulling of ropes, and placing of ordnance, he burst out into these, or such like abrupt speeches: Oh hellish slavery to be thus subject to dogs to labor thus to enrich infidels, and maintain their pleasures to be ourselves slaves, and worse than the out-cast of the world: is there no way of release? no devise to free us from this bondage? no exploit, no action of worth to be put in execution, to make us renowned in the world, and famous to posterity? Oh God strengthen my heart and hand, and something shall be done to ease us of these mischiefs, and deliver us from these cruel Mahumetan dogs. The other slaves pitying his distraction (as they thought) bade him speak softly, left they should all fare the work for his distemperature. The worse, (quote Rawlins) what can be worse? death is the determiner of all misery, and torture can last but a while: but to be continually a dying, and suffer all indignity and reproach, and in the end to have no welcome but into the house of slaughter or bondage, is insufferable, and more than flesh and blood can endure: and therefore by chat salutation which Christ hath brought, I will either attempt my deliverance at one time, or another, or perish in the enterprise: but if you would be contented to hearken after a release and join with me in the action, I would not doubt of facilitating the same, and show you a way to make your credits thrive by some work of amazement, and augment your glory in purchasing your liberty. I prethee be quiet (said they again) and think not of impossibilities: yet if you can but open such a door of reason, and probability, that we be not condemned for desperate and distracted persons, in pulling the sun as it were out of the firmament, we can but sacrifice our lives and you may be sure of secrecy and taciturnity. Now blessed be my Genius, said Rawlins, that ever this motive was so opportunely prefer, and therefore we will be quite a while, till the iron be hotter, that we may not strike in vain.

The 15 of January the morning water brought us near Cape de Gatt, hard by the shore, we having in our company a small Turkish ship of war, that followed us out of Argier the next day, and now joining with us, gave us notice of seven small vessels, six of them being Sattees, and one Pollack, who very quickly appeared in fight, and so we made toward them; but having more advantage of the Pollack, than the rest, and loathe to lose all, we both fetch her up, and brought her past hope of recovery, which when she perceived, rather than she would voluntarily come into the slavery of these Mahumetans, she ran herself ashore, and so all the men forsook her; we still followed as near as we dare, and for fear of splitting, let fall our anchors, making out both our boats, wherein were many Musketeers, and some English and Dutch renegades, who came aboard home at their Conge, and found three pieces of ordnance, and four Murtherers, but they straight way threw them all overboard to lighten the ship, and so they got her off, being laden with hides, and logwood for dying, and presently sent her to Argier, taking nine Turks, and one English Nave, out of one ship, and six out of the less, which we thought sufficient to man her.

But see the chance, or if you will, how fortune smiled on us; in the rising of this Catclaynia, our Turks fell at variance one with another, and in such a man that we divided ourselves, the lesser ship returned to Argier, and our *Exchange* took the opportunity of the wind, and plied out of the Straights, which rejoiced John Rawlins very much, as resolving on some stratagem, when opportunity should serve: In the mean while the Turks began to murmur and would not willingly go into the *Mary Granda*, as the phrase is amongst them: notwithstanding the Moors, being very superstitious, were contented to be directed by their Hoshea, who with us signified a witch, and is of great account and reputation amongst them, as not going in any great vessel to sea without one, and observing whatsoever he concluded out of his divination: the ceremonies he used are many, and when they come into the ocean, every second or third night he made his conjuration; he began and ended with prayer, using many characters and calling upon God by diverse names: yet at this time, all that he did consisted in these particulars.

Upon the sight of two great ships, and as we were afraid the chasing, being supposed to be Spanish men of war, a great silence is commanded in the ship, and when all is done, the company gives as great a scratch; the captain still coming to John Rawlins, and sometimes making him take in all his sails, and sometimes causing him to hoist them all out, as the witch finds by his book, and presages; then have they two arrows, and a curtilage, lying upon a pillow naked; the arrows are one for the Turks, and the other for the Christians; then the witch reads, and the captain or some other taketh the arrows in their hand by the heads, and if the arrow for the Christians come over the head of the arrow for the Turks, then do they advance their sails, and will not endure the fight, whatsoever they see: but if the arrow of the Turks is found in the opening of the hand upon the arrow of the Christians, then will they stay and encounter with any ship whatsoever: the Curtilage is taken up by some child, that is innocent, or rather ignorant of the ceremony, and so laid down again; then do they observe, whether the same side is uppermost, which lay before, and so proceed accordingly. They also observe lunatics and changelings, and the conjurer writes down their laying in a book, groveling on the ground, as if he whispered to the Devil to tell him the truth, and so expounded the letter, as it were by inspiration. Many other foolish rites they have, whereon they do dote as foolishly, and whereof I could entreat more at large, but this shall suffice at this time.

Whilst he was thus buried, and made demonstration that all was finished, the people in the ship gave a great shout, and cried out, a sail, a sail, which at last was discovered to be another man of war of Turks: for he made toward us, and sent his boat aboard us, to whom our captain complained that being becalmed by the Southern Cape, and having made no voyage, the Turks denied to go any further North-ward: but the captain resolved not to return to Argier, except he could obtain some prize worthy his endurances, but rather to go to Salle, and fell his Christians to victual his ship; which the other captain apprehended for his honor, and so persuaded the Turks to be obedient unto him; whereupon followed a pacification amongst us, and so that Turk took his course for the Straights, and we put up Northward, expecting the good hour of some beneficial bootie.

All this while our slavery continued, and the Turks with insulting tyranny set us still on work in all base and servile actions, adding stripes and inhumane reviling's, even in our greatest labor, where upon John Rawlins resolved to obtain his liberty, and surprise the ship; providing ropes with broad specks of iron, and all the iron crows, with which he knew a way, upon consent of the rest, to ram up or tie fast their scuttles, gratings, and cabins, yea to shut up the captain himself with all his consorts, and so to handle the matter, that upon the watchword given, the English being masters of the gunner room, ordnance, and powder, they would either blow them into the air, or kill them as they adventured to come down one by one, if they should by any chance open their cabins. But because he would proceed the better in his enterprise, as he had somewhat abruptly discovered himself to the nine English slaves so he kept the same distance with the 4 Hollanders that were free men, til finding them coming somewhat toward thein, he acquainted them with the whole conspiracy, and they affecting the plot, offered the adventure of their lives in the business. Then very warily he undermined the English renegades, which was the gunner, and three more his associate, who at first seemed to retract: Last of all were brought in the Dutch renegades, who were also in the gunner room, for always there lay 12, there, five Christians, and 7 English and Dutch Turks: so that when another motion had settled their resolutions, and John Rawlins his constancy had put new life as it were in the matter, the 4 Hollanders very honestly according to their promise sounded the Dutch renegades, who with easy persuasion gave their consent to so brave an enterprise; whereupon John Rawlins not caring whether the English gunners would yield or no, resolved in the captains morning watch, to make the attempt: But you must understand that where the English slaves lay, there hung up always four or five crows of iron, being still under the carriages of the pieces, and when the time approached being very dark, because John Rawlins would have his crow of iron ready as other things were; and other men prepared in their several places, in taking it out of the carriage by chance it hit on the side of the piece, making such a noise, that the soldiers hearing it awakened the Turks, and had them come down whereupon the boatswain of the Turks descended with a candle, and presently searched all the slaves places, making much ado of the matter, but finding neither hatcher nor hammer nor anything else to move suspicion of the enterprise, more than the crow of iron, which lay flipped down under the carriages of the pieces, they went quietly up again, and certified the captain what had chanced, who satisfied himself, that it was a common thing to have a crow of iron slip from his place.

But by this occasion we made stay of our attempt, yet were resolved to take another or a better opportunity only I must tell you, what John Rawlins would have done, if this accident had not happened: he was fully minded with some others with their naked knives in their hands, to press upon the gunners breast, and the other English renegades, and either force them to consent to their designs, or cut their throats, first telling them plainly, that they had vowed to surprise the ship, and by God's assistance to obtain their liberty, and therefore either die or consent, that when you hear the watchword given, for God, and King James's, and St. George for England, you presently keep your places and advise to execute what you are commanded.

But as you have heard, God was the best physician to our wounded hearts, and used a kind of preventing physique, rather than to cure us so suddenly: so that out of his providence perceiving some danger in this enterprise, he both caused vs to desist, and at last brought our business to a better period, and fortunate end. For we sailed still more northward, and Rawlins had more time to tamper with his gunners, and the rest of the English renegades, who very willingly, when they considered the matter, and perpended the reasons, gave way unto the project, and with a kind of joy seemed to entertain the motives: only they made a stop at the first onset, who should begin the enterprise, which was no way fit for them to do, because they were no flaws; but renegades, and so had always beneficial entertainment amongst them. But when it is once put in practice, in they would be sure not to sail them, but venture their lives for God and their country. When Rawlins had heard them out, he much liked their contradiction, and told them plainly, he did require no such thing at their hands, but the slaves and himself would first found the channel, and then adventure the water, and so after reciprocal oaths taken, and bands given, Rawlins once again lay in wait for the first opportunity, but once again he is disappointed, and a suspicious accident brought him to recollect his spirits anew, and study on the danger of the enterprise, and thus it was.

After the *Renegado* Gunner had protested secrecy by all that might induce a man to bestow some be lease upon him, he presently went up the scuttle, but stayed not aloft a quarter of an hour, nay he came sooner down, and in the gunner room sat by Rawlins, who tarried for him where he left him: he was no sooner placed, and entered into some conference, but there entered into the place a furious Turk with his knife drawn, and presented it to Rawlins his body, who verily supposed, he intended to kill him, as suspicious that the gunner had discovered something, whereat Rawlins was much moved, and so hastily asked what the matter meant, or whether he would kill him or no, observing his countenance, and according to the nature of jealousy, conceiting that his color had a passage of charge, whereby his suspicious heart, condemned him for a traitor: but that at more leisure he swore the contrary, and afterward proved faithful and industrious in the enterprise. And for the present he answered Rawlins in this manner, no master be not afraid, I think he doth but jest. With that John Rawlins gave back a little and drew out his knife, stepping also to the gunners sheath and taking out his, whereby he had two knifes to one, which when the Turk perceived, he threw down his knife, saying he did but jest with him. But (as I said) when the gunner perceived Rawlins took it so ill, he whispered something in his care, that at last satisfied him, calling heaven to witness, that he never spoke word of the enterprise, nor ever would, either to the prejudice of the business, or danger of his person: Notwithstanding Rawlins kept the knifes in his sleeve all night, and a was somewhat troubled, for that he had made so many acquainted with an action of such importance: but the next day when he perceived the coast clear, and that there was no cause of further fear, he somewhat comforted himself, and grew bolder and bolder in disposing the affairs of the ship, only it grieved him, that his enterprises were thus procrastinated, whereby the Mahumetane tyrannical increased, and the poor slaves even groaned again under the burthen of their bondage, and thought every day a year till something were put in execution for their deliverance: for it was now full five weeks, since Rawlins first projected the matter.

All this while Rawlins drew the captain to lie for the Northern Cape, assuring him, that thereby he should not miss purchase, which accordingly fell out, as a wish would have it: but his drift was in truth to draw him from any supply, or second of Turks, if God should give way to their enterprise, or success to the victory: yet for the present the 6 of February being 12 leagues from the Cape, we descried a sail, and presently took the advantage of the wind in chasing her and at last fetch her up, making her strike all her sails, whereby we knew her to be a bark belonging to Torbay near Dartmouth, that came from Auerare laden with salt: ere we had fully dispatched, it chanced to be foul weather, so that we could not, or at least would not make out our boat; but caused the master of the bark to let down his, and come aboard with his company, being in the bark but 9 men, and one boy; and to the master leaving his mate with two men in the same, came himself with 5 men, and the boy unto us, whereupon our Turkish captain sent 10 Turks to man her, amongst whom were two Dutch, and one English Renegado, who were of our confederacy, and acquainted with the business.

But when Rawlins saw this partition of his friends, before they could hoist out their boat for the bark, he made means to speak with them and told them plainly, that he would prosecute the matter either that night, or the next, and therefore whatsoever came of it they should acquaint the English with his resolution, and make toward England, bearing up the helm, whiles the Turks slept, and suspected no such matter: for by God's grace in his first watch about midnight, he would thew them a light, by which they might understand, that the enterprise was begun, or at least in a good forwardness for the execution: and so the boat was let down, and they came to the bark of Torbay, where the masters mate being left (as before you have heard) apprehended quickly the matter, and heard the discourse with amazement. But time was precious, and not to be spent in disputing, or casting of doubts, whether the Turks that were with them, were able to master them, or no, being seven to six, considering they had the helm of the ship, and the Turks being soldiers, and ignorant of sea affaires, could not discover, whether they went to Argier, or no; or if they did, they resolved by Rawlins example to cut their throats, or cast them overboard: and so I leave them to make use of the Bevegadaes instructions, and return to Rawlins again.

The master of the bark of Torbay, and his company were quickly searched, and as quickly pillaged, and dismissed to the liberty of the ship, whereby Rawlins had leisure to entertain him with the lamentable news of their extremities, and the adventure of their voyages, whereby he understood of his first setting out from the west country, of his taking and surprising at sea by Villa Rise, of his twice being sold as a slave, and so continuing to his heart-burning and excruciation; of the making the *Exchange* of Bristow a man of war, which they were now in; of the captain and master, who were both English Renegadoes; of the cruelties of the Turks in general, and his own fortunes in particular; of his admission into the ship as a pilot; of the friendship which passed between him and the Hollanders; of the imparting the secret of surprising the ship both to the slaves and Christian Renegadoes; of their consent and courageous apprehension of the matter; of the first attempt, and their twice disappointing; of his still resolution presently to put it in practice of his last acquainting the Dutch Renegadoes, who went aboard his bark; and in a word, of every particular which was befitting to the purpose: yea he told him, that that might he should lose the sight of them, for they would make the helm for England, and he would that night and evermore pray for their good success, and safe deliverance.

When the master of the bark of Torbay had heard him out, and that his company were partakers of his story, they became all silent, not either diffident of his discourse, or afraid of the attempt, but as wondering at the goodness of God, and his mercy, in choosing our such weak instruments to set forth his glory. True, quote Rawlins when he found them coming toward him, it is so. For mark but the circumstances of the matter, and you shall see the very finger of God to point us out our deliverance. When we came into the main ocean to hunt after prizes, according to the nature of pirates, and that I resolved on the enterprise, there were 65 Turks in our ship, and only 17 of our confederacy; then it pleased God to abate us 10 of the Turks who were sent to Argier with the Pollaker before recited; and when we were disappointed again of our purposes, you see now what has changed, we are rid of more Turks, and welcome you as a new supply; so that if you please, we shall be 24 strong, and they in all are but 45. Be therefore courageous, and let us enjoy heart, hand, and foot together, that we may execute this brave attempt, for God's glory, our countries honor, the good example of other, our own deliverance, and if we may not be counted vain-glorious, our everlasting memory.

By that time he had finished this discourse also; the master of the bark and his company resolved to assist him, as projecting the misery and wretchedness they should endure by being slaves to the Turks, and the happiness of their liberty, besides the reputation of the enterprise; as for death, it was in community to all men, and so in the hands of God to dispose at his pleasure, and either could not happen before the hour of limitation, or could not be prevented for humane policy must submit to divine providence? yet to show himself an understanding man, he demanded of Rawlins, what weapons he had, and in what manner he would execute the business, to which he answered, that he had ropes, and iron hooks to make fast the scottels, gratings, and cabins, he had also in the gunner room two curtleaxes, and the slaves had five crows of iron before them, besides, in the scuffing they made no question of some of the soldiers weapons: then for the manner, he told them, they were sure of the ordnance, the gunner room, and the powder, and so blocking them up, would either kill them as they came down, or turn the ordnance against their cabins, or blow them into the air by one stratagem or other, and thus were they contented on all sides, and resolved to the enterprise.

The next morning being the seventh day of February the prize of Torbay was not to be seen or found, where at the captain began to storm and swear, commanding Rawlins to search the seas up and down for her, who bestowed all that day in the business, but to little purpose: whereupon when the humor was spent, the captain pacified himself, as conceiting he should sure find her at Argier: but by the permission of the ruler of all actions, that Argier was England, and all his wickedness frustrated: for Rawlins being now startled, left he should return in this humor for the straits, the 8 of February went down into the hold, and finding a great deal of water below, told the captain of the same, adding, that it did not come to the pump, which he did very politically, that he might remove the ordnance. For when the captain asked him the reason, he told him the ship was too far after the head: then he commanded to use the best means he could to bring her in order: sure then quote Rawlins we must quit our cables, and bring 4 pieces of ordnance after, and that would bring the water to the pump, which was presently put in practice, so the pieces being usually made fast thwart the ship, we brought two of them with their mouths right before the byticle, and because the Rengadoe Flemings would not begin, it was thus concluded: that the ship having three decks, we that did belong to the gunner room should be all there, and break up the lower deck. The English slaves, who always lay in the middle deck, should do the like, and watch the scuttles: Rawlins himself prevailed with the gunner, for so much powder, as should prime the pieces, and so told them all there was no better watchword, nor meanies to begin, then upon the report of the peace to make a cry and scratch, for God, and King James, and Saint George for England.

When all things were prepared, and every man resolved, as knowing what he had to do, and the hour when it should happen, to be two in the afternoon, Rawlins advised the master gunner to speak to the captain, that the soldiers might attend on the poop, which would bring the ship after: to which the captain was very willing, and upon the gunners information, the soldiers got themselves to the poop, to the number of twenty, and 5 or 6 went into the captain's cabin, where always lay diverse curtleaxes and some targets, and so we fell to work to pump the water, and carried the matter fairly till the next day, which was spent as the former, being the ninth of February, and as God must have the praise, the triumph of our victory.

For by that time all things were prepared, and the soldiers got upon the poop as the day before: to avoid suspicion, all that did belong to the gunner room went down, and the slaves in the middle deck attended their business, so that we may cast up our account in this manner. First, nine English slaves, besides John Rawlins: five of the Torbay men, and one boy, four English Renegadoes, and two Dutch, four Hollanders: in all 24 and a boy: so that lifting up our hearts and hands to God for the success of the business, we were wonderfully encouraged, and settled ourselves, till the report of the peace gave us warning of the enterprise. Now you must consider, that in this company were two of Rawlins men, James Roe and John Davies, whom he brought out of England, and whom the fortune of the sea brought into the same predicament with their master. These were employed about noon (being as I said the ninth of February) to prepare their matches, while all the Turkeys or at least most of them stood on the poop to weigh down the ship as it were, to bring the water forward to the pump: the one brought his match lighted between 2 spoons the other brought his in a little piece of a can: and so in the name of God, the Turks and Moors being placed as you have heard, and 45 in number, and Rawlins having purloined the Tuch-holes, James Roe gave fire to one of the pieces, about two of the clock in the afternoon, and the confederates upon the warning, shouted most cheerfully: the report of the peace did tear and break down all the Bitickell, and compasses, and the noise of the slaves made all the soldiers amazed at the matter, till seeing the quarter of the ship rent, and feeling the whole body to shake under them: till understanding the ship was surprised, and the attempt tended to their utter destruction, never bear robbed of her whelps was so fell and made. For they not only cat vs. dogs, and cried out, Vsance de Lamair, which is as much as to say, the fortune of the wars: but attempted to tear up the planks, setting a work hammers, hatchets, knifes, the oars of the boat, the boat hook, their curtleaxes, and what else came to hand, besides stones and bricks in the cook room; all which they threw amongst us, attempting till and fill to break and rip up the hatches, and boards of the steering, not desisting from their former execrations and horrible blasphemies and revealing.

When John Rawlins perceived them so violent, and understood how the slaves had cleared the decks of all the Turks and Moors beneath, he set a guard upon the powder, and charged their own muskets against them, killing them from diverse scout holes, both before and behind, and so lessened their number, to the joy of all our hearts, whereupon they cried out and called for the pilots and so Rawlins, with some to guard him, went to them, and understood them by their kneeling, that they cried for mercy, and to have their lives saved, and they would come down, which he bad them do, and so they were taken one by one, and bound, yea killed with their own Curtleaxes; which when the rest perceived, they called us English dogs, and reviled us with many opprobrious terms, some leaping overboard; crying it was the chance of war, come were manacled, and so thrown overboard, and some were slain and mangled with the Curtleaxes fill the ship was well cleared, and our selves assured of the victory.

At the first report of our peace, and hurly-burly in the decks, the captain was a writing in his cabin, and hearing the noise, thought it some strange accident, and so came out with his curtleaxe in his hand, presuming by his authority to pacify the mischief: but when he cast his eyes upon us, and saw that we were like to surprise the ship, he threw down his curtleaxe, and begged us to save his life, intimating unto Rawlins, how he had redeemed him from Villa Rise, and ever since admitted him to place, of command in the ship, beside honest usage in the whole course of the voyage. All which Rawlins confessed, but with all added, the fearfulness's of his Apostle from Christianity, the unjustifiable course of piracy, the extreme cruelty of the Turks in general, the fearful proceedings of Argier against us in particular, the horrible abuses of the Moors to Christians, and the execrable blasphemies they use both against God and men. I will not dwell on his reply, nor on the circumstances of atonement, only I am sure Rawlins at last condescended to mercy, and brought the captain and five more into England. The captain was called Ramtham Rise, but his Christen name Henry Chandler, and as they say, a Chandlers son in Southwark. John Goodale was also an English Turk. Richard Clarke, in Turkish, Lasar; George Cooke, Ramdam; John Browne, Mamme; William Winter, Mustapha; besides all the slaves and Hollanders, with other Renegadoes, who were willing to be reconciled to their true Savior, as being formerly seduced with the hope of riches, honor; preferment, and such like devilish baits, to catch the souls of mortal men and entangle frailty in the carriers of horrible abuses, and imposturing deceit.

When all was done, and the ship cleared of the dead bodies, John Rawlins assembled his men together, and with one consent gave the praise unto God, using the accustomed service on shipboard, and for want of books lifted up their voices to God, as he put into their hearts, or renewed their memories: then did they sing a Psalm, and last of all embraced one another for playing the men in such a deliverance, whereby our fear was turned into joy, and trembling hearts exhilarated, that we had escaped such inevitable dangers, and especially the slavery and terror of bondage, worse than death itself. The same night we washed our ship, put everything in as good order as we could, repaired the broken quarter, set up the biticle, and bore up the helm for England, where by God's grace and good guiding, we arrived at Plymouth, the 13 of February, and were welcomed like the recovery of the lost sheep, or as you read of a loving mother, that run with embraces to entertain her son from a long voyage, and escape of many dangers.

Not long after we understood of our confederates, that returned home in the bark of Torbay, that they arrived in Penance in Cornwall the 11 of February: and if any ask after their deliverance, considering there were ten Turks sent to man her, I will tell you that too: the next day after they lost us, as you have heard, and that the three Renegadoes had acquainted the masters mate, and the two English in her with Rawlins determination, and that they themselves would be true to them, and assist them in any enterprise: then if the worst came, there were but 7 to 6, but as it fell out, they had a more easy passage, then turmoil, or man-slaughter. For they made the Turks believe, the wind was come fair, and that they were sailing to Argier, till they came within sight of England, which one of them amongst the rest discovered, saying plainly, that that land was not like Cape Vincent; yes said he that was at the helm, and you will be contented, and go down into the hold, and trim the salt over to wind-ward, whereby the ship may bear full sail, you shall know and see more tomorrow. Whereupon five of them went down very orderly, the Renegadoes fairing themselves asleep, who presently start up, and with the help of the two English, nailed down the hatches, where at the principal amongst them much repined, and began to grow into choler and rage, had it not quickly been over passed. For one of them stepped to him, and dashed out his brains, and threw him over-board: the rest were brought to Exeter, and either to be arraigned, according to the punishment of delinquents in such a kind, or disposed of, as the king and council shall think meet: and this is the story of this deliverance, and end of John Rawlins voyage.

Now gentle reader, I hope you will not call in question the power and goodness of God, who from time to time hath extended his mercy to the miraculous preservation of his servants, nor make any doubt that he hath still the same army and vigor, as he had in times past, when Gideon's 300 men overcame the Midianites: and many ancient stratagems are recorded to have had a passage of success, even within our memories, to execute as great a wonder as this: nor do I think you will be startled at anything in the discourse, touching the cruelty and inhumanity of Turks, and Moors themselves, who from a native barbarous do hate all Christians and Christianity, especially if they grow into the violent rages of piracy or fall into that exorbitant course of selling of slaves, or enforcing men to be Mamertines. Nor can I imagine, you will call in question our natural desire of liberty, and saving of our lives, when you see from instinct of nature all the creatures of the world come to the law of preservation; and our Savior himself allows the flying out of one city into another in the time of persecution; and Paul by saying he was a Roman procured his delivery. Well then: it is only the truth of the story you are amazed at, making doubt, whether your belief of the same may be bestowed to your own-credit: I can say no more; the actors in this comic tragedy are most of them alive; the Turks are in prison; the ship is to be seen, and Rawlins himself dare justify the matter. For he had presented it to the Marquise, a man not to be dallied withal in their things, nor any way to be made partaker of deceit. Nay, I protest, I think, he durst not for his ears (concerning the substance) publish such a discourse to open overlooking, if it were not true. As for illustration, or cementing the broken pieces with well tempered mortar, blame him not in that: for precious stones are worn enameled, and wrought in gold, which otherwise would be still of value and estimation; but polished and receiving the addition of art and cunning, who doth not account the better, and esteemed himself the richer for their possession? So then; entertain it for a true and certain discourse: apply it, make use of it, and put it to thy heart for thy comfort. It taught the acknowledgment of a powerful, provident, and merciful God, who will be known in his wonders, and make weak things the instruments of his glory. It instructed us in the practice of thanksgiving, when a benefit is bestowed, a mercy shown, and a deliverance perfected. It makes us strong and courageous in adversity, like cordial restoratives to a sick heart, and our patience shall stand as a rock against the impetuous assaults of affliction. It is a glorious sun to dissipate the clouds of desperation, and cheer us thus far, that God can restore us, when we are under the pressure of discomfort and tribulation: for preferment comes neither from the East, nor the West, but from him that holds the winds in his hands, and puts a hook in the nostrils of Leviathan: so that if he do not give way to our contentment, it is because he will supply us with better graces, or keep us from the Adders hole of temptation, whereat if we carry, we shall be sure to be flung unto the death. In a word, it is a mirror to look virtue in the face, and teach men the way to industry and noble performances, that a brave spirit and honest man shall say with Nehemiah shall such a man as I fly? Shall I fear death or some petty trial, when God is to be honored, my country to be served, my king to be obeyed, religion to be defended, the common-wealth supported, honor and renown obtained, and in the end the crown of immortality purchased?

Famous and Wonderful Recovery of a Ship of Bristol, Called the Exchange *from the Turkish Pirates of Argier.* p. 6-43.

Pelham's Narrative of the Eight Seamen of the *Salutation*, 1630.

Edward Pelham shared his experiences in a northern voyage and is more remarkable for the hardships which the unfortunate mariners underwent than other rare accounts. In 1596, the Dutchmen under Barentz and Heemskirk, wintered in Nova Zembla in 76° north, and the greater part of their number returned home, but they had access to their ship and her stores which made life slightly better.

The only resource these seamen had was their own ingenuity fueled by the desire to survive and lived to share their story. They were really at Spitzbergen on the west side, though we now know it as Greenland, in latitude 77° 40' north.

Captain Parry had shown how easy it was to winter in high latitudes in a ship well provided with necessaries, and the Dutchmen had their vessel "the present is therefore one of the most extraordinary instances of preservation shared. It must be granted, however, that the mariners periled, some of them had been men of sound judgment, from the steps they adopted to guard against cold and famine, as may be observed during the narrative. They yielded not to despair, but determined to meet the danger by corresponding efforts, and if they perished, to die with the reflection, that human prudence had done its utmost for self-preservation."

In 1633, seven Dutch sailors, left in Mayen's Island in 71° or 72° north, provided with a hut and most things they required, perished of cold. The truth seems to be, that the real nature of the evils with which man has to cope in these high latitudes was not understood in those days. Scurvy and excessive cold seem to be the two terrible enemies they had to combat. Yet a store of lemon-juice and moderate exercise would have prevented the first, and burying their hut, as the Esquimaux do, under a few feet of snow on its first setting in, contriving a passage with an angle in it through the snow, and covered in with a thick snow roof also, would have enabled them to bear the cold, especially when keeping up a good fire. These resources were unknown to the Dutchmen. The English seamen, who built one hut within another, perhaps unwittingly, hit upon the best mode that could be adopted, of warding off the external cold. How they succeeded in escaping the scurvy does not so well appear. That these things are true, may be learned from a sort of preface to the relation of Pelham, wherein he says that, while the Dutch had bread, beer, and wine, (he refers to those who wintered in Nova Zembla, in 1596 and 1597, and reached Holland alive,) victuals and clothes, the English seamen had filthy whale fritters, bears, and anything they could get. With the bears that the Englishmen killed it was frequently a question who should be master.

The Dutch had coals, and baths, and wine, and though they complained that the nails they used stuck to their flesh from the cold, the Englishmen were forced to keep two fires to prevent their mortar freezing while they used it. The Dutch complained that their hut walls were frozen two inches within side; the Englishmen state theirs were not so, from their pains and industry in building them, which they seem to have managed with great skill, making them in fact double. If the Dutchmen's clothes froze upon them, it was owing to their own ignorance, from not knowing how to manage to prevent it under their circumstances. The Englishmen were farther to the north, but the reason Pelham gives, that they had abler bodies than the Hollanders, is hardly satisfactory; the real truth was, they had a vast deal more sagacity. In comparing the two narratives, and seeing the conveniences of one party, and the privations of the other, the conclusion in every enlightened mind must be, that superior instruction and knowledge, or both, were on one side, and these are not only strength, as is commonly remarked, but safety.

The names of the seamen who were left in Greenland nine months and twelve days were, William Fakeley, gunner; Edward Pelham, gunner's mate (the narrator); John Wise and Robert Goodfellow, seamen; Thomas Ayres, whale-cutter; Henry Bett, cooper; John Dawes and Richard Kellet, landsmen. The foregoing eight men were in the service of the Muscovy Company of merchants, and sailed in the *Salutation* of London, for Greenland, on May-day, 1630. They arrived at their destination on the eleventh of June, moored their vessels, and got ready their boats for the fishery. There were three ships in company; they were to remain together until the fifteenth of July, when, if they did not succeed according to their wishes, they were to separate. Two of the ships were then to sail, one about eight leagues off, where whales resorted in great numbers, another to Green harbor, a place about fifteen leagues to the southward, while the *Salutation* was to remain at the Foreland until the twenty-sixth of August. They now appear to have sent out their boats to fish; and the captain of the *Salutation*, having succeeded to his wishes, ordered a boat to direct the ships to a place called Bell Sound, that they might take in train oil. They would thus be more united by sailing in company, and better able to secure themselves from capture on their return, the privateers of Dunkirk being on the look out to capture the returning whale-ships.

On the eighth of August, they set sail to the south-ward, in order to make Green harbor, and take in some men belonging to the ships, who were on shore there. The wind blew contrary, and the ship could not make way. On the fifteenth of the month, upon a calm and clear day, the ship being about five leagues only from a place noted for good venison, the master sent ashore eight men with two dogs, a matchlock, two lances, and a tinder-box, that they might hunt deer for the ship's provision. They succeeded in killing fourteen deer, the weather being fine and favorable. They were now tired, and ate their meal, agreeing to rest where they then were for that night, the next day to hunt again, and then go on board. But the following morning was thick and foggy; the ship, from a southerly wind coming on, was obliged to stand off to sea, and was not in sight. The weather continuing the same, they agreed to hunt along the shore towards

Green harbor, where they expected to find their ship. They killed eight deer more, loaded their boat with the venison, and reached Green harbor on the seventeenth, where they found their ship gone, together with the twenty men who had been left there. Knowing the ships were short of provisions, they wondered at the cause of their departure, but there was no help for them at that place. The time had arrived, within three days, when the vessels usually left the coast. The seamen now thought it best to get to Bell Sound, where they imagined they should find the ship. To lighten their boat they hove the venison into the sea, and proceeded as rapidly as possible towards the spot they intended to visit, about sixteen leagues off. They were compelled to lie to in a cove, owing to the thickness of the weather, from the night of the seventeenth, until noon on the eighteenth, when they again steered, as they supposed, for Bell Sound, but overshot it at least ten leagues to the southward. They now, judging they were wrong, returned northward, and the weather clearing up, they saw the top of the mountains, yet one of the boat's crew insisted they were wrong, contrary to those who judged better, and by his influence the boat was again put round to the southward.

This was on the twentieth of August, and they now began to feel what miseries they must endure if they were left behind. They ran as far to the southward as before, and at last providentially discovered they were again in error. Vexatious as it was thus to be delayed, when every moment was of so much importance, they put the boat's head to the northward again; an easterly wind sprung up, and hoisting a sail, they ran so swiftly before it, that the next day they made Bell Point, and soon entered the sound, but no vessels were there. Their prospects were now gloomy indeed. The shallop was secured, and two of the party went in vain, over land, to see if the ships were at a place called the Tent. They next searched for them at Bottle Cove, three leagues on the other side of the sound, without success. All now seemed to be hopeless. They had neither pilot, chart, nor compass. Their fears, as they reasonably might do, now grew stronger. They debated whether it was best to stay where they had now landed, or to set sail. The ice was an obstacle to the latter step; yet at Bottle Cove nothing could be expected but a lingering and painful death, for the place was no way habitable. The minds of these unfortunate men were now terribly distracted. They felt they were alone upon a spot where man had never dwelt; where winter was a scene of darkness, horror, and desolation, only to be imagined by those who had witnessed its frightful aspect approaching, on board the last of the whale-ships. They had heard that the merchants had offered great rewards to those who had expressed a willingness to remain a winter in that climate, to pay them handsomely, furnish them provisions, and all the necessaries required, and yet that, when it came to the point, none would encounter the hazard the boldest spirits had shrunk from the undertaking.

Even condemned criminals had preferred returning home to execution, rather than venturing on perils which they had volunteered to meet, and which, in the present day, have been encountered with so little danger. It cannot be wondered, that these reflections among themselves, if they were little calculated to allay their fears at the view of their situation, made them more cautious in their conduct, and more inclined to exert a resolute perseverance in the measures to which they were ultimately indebted for their safety. They saw all and much more than the dangers they must dare, but they met them like men. What most affected them, was the fate of nine men left in the same place before, and by the same barbarous master who had now left them behind. The poor fellows had all perished miserably. This had happened at Bottle Cove, where they now stood like men overcome with their calamity, and not knowing what to do.

They looked into each other's faces with an expression of pity, at the inevitable end of him whom they beheld. They considered their destitute state, the want of everything necessary to keep themselves alive during the approaching winter, lacking even clothing and every kind of shelter. Silent they stood for a short time, as if combating inwardly with their despair. At length they reflected that what little hope remained for them, must perish by delay, and that they must endeavor immediately, or not at all. Their passage to England was now out of the question. They wisely determined to shake off all fear. God having given them the hearts of men, they determined to be resolute, and resist despairing thoughts. They agreed to go to Green harbor, and to hunt venison for their winter's subsistence. On the twenty-fifth of August, they set sail for Green harbor, and in twelve hours reached it in safety. They landed, and made a sort of tent with the boat's sail spread upon their oars, designing, after taking sufficient rest, to set out hunting. They rose early and steered in their boat for a place called Cole's Park, well known to one of them as abounding in deer. It was about two leagues distance. There they killed seven deer and four bears that day, after which, the sky not looking favorable, they returned to where they had slept the night before, rigged up their tent again, and spent the night.

The next morning, the weather being fine, they left two of their number behind, to cook their provisions, and returned to their hunting ground. On their way, seeing deer feeding on the shore, they landed, and killed twelve in the whole, when it began to rain and blow, and they determined to return to their tent, and proceed no farther. The following day the weather would not admit of their hunting again. They therefore loaded their boat with bears and venison; and finding a second boat, which was drawn up to be ready for the whalers the next season, they loaded that with greaves of the whales, which had been left in heaps on the ground, by the last ships, and dividing themselves into two companies, manned both boats, and set out for Bell Sound, at which place they intended to winter, in a building used by the whalers, and called the "Tent." They there purposed to lay up their present stock, and then set out again to hunt more, that they might be under no apprehension on the score of their winter-provision. Night came on them before they could get ready to set out, and the following day being Sunday, they determined to do no work, taking the best mode they could to show their devotion to the Almighty, though Bible or book of prayer they had none.

On the Monday they arose early, but from foul weather they could only get half-way to Bell Sound, before the evening came upon them; but they lay to in Bottle Cove that night, going on shore and anchoring their boats in the cove. In the night the sea blew right into the cove, owing to a south-west wind; the grapnel that secured the boats came home, and both were driven on shore, so that their stock of provisions was part wetted, and part beaten out of the boats into the sea. This was a fearful accident at such a time. The only hope upon which depended their lives was well near being lost, or rendered unfit for food. They got through the surf to the boats; got a hawser on shore, and with a purchase, by main force heaved them upon the land. They then collected such of their provisions as had been washed out of the boats. They determined not to venture afloat again, until the weather would allow them to go over to Bell Sound.

On the third of September, they launched their boats, and reaching their destination in safety, secured their provisions, taking them into the shed called the Tent, already mentioned. This shed or house, in which they designed to winter, was built very substantially of beams and boards, and covered with Flemish tiles, having been formerly erected by the Flemings at the time their ships came thither. It was eighty feet long and fifty broad. The coopers, of the whalers used to live and work in it, while they made the casks for holding the train oil. The weather now began to change; the nights lengthened, and the frosts set in upon them. They were afraid to venture by sea upon another hunting excursion, lest the Sound should freeze up and prevent their return. On land, the country was so mountainous, there was no travelling that way. They therefore deemed it best to remain at the "Tent," and provide for the coming winter. They determined with great sagacity and sound judgment to build themselves an apartment within the large house or tent, close to the south side of it. A smaller house had been built for other laborers from the whalers, hard by the large one already mentioned. This they took down.

With the materials they proposed to build that which they had resolved upon, within the large building, by which means their walls would be double. The materials thus obtained furnished them with deal boards, rafters, and posts, while the chimney furnaces used for boiling the whale oil, supplied them with bricks. They found three hogsheads of fine lime hard by, and knowing another was stored up at Bottle Cove, three leagues off, they fetched home that also. This lime they mixed with the sea-sand and formed excellent mortar for laying their bricks, but the weather was already so cold they were obliged to keep up two fires to prevent their mortar from freezing. Two of the party employed themselves in raising a wall a brick thick against the inner side of the large shed, which was of wood. While these two were thus employed, others were bringing in bricks or cleaning them, some at the same time were making the mortar, or hewing the boards intended to be used. Two hands at the same time flayed the venison, so that all proceeded together, as fast as it was possible, a plan reflecting great credit upon the judgment of these men. There were only bricks sufficient for two of the walls, and a few to spare. The other two walls, within the large building, they built of boards nailed close together, upon stanchions a foot in depth, the space between they filled up with sand, and it was found so tight, that not a breath of air passed through to inconvenience them. The chimney they made about nine inches wide, and four feet long, opening into the large building. Their apartment thus ingeniously constructed, was twenty feet long, by seventeen wide, and ten high.

The ceiling was composed of deal boards doubled five or six times over the joints of those beneath, the middle of one board pressing on the joining of two beneath, so close that no air could enter. Their door they lined with a bed, which they found in the place, lapping over the opening and shutting of it. They made no windows, but removing two or three tiles in the roof of the outer building directly over their chimney, it gave them all the light they thought it needful to admit while they had the sun in the horizon. They next built up four cabins, to hold two in each cabin, and made their beds of deer skins dried, which they found very warm and comfortable. Their next object was to provide themselves with firing. For this purpose they examined the boats which had been left on shore by the whalers, and finding seven of them too crazy to be used the ensuing year, they broke them up, and stowed them over the cross beams of the outer house, in the manner of a floor, to prevent any snow which might drive in between the tiles, from getting into the outer shed, and incommoding them when they wanted to reach any of their stores, which were laid up there.

When the weather began to get colder, and the day almost to disappear, they stove some empty casks which had been left behind by the shipping, and used several other things for fuel, always endeavoring to injure, as little as possible, anything which would be of service during the ensuing fishing season, for they could easily have rendered abortive the next year's voyage, by any wanton waste. They determined to husband their stock of fuel, as they seemed still to have one too small for the long and cold season which had just begun. They also hit upon the expedient, at night when they raked up their fire and it had a good quantity of ashes and embers, to place in the midst of it a piece of elm wood, and after it had been sixteen hours thus covered up, they found in it a good body of fire and heat. By this means their fire never went out for eight months, and they found it a plan of great economy in fuel.

On the twelfth of September, drift ice came floating into the sound, on which they espied two seahorses, a young and old one asleep, and taking an old harpoon iron which they found in the shed, they fastened a grapnel rope to it, and launched their boat in pursuit. Approaching warily, they struck the old one, and secured it. The young one, unwilling to abandon its parent, was also killed. This was a fortunate addition to their stock of provisions, with which these two animals were speedily placed. A third was captured on the nineteenth of the same month. The nights now began to be so long, and the weather so cold, that there was little hope of their getting any addition to their provisions, unless a chance bear might stray near them. They therefore took a survey of their stock, and found it not more than half the quantity which they estimated they should need. They therefore agreed to stint themselves to one reasonable meal a day, and to keep Wednesdays and Fridays as a sort of fast, upon the loathsome greaves of the whale, which are the scraps of fat flung away after the oil is extracted; this mode they pursued for three months. ·

They had now done all which human prudence could suggest in their situation to provide for their future wants. The coming time appeared dismal and gloomy enough to them. Their clothes and shoes were nearly worn out, and they endeavored to repair them with rope yarn for thread, using whale-bone needles. The sea was frozen over by the tenth of October, and the cold was so severe, that it might bend down the boldest spirit. Now came the moment of trial, when they could be no longer active, and they were to be left to the reflections and imaginations of a situation where solitude was rendered more painful by idleness, and the mind, no longer employed in casting about for the means of preservation, was flung back upon itself. Their heads were filled with a thousand troubles and complaints. Their wives and children appeared before them in affliction, at their supposed unhappy fate. Some had parents, whom they fancied to be broken-hearted at their doom. Thus they in their leisure intermingled their apprehensions and bewailing, until hope would for a time again revive, and a prospect of surviving and returning home would cheer them. At one time they would complain of the conduct of their master, who had left them to their fate, and then they would find excuses for him, imagining he and his ship had been lost among the ice, and even lament his miserable end. At length tormented in this manner, and suffering from cold and privation, they seemed on the point of giving way to despair. They endeavored with some success to resist their grief, and they supplicated God for strength and patience to bear their miseries. Soon they would cheer up again, fancying their prayers were heard, and determine to use the best means in their power to prolong their lives.

They now apprehended their firing might fail them before the winter was over, and they every day roasted half a deer, which they stowed away in hogsheads, leaving only so much in a raw state, as would furnish them a quarter every Sunday, and also one for Christmas day. This employment finished, again they began to dwell upon their miseries and their hardships, that, though they were preserved, they must still be as banished men bereft of all society. They thought of the hunger they might have to sustain, and in examining the greaves of the whale they had in store, discovered they were most of them injured by the wet they had taken from the sea water, having grown moldy. Their bear and venison they found would not allow them so much as they had before estimated, so that they could only feast upon it three days a week, and were obliged to eat the spoiled greaves the other four, or go without food. They had now no more light from the fourteenth of October to the third of February, the sun did not appear above the horizon, though the moon shone as bright as in England both day and night, except when, during the thick and dark weather, which was frequent, she could not be seen.

The day which had seemed to glimmer for eight hours in October, did not appear at all from the first to the twentieth of December, and prior to that time, the light had shortened with great rapidity. From the twentieth of December to the first of January, a little white glare appeared in the south, but no light, though, on the first of January, the day seemed to approach. The darkness rendered the times of day and night uncertain. Pelham tried to keep an account in his mind, by first recollecting the number of the epact. He then made his addition by the supposed, though uncertain daylight, from which he judged the moon's age; and this enabled him to make a rule for the passing time. He was so correct as it happened, that, on the arrival of the ships in the next whaling season, he told them the day of the month correctly. The continual darkness became so irksome to them, and the time hung so much heavier on their hands, that they endeavored to find means of preserving a light. A piece of sheet lead which they found, they shaped into three lamps, rope-yarn serving them for wicks. Train-oil they found in sufficient quantity in the outer building, left by the ships. These lamps they kept constantly burning and they found them a great relief in their dreary situation. Yet all could not secure them from desponding thoughts at times. They accounted themselves dead men, and their hut the dungeon where they awaited their doom. They would burst out into repining at their state of suffering, and in their impatience arraign the causes of their misery. Then their consciences would tell them it was in consequence of their own former loose lives, and that they were either reserved as examples in their punishment, or else to be objects of divine mercy in their deliverance. Then they fell to prayer, and humbling themselves two or three times a day. The same course they followed during the whole time of their confinement in the hut.

When the New Year commenced, they found the cold increase so much, that at last it raised blisters on their skin, and on touching iron, it stuck like bird-lime to their fingers. When they went out to fetch water or snow, the cold would so chill them, that they felt as sore as if they had been beaten. Until the tenth of the month of January, they found water issuing out of an ice cliff, in a hollow near the sea shore, which they obtained by digging through the surface of the ice with a pickaxe. When the cold became too intense for this, they had recourse to snow water, which they melted by putting red hot irons into it, and this they were obliged to do until the end of May.

At the end of January, the days were several hours long; this enabled them more conveniently to survey their stock of victuals, when they found, to their dismay, it could not last them more than six weeks longer. They now began to dread that they were reserved to perish of famine, and they saw no hope of relief. On the third of February, they once more beheld the sun, the day was fair, clear, but exceedingly cold. The tops of the lofty mountains near them once more reflected the glorious beams of the orb of day. The bright appearance of the light upon the dazzling white of the snow filled their hearts with the liveliest joy; "it seemed enough," they said, "to revive a dying man." By this welcome light they perceived a bear and her cub approaching the tent. They took their lances, the bear rushing upon them angrily, and they succeeded in destroying her very quickly: the cub, on seeing the fate of its dam, fled. They were driven into their hut by the cold, and obliged to warm themselves before they could cut up the animal. This served them for twenty days provision, and they found the flesh better than their venison. Some of them, however, ate the liver, after which they observed that their skins peeled off. Still they were afraid of being straitened again before the ships should arrive from England.

The bears, however, continued to visit them, and they were fortunate enough to kill seven. One of these, which they dispatched on the tenth of March, was of enormous size. They flayed and roasted them upon wooden spits, for their only cooking utensil was a frying pan, which they had found in the hut. Having now so good a stock of provisions, they ate two or three meals every day, and found their strength and spirits increase. The season soon became more cheerful. One of their two dogs left them on the sixteenth of March, and never returned, having perhaps been devoured by bears. The wild fowl that resorted to the coast in spring to breed, and feed on the small fish, began to appear, and the foxes to come forth from the holes in which they burrow, and remain during the winter. The fowls being the food of the foxes, the seamen prepared three traps, baited with their skins, having caught some of these birds on the snow, where they had fallen and were unable to rise on the wing again.

In these traps they caught fifty foxes, which they found good food, and with another kind of trap they captured sixty of the fowls, so that they were no more anxious about provisions. On the first of May the weather got so much warmer, that they were able to go to a distance in search of their food: they met with nothing until the twenty-fourth, when they saw a fat buck, which their dog, from his idle life during the winter, could not hunt down, he being grown fat and lazy. They succeeded in getting about thirty bird's eggs, but the cold coming in again suddenly, prevented their obtaining more.

The twenty-fifth of May, the cold being very severe, they were obliged to keep in their hut all day. They had been accustomed after the fine weather commenced to go frequently to the top of a mountain, to see if they could discern the water of the sea; the outermost ice had broken up and been carried away, but the sea was still three miles out from the shore near the hut, when it was last observed. The very day they thus remained in their hut, two vessels from Hull entered the Sound. The master well knew that the men had been left there the year before, and was anxious to discover if they were alive. He sent his boat from the ship, with orders, in case they could not reach the shore, to haul up the boat on the ice, and walk over it to the hut or tent. These men saw the boat belonging to the seamen in the tent, and that it was prepared for sea the moment it was practicable, being dragged down to the water for that purpose. The sight of the preparations inside made them think, though they could not at first believe it, that those they came in search of were alive. They took the lances out of the boat, which had been put there with the intention, when the owners could go out, of searching for sea-horses. The sailors newly landed came towards the tent without being perceived by its inmates, who were just about to go to prayers. They hailed it with a seaman's "Hoy!" and were answered with a "Ho!" which startled them, and made them halt, not crediting their senses. The men from the inner hut now appeared, in tatters and black with smoke.

The Hull men were yet more amazed at the, uncouth figures they cut; but soon recognizing them for comrades, they went into their dwelling, drank a glass of water, and eat some of the venison cooked four months before. The seamen now accompanied their old friends to the ship, where they remained until the London fleet came. They were impatient for news from their friends and relations, and their inquiries were earnest and reiterated respecting them. After fourteen days' nursing and good treatment on board ship, they grew perfectly well. Four of them went into the vessel again that had left them behind, the captain of which, notwithstanding their sufferings, treated them unkindly.

Pelham, from whose narrative the present is taken, remained in the vessel they first boarded, commanded by William Goodler; and leaving the coast of Greenland on the twentieth of August, reached the Thames in safety. The Muscovite Company treated them very kindly on their return home, as the feat they had performed was almost without precedent. *A History of Shipwrecks and Disasters at Sea,* Volume I, p. 112-133

Account of Captain Norwood.

Captain Norwood was a member of the royalist party during the time of Charles I. This account paints a horrific portrait of what starving desperate people will do to survive:

He engaged with other royalist officers to embark for America, seeing the affairs of the crown were not likely to amend, and that the monarchy existed no longer. He agreed in the year 1649, to meet two other officers who were royalists, and to arrange their immediate departure from England. A great many had already embarked for the colonies in different parts of the western world, and the captain with his two friends fixed upon Virginia for their residence. Captain Norwood was nearly related to Sir William Berkeley, the governor of that colony for the king, of whom it is handed down, that, reporting on the state of things in Virginia, he wrote, "I thank God there is no free schools, or printing here, and I hope we shall not have either, these hundred years." It was in the month of September, that Captain Norwood and others took their passage in a vessel called the *Virginia Merchant*, of three hundred tons, and thirty guns. He and his friends agreed, for six pounds sterling each, to be transported to James River, in the colony already mentioned. On the fifteenth of the month, they met the ship at Gravesend, and having gone through the necessary forms previous to the embarkation as passengers, and paid their money, they posted to the Downs.

On the twenty-third, upon the vessel's coming round, they embarked at Deal, and in three days had cleared the Channel. They had a prosperous voyage for twenty days towards the Western Islands, where they designed to touch. The cooper first began to complain that they were short of water, there not being enough to last out the month for the number of three hundred and fifty souls, which were on board. This occasioned great alarm in the ship, and the master thought it necessary to consult his officers on so fearful a situation. They were now, according to their calculation, off, or very near the Western Islands, and expected to make Fayal, where they might replenish. The passengers were all rejoiced at the thought of seeing the land. At day-break, on the fourteenth of October, they saw the peak of Fayal, the most conspicuous in the Atlantic, except that of Teneriff, with which seamen are acquainted. They soon made the harbor, and on anchoring, were speedily invited to dine on shore, by the English merchant's resident there. They refreshed themselves with the fruits of that delightful island; but they lost their long-boat, owing to the neglect of the sailors, who got drunk, and lay up and down in all quarters, in a very bad condition. The loss of the long-boat was a most serious inconvenience to them. In their revels they drank the two kings, of Portugal and England, although the latter was an exile, and cannon were fired in honor of the occasion. The sailors who were on shore continued their carousing, and water was got into the ship very slowly. The consumption of liquors on board made great havoc with the stock.

On the twenty- second of October they sailed from Fayal, with a store of pigs and fruit to supply them at sea. The wind was easterly a topsail breeze which carried them into the trade wind; and they swept along at the rate of fifty or sixty leagues a day, until they made the Bermudas. In this latitude the seas were often stormy. The officer on the watch pointed out a water-spout to Norwood, which he seems to have viewed with thankfulness to God's providence, that it did not "hoist the ship out of her own proper element." The passengers and crew were equally pleased at the sight of land. The latter knew it by the true bearing from Cape Hatteras, and they all hoped to put their feet soon again upon dry land. The weather was fair until the eighteenth. The water was then observed to change color. They hove the lead, and found thirty-five fathoms, at which they were glad, having consumed almost all the stock on board. It was about break of day that Captain Norwood visited the watch in charge of the mate, whose name was Putts. The captain offered him some brandy, which he refused, unless he could have tobacco with it: he observed it was break of day, and that he would see what change there was in the water. No sooner had he looked, than he called out to the sailors, "All hands aloft! Breakers, breakers on both quarters!"

The seamen sprang to the deck in a moment, but when they saw how the ship lay, they desponded and fell on their knees. The captain, who came on the first alarm, was as much dismayed as his men. The mate was a stout-hearted sailor, and instead of remaining still, called out, "Is there no good fellow who will stand to the helm and let go a sail?" Yet of all the crew, only two foremast men dared from fear to obey the command; one was named Thomas Raisin, the other John Smith, sailors of undaunted courage. One went aloft and loosened the foretopsail; the other stood to the helm, and shifted it at the critical moment, for the ship was in the very act of dashing among the breakers to the starboard. This was the more remarkable as the vessel was generally noted for not feeling the helm. She now fell off from the danger manfully. On the larboard bow was another rock ready to receive her. By this time the crew were ashamed of their dastardly behavior, and taking heart from the examples of Raisin and Smith, went to work, when the ship fell off again and escaped this new peril. Daylight showed them the full hazard of their situation. Breakers surrounded them, and the sea was white with the foam of the raging water. There did not seem to be any channel among the rocks by which the vessel could be worked out of the labyrinth in which she was involved. There was no time for deliberation, and in these miserable circumstances the ship struck, though fortunately only on a sand-bank. The water and sand rose together in foam, and fell into the vessel; yet though there seemed but little hope, the sailors were now all under command, and omitted nothing which could contribute to their preservation.

The ship still floated, and appeared to go ahead-most cheering circumstance. Raisin, the man who before displayed so much activity, seized the helm, and afterwards hove the lead. After a little further progress, beyond their most sanguine hopes, there was still more water than the ship drew; and it began to deepen, the lead showing twenty feet. They kept the vessel in this channel, until the light was strong enough to enable the quarter-master to con her. At last they got clear of the formidable breakers of Cape Hatteras, and stood out to sea. No sooner was the ship clear of the rocks and in the offing, than the seamen surveyed each other for a moment, like so many ghosts, in silence and wonder. They seemed to doubt whether they were really in safety. They shook hands with each other as if they were strangers, or had just arisen from the grave, and met they knew not how. They could scarcely believe that they were still in an existence of flesh and blood. When they recovered themselves, they made from the land with all the sail they could carry. But they had only escaped one danger to get into another. A storm from the north-west now came on to blow with great violence. They left the land behind them, at the rate of eight miles an hour, with the fore-courses only set. It was soon thought necessary to slacken their way. The ship was ordered to be put about, the sails to be furled, and to try with the mizzen. The sea ran so high that the sailors were puzzled how to put about the vessel, yet they were running at such a rate off the land, that it was absolutely necessary to control the rapidity of their course.

They lowered the main-yard to ease the mast, but found it difficult to handle the foresail, as all hands were not strong enough to haul home the sheet to bring the vessel round. They shipped several heavy seas, and one broke with such violence aft, that a ton of water at least entered the round-house. The noise was like the report of a cannon, as it struck the deck, and put the passengers in terrible fear.

The ship was at length got about, and they lay trying under their mizzen. Porpoises in immense numbers now appeared around the vessel, so that the oldest seamen on board declared they had never seen so many. They are generally supposed to be the forerunners of a storm, though in the present instance Captain Norwood observes the tempest was raging at the time they were first noticed. The ocean was covered with hissing foam. The wind appeared to rise still higher, so that the officers began to think they could not be long without some disaster in the rigging. Between ten and eleven o'clock a crash was heard aloft, and the cry that the fore-topmast had come by the board. It had indeed been carried away, and with it had broken off the foremast head, just under the cap. The crew were now in great straits. Putts, the mate, had the watch at the time, and apprehended that worse damage must soon follow. Between twelve and one the following morning, a tremendous sea broke into the ship forward, and so deluged the deck where the mate happened to be walking, that he retired aft with prayers on his tongue. He imagined that the ship was on the point of foundering. The blow seemed to be a stroke of death to the vessel, which remained stock still with her head in the wave, and then seemed to bore her way through it, and free herself. The passengers, men, women, and children, took leave of each other. A melancholy cry was heard throughout the ship, from the apprehension of immediate death. The mate, however, seeing that the water cleared away from the deck, called all hands to the pumps.

Upon examining the mischief which had been done by the sea, it was found that the forecastle, six guns, all the anchors but one, which was bent to the cable, together with the two cooks, of which latter one was miraculously saved, were carried overboard. The breach made forward for the sea to enter, opened a passage to the hold for the water. All on board who were able set to work to construct a platform of wood that would keep off an ordinary sea, to render the vessel as secure as it was possible to do in such distressing circumstances. In fact the storm cut out sufficient labor for all who were able to work every hour in the twenty-four. The bowsprit got loose, having lost the stays and rigging, so that they were obliged to cut it away. The stays of all the masts were gone, and, the shrouds loose and useless. The main-topmast, it was next seen, would not stand long; and Raisin, still the most active fellow on board, ran aloft with an axe to cut it away, hoping to save the mainmast by that means. The danger of the operation seemed so clear to those below on deck, that he was called down urgently. He was scarcely on the deck, when the mainmast and topmast came down at once, and fell into the sea to windward. Fortunately no one was hurt by their fall. The mast was still attached to the ship by the shrouds, and struck her like a battering ram at every motion of the waves. The rigging, therefore, was with difficulty cut away, and the mast set free. In this state several of the seamen fell overboard. Their loss was the less regarded by those who were safe, as they expected the same fate. The mizenmast was now left, by which alone they could hope to bring about the ship, whenever it became needful.

Two days were passed in this distressing state, the tenth and eleventh of November. On the twelfth they saw an English merchant vessel, which showed his flag, but avoided speaking, fearing he might be compelled to lend assistance, as his force in guns was the weakest. He fired a shot to leeward, and stood away. It was now absolutely necessary to bring about the ship. The sailors were exhausted from toil and want of rest, and for some days had been unable to get their meals. The passengers had no appetite, but all were likely to fall short, for the bread was wetted by the sea; the cook-room was carried away, so that nothing could be dressed as usual, and they were compelled at length to saw a cask asunder, fill the half of it with ballast, and thus make a hearth to parch peas and boil their salt beef between decks. This was executed with difficulty, for the whole apparatus was often upset, to the great grievance of those who were in expectation of satisfying their hunger.

On the seventeenth of the month the sea grew calmer, and they saw several English vessels, none of which, save one which was in as bad a condition from the storm as themselves, and felt a community in misfortune, would speak with them. The vessel which accosted Norwood's ship lay to, for the boat which paid him a visit. The master of the stranger proposed that he should be spared hands to aid him at his pumps, in lieu of other things he might give in return. He promised to keep in company, and, if possible, to take the *Virginia Merchant* in tow to weather the cape; but he disappeared in the night, forgetting his promises, although he was bound to the same port.

On the thirteenth of November, the weather being fine, they thought it a good opportunity to get the ship about with the mizzen. This they succeeded in effecting, but the next consideration was how they should make sail. The foremast, as high as to where it had lost its cap, still remained, and it was necessary that a yard should be fixed to it. The difficulty was to climb the bare and greasy stump, for there was nothing of which to take hold for support in ascending. The ship's crew were at a loss, until Tom Raisin, who was apparently a genius born with great resources, undertook to make the attempt. The passengers, to encourage him, promised to present him with a stock of Virginian tobacco upon their arrival in port, should they be so fortunate as to reach it in safety. They set down on paper the proportions each would bestow on the gallant fellow, and many of them were not nice as to the quantity, for they never expected to reach the place of payment. Raisin selected from the ship's stores half a dozen spike nails. He drove one of them into the mast as high as he could reach. He next took a ten-foot rope, and threaded a block with it, which divided it equally. He then made both ends of the rope meet in a knot over the spike. The block hanging on the opposite side of the mast served for a stirrup to stand in for driving the next spike, and so on until he was as high as he wanted. He was careful to strike with his hammer at the time of the smoothest sea. He soon managed to receive help from others of the crew, and they got up a yard and tackle in a few hours, so as to be able to carry sail towards their destination. The main-yard, which they had lowered at the commencement of the gale, was now made to serve the purpose of a main-mast, being lashed to the stump, which still remained eight or ten feet above the deck.

They, not without difficulty, contrived to rig their masts with spare top-sails. The sea grew still calmer, and all seemed to promise well. The crew indulged a hope of seeing the capes, and making their destined port in safety. They now fell in with another ship bound to Virginia, which promised to remain near them. They endeavored to get to the weather side of Cape Henry, thinking they were to the southward of Cape Hatteras; but they found, by an observation, that they were carried by a current to windward, far beyond all their reckoning or allowances for sailing; in fact so far, that when they thought they were to the southward of the cape, they were in reality to the north of Achomack, according to their mate, whose opinion no one was capable of disputing. He averred, that if the wind remained as it was, there was no doubt they would all dine the next day within the capes. This expectation was the more agreeable as their water was again nearly gone, their meat spoiled and useless, and only a biscuit a day per head, and of that not enough to last much longer. The mate fancied he saw the usual landmarks, being hummocks of trees, of which his twenty-third voyage had given him, as might be supposed the capacity of judging rightly. The error was afterwards discovered, and was a sad disappointment.

Had their sails and rigging been in a sound state, the mischief might have been of less importance: both capes were in sight, but the ship would not lie within eleven or twelve points of the wind, and they were compelled to run from the land which they were so eager to make, and a short time previously so certain among themselves of making in a few hours. There was only an allowance now of half a biscuit to each person on board, five of which made a pound. Of drink there was none except Malaga wine, which inflamed their thirst. Towards night the wind grew fresher, and they were carried away at a swift rate of sailing; the mate Putts being much cast down at the consequence of his error. For days and nights together the wind set them out to sea so rapidly, that they were at least a hundred leagues from the capes before they could settle what should be done. They tried every method, by the help of top-gallant sails, and little masts wherever they could be fixed, to keep to windward; but for want of bowlines and tackle to force the sails stiff, the wind would at times take them and rend them in pieces. The ship would then be tumbling about on the ocean until they were repaired.

For not less than forty days they were tossed about after they had lost the land. On the nineteenth of November the wind shifted to the eastward, but came back again in a short time to the north-west. The sea began to run high. They feared the guns would break loose when the ship rolled, while they mended the sails, the lashings being rotten. They at last were enabled to get rid of this fear by moving them into the hold. By placing them, too, thus lower in the vessel, she had a tendency to lie steady in the water. They got a little rain water for drink, but for provisions they were in a famishing condition. In a week they had run two hundred leagues to the east. There were differences of opinion among the crew upon the subject. Some thought they had gone a good deal to the south, and recommended the making Bermuda. In the midst of a contrariety of opinion, it was at length resolved to make any part of the American coast they were able to fetch, even if it were as far to leeward as New Fagland. In the meantime hunger began to press heavier than ever upon both crew and passengers. The women and children made the ship resound with their cries and complaints.

The rats which were caught were all eaten, and the price of one on board was sixteen shillings. One woman, far gone with child, offered a man twenty shillings for a rat, which was refused, and the poor creature died.

Miserable days were thus passed until Christmas came, which, according to the custom of the times, must needs be kept with merriment amidst the most depressing calamity. They scraped and ransacked their meal-tubs to compose a pudding. Malaga sack, sea water, fruit and spices well fried in oil, were the luxuries with which the officers and passengers regaled themselves, and upon which the crew looked with longing and greedy eyes. Captain Norwood says, that the greatest suffering he experienced was from thirst. At night in his slumbers he dreamed of nothing but overflowing cellars and their contents, in which he imagined he was refreshing himself, and the effect of which in his waking moments he found very prejudicial by tantalizing his fancy. The captain had a small store of claret in secret, of which he made Norwood a partaker, but it wanted the qualification of water to quench the thirst; notwithstanding which, it was a very great refreshment.

One day the captain took Norwood into the hold to seek a draught of fresh water in the bottoms of the casks. They found just enough to satisfy their longing, though it was so thick as hardly to be palatable. They then got astride upon a butt of Malmsey, and swallowing some of it found it preferable to the water, and the effect on Captain Norwood was cordial and beneficial. The captain became more gloomy, trembling for his position, and then, confessing how much he felt for having been the means of bringing so many into trouble by a false confidence in the goodness of his ship, he burst into tears. Captain Norwood comforted him as well as he could, and recommended that they should rely upon Providence, and hope for the best. They were now making for the nearest land, and suffering much from hunger, fatigue, and thirst. In eight days they got once more into soundings, and on the fourth of January saw the land, but in what latitude none could tell. The persons who should have kept the reckoning had neglected the duty for some days. The sun had not been seen a good while. The desperate situation in which the vessel had been, and the little hope they had of reaching the shore, together with the idea that they must very quickly render up an account in a different state of being, made them neglect both log and journal.

One day, about three in the afternoon, they were fairly set in for the shore; the weather was calm and the sea smooth, the land was seen about six miles distant, and they had twenty-five fathoms of water. They had only one anchor on board, which was not let go, because if it were lost there was no chance of saving the ship, in case an absolute necessity for its use should arise, and moreover the cable was too short for such a depth of water. The necessity of the crew and passengers was so great, that it was at length agreed the ship should lie to, and a boat be sent off to examine if there was a harbor for anchoring. Twelve or thirteen of the more sickly on board, one of whom was a Major Morrison, embarked in it, determined to risk any chance on shore, rather than remain longer in the vessel. In a short time the boat returned with the tidings of there being a creek where the ship might anchor, and also fresh water, whereof a bottle was brought to the vessel. There were also plenty of fowls observed, which would serve for food. The captain was eager to save the lives of the remaining passengers; and not relying wholly on his mate's report, he set off for the shore himself with Captain Norwood and a few others to examine the spot. As night came on, they saw the fires of those on shore, which guided them to the place. The weather was very cold. As soon as they landed, they rushed to the water, as if it were the most delicious beverage they had ever tasted. They then shot a duck, which was cooked and eaten on the spot. They found a bed of oysters hard by, some of which made an agreeable addition to their repast. The duck was soon devoured, the head, legs, and entrails, being given to the cook as his share. The captain now examined the water on the bar of the creek, and seemed satisfied of its depth.

When day broke, though he appeared determined to come in and anchor, he still wanted Captain Norwood to go back with him to the ship. The latter replied that he did not see any necessity, as the ship would so soon be in herself. Borrowing a coarse cloak of one of the party, Norwood remained behind, and the captain re-embarked. No sooner had the boat pushed off, than the ship was seen under sail with all canvasses spread. This it is probable the captain had noticed when he asked Norwood to go with him. The vessel had set sail without orders from the captain, who had difficulty in getting on board; and but for the mate, who saw the boat from the tops, and got the seamen to lay by until it came alongside, the captain would have been abandoned as those on land were, and probably to a worse fate, words cannot paint the anguish and horror of the party left on shore in this unforeseen manner. They were without food or necessaries of any kind, and they had not the slightest shelter. They consulted together on their miserable condition without being able to determine on anything. They prayed Heaven to have mercy upon them, and finally requested Captain Norwood to be their leader, and to advise them in what was most likely to contribute to their preservation. It fortunately happened that Captain Norwood's Dutch servant had saved from his own wants a hoard of thirty biscuits, which he had starved himself more than he need have done, to preserve for an hour of yet more pressing want. They were in a bundle he had put into the boat when his master came on shore. Captain Norwood divided them into nineteen portions, being one for each individual on shore.

It was now the fifth of January, and the weather was severely cold. The whole party considered that nothing but death after protracted misery was before them. Each man was mustered with a fowling-piece who had ever been accustomed to its use; and powder and shot, which had fortunately been brought on shore, were delivered to each, by which means some geese were killed that day for their supper. In the mean time Mr. Francis Cary, the cousin of Captain Norwood, was sent to explore the creek, and see if he could discover any Indians or other inhabitants, from whom it was likely the wants of the party might be relieved. It was possible they might find enemies, and in that case it was resolved to sell their lives as dearly as possible. Cary returned in no longer time than an hour's absence, with the unfortunate intelligence that they were upon a small island. He had seen no traces of natives, and the water between the island and the main was deeper than his head, as far as he could observe. The fowls of the air were the only living things he had seen. This melancholy intelligence filled them with dismay, as it well might, and they with difficulty kept themselves from utter despair. The likelihood of perishing by a lingering death was considerably increased; they were wholly without food. Cary now disappeared from among them, and no one knew where he was gone. In a little time he came back with a quantity of oysters in his hands, which he found by accident in the bed of a current, contiguous to a large bank of the same species of shellfish.

These oysters were the main subsistence of the party; though, while the cold weather remained, great quantities of wild fowl frequented the island, many of which they killed and roasted upon sticks, devouring every part of them but the feathers. As the weather grew warmer, the number of these fowls diminished, and then they were compelled to subsist upon oysters alone. They also met with a sort of weed, about five inches long, and thick like a house-leek, that they boiled with a little pepper, of which they happened to have a brought on shore about a pound, and then with five or six oysters it became occasionally a kind of feast to them. They erected huts to shield themselves from the weather, and made one for every six. There were three weak women among their number. The endeavors of the party to procure food were unremitting. One morning, Captain Norwood killed a great number of small birds called "oxeyes" in the country, which afforded the party a banquet, but these birds soon afterwards disappeared, and hunger again pressed upon them. All their efforts were directed to spin out their miserable lives a little longer, for they had a presentiment that famine was to close their career, and that what they had hitherto obtained towards supporting their existence was but a feeble means of protracting that which was inevitable. A spring-tide and heavy rains for a time made the oyster bank less accessible, and they began at last to grow so weak, that they could hardly tear away the oysters from the bank when they were able to reach them. All the birds they could see began to get shy. Their guns were soon out of order, and their powder damp.

One of the women died, and the other two were constrained to feed upon her remains. Four of the men died about the same time; and their bodies, horrible to relate, became the chief subsistence of those who survived. The deceased had perished of hunger, but death was hastened by a severe storm of cold attended with snow. Those who were still alive suffered greatly from its effects. It was now an effort of labor almost past the power of the strongest to collect fuel sufficient to keep a fire, without which they must have very quickly succumbed. Captain Norwood took off his cloak and made it a sort of screen against the wind, having found it necessary to move to some more sheltered spot than that where they had at first taken up their quarters. Behind the cloak a portion of the number were huddled together: those who could not be thus accommodated suffered more severely, for want of some similar security. With a fire having two or three loads of wood upon it, they could not keep themselves warm. On one side even their clothes were scorched, while on the other they were frozen. They now considered what could be done to give any of them a chance of ultimate safety. Some of them, though they still retained more vigor than others, were not adequate in strength to struggle with the difficulties of their situation much longer.

The being cooped in a small island seemed to deprive them entirely of hope. Major Morrison, who was one of the main props of the party, could no longer stand on his legs. Captain Norwood was still in the enjoyment of tolerable strength, and he could think of no other plan than attempting to swim the creek between the island and the main land. The water was not more than a hundred yards across; and having passed it, he thought, by coasting the woods to the south-west, he might meet with Indians who would either relieve or destroy him. Death at their hands would be better than dying of famine. The party agreed, upon deliberation, that it was the only rational scheme which could, in their circumstances, afford any hope of relief. The enterprise was desperate, and so was the present situation of the party.

It was now the thirteenth of January, and they had been nine days on the island, in the open air, for their huts excluded neither wind nor rain. They had been landed from a vessel where they had endured hunger, thirst, and fatigue, for several months. A last effort it was therefore necessary to make. They gathered as many oysters as would fill two quart bottles, to be boiled in their own liquor, and given to Captain Norwood for his travelling stock. Everything was ready for setting out on this forlorn adventure, and the cooking of the oysters was nearly effected, when Cary, who had been out rambling, declared that he saw Indians on the main land. Captain Norwood set out, but could not get a glimpse of any, and treated the matter as some deception of Cary's sight, thinking that what he wished, he had fancied or persuaded himself he actually saw. Captain Norwood now returned again to the task of completing his cookery, and had filled one bottle, when he was tempted to go out with his gun, hearing the noise of geese. He had the good fortune to shoot one without a witness, and determined to eat it alone, hoping to be so much the stronger for swimming the creek in consequence. He therefore hung the goose on a tree, while he went to call the cook to dress it secretly: from him the head, bones, and entrails, would have secured secrecy. When the captain came back, he found all the bird but the head was carried off. This, as he learned afterwards from the Indians, was done by foxes or wolves, which abounded in the island. The loss was looked upon by the captain with a sad heart, and, with a hungry stomach, he was obliged to return to the cooking of his oysters.

On the tenth day of his being on the island, all was ready to begin the journey, when a canoe was found lying on the south of the island, and it was soon found that the Indians had discovered the women's hut in the night, and had given them shell-fish to eat. The men had, as already observed, removed to some distance from the spot where they had been quartered at first, in order to be less exposed to the cold; the poor women, it would seem, had remained. They said that the Indians pointed to the south-east, but they did not understand their signs, and only thought that they intended to intimate they would come again the next day. This intelligence respecting the Indians gave the suffering party new life. Many had lain down in despair, determined they would rise no more. They now began to think of the best mode of receiving the Indians on their arrival; and it was agreed that each man should have his gun by his side, loaded, and rendered fit for use, so that if the Indians showed themselves inimical, which was not very probable, their lives might be disposed of as dearly as possible. In this way did every eye look out keenly for the strangers.

When the sun was in the south-east, each man looked through the avenues of the woods in hopes to see them approach. The sun came to the south, but they were not seen; and then the sufferers were tortured with doubt and uncertainty, in a manner impossible to describe. All the forenoon they watched; those who were able going out as scouts to try and discover them in vain. The necessity of their case increased their anxiety. They felt too deeply that their doom depended on the appearance of the Indians-it was the last stake for life. To swim the creek in the severe cold which then prevailed was a dangerous experiment in respect to life, yet Captain Norwood began again to think of it. It was between two and three o'clock in the day when the Indians appeared from behind a tree, without arms, and with kind countenances. There were men, women, and children, who all appeared to pity the wretched situation of the English, shaking hands with them heartily. They repeated frequently the word Nytop! which was thought to have a friendly signification, and in fact to mean "My friend." Beyond this they could not understand each other, and their interview was a mere jargon of unintelligible sounds. They then gave the English ears of Indian corn, to satisfy their hunger for the moment. The Indian women, in particular, seemed to feel deeply for the sufferings of the emaciated beings before them; and one of them presented Captain Norwood with the leg of a swan, which he remarked he thought the best, because it was the largest, he had ever seen.

The Indians remained two hours, and parted with the promise, as well as signs could be understood, that they would come again on the following day. They pointed to the sun, to indicate the hour of two in the afternoon. Some ribbon, and a few similar articles which Captain Norwood happened to possess, were presented to the chief. They then pointed again at the sun, and took their leave, having left a sufficiency of Indian corn and bread to supply the calls of appetite among the party, which did not see them go away without regret. The next day these charitable Indians came again, men, women, and children, bringing bread and corn enough for all: many of them asked for beads and a few similar things of those who had brought them on shore, and they were given to them freely. Those who had none to give in exchange, received food from these kind Indians without any return. One of them, an old man, applied to Captain Norwood by gestures, as if he wished to be informed of what country Norwood and his friends were. Signs in reply were given, but both parties were equally unintelligible to each other. At last the captain recollected having read that 'werowanee', which the old man had frequently pronounced, meant king in English. Speaking the word to the old man emphatically, seemed to please him, and he led Norwood to the sea side, when he embarked in a canoe for a place where a much larger one was laid up. This was set afloat, and the party got into it, being six short of the number which had come ashore from the ship.

Four men and one woman were known to be dead, and one other woman was absent, but the Indians hinted they knew it, and would take care of her. They were now carried to the home of an Indian, and welcomed with great hospitality, after the manner of that people. Their arms and powder were placed in security, food supplied to them, and a large fire. Furs and deer skins were placed over them for warmth; in short, no kindnesses which their unaffected hosts could show or obtain were omitted towards them. Compassion and tenderness were visible in everything these children of nature did. To Christians it was felt as a reproach, that they frequently, so far from affording succor to persons shipwrecked, too often neglected them wholly, or treated them with barbarity. In the woods of America, the brave, but simple Indians practiced those virtues of which Christians only talked. They neither plundered, nor did they seem to covet anything in the possession of the shipwrecked men. In a hut of mat, bark, and reeds fixed on poles, the party were thus entertained, and treated with a boiled swan for their supper. Refreshed by a sound sleep upon a stomach no longer craving, Norwood and his companions in misfortune awoke, as it seemed to them, in an earthly paradise. A good breakfast was provided for them, their fire-arms restored, and they set off to where the king or chief resided, leaving the two women to the care of the Indians, who were so weak that they could not accompany them, until means could be adopted of getting them to Virginia, where they ultimately arrived in safety, and were afterwards married.

The travelers had not gone far upon their journey, when they were stopped by orders from the chief, and sent back to their old quarters, he having heard of their weak and emaciated condition. The chief would not suffer them to walk, but had sent canoes to the creek for them to come to him by another route. They went back accordingly, and embarked, passing about three miles through another branch of the creek they had formerly entered; and they landed near the residence of the chief's wife, who treated them with food of various kinds. They then set out for the chief's own residence, which was built of matting and reeds. Posts of wood were sunk in the ground at the corners, to sustain the fabric and render all secure. The roof was tied down with strong rushes. The breadth of the house or palace was about twenty feet, and the length sixty. The only furniture were platforms for reposing upon, each about six feet long, placed on both sides of the building, about five feet from each other. A hole in the midst of the roof served for the chimney, through which all the smoke did not issue, enough being left to be troublesome to those seated below, who were divided into two ranks, disposed one on each side of the house.

Fourteen fires were lighted at once. The apartment of the king, or chief, was twice as long as that of the rest; and he sat upon a bed of deer skins, otter furs, and beaver, the finest that could be procured. The party of Captain Norwood was conducted to a fire by themselves, to which no Indians came but those who were bent upon some friendly office. The chief sent his daughter, about twelve years old, with a bowl of refreshments, which were delivered out of a mussel shaped shell. After the visitors had eaten, the chief sent to Captain Norwood, requesting he would come to him. He was made to take his place by the chief, who called him his brother. A consultation was then held among the Indians present, which seemed to relate to the situation of the shipwrecked people. Captain Norwood presented the chief with a sword and belt, which he put on, and with which he was much delighted. After mutual civilities, and having received much kindness, Captain Norwood parted, without making any progress in getting their Indian friends to understand they wished to set out for Virginia.

Thus kindly treated, they gained strength daily, and became more and more anxious to get away. They thought Virginia could not be at any very great distance, and that it bore from them south by west, to south-west. They were ignorant of the latitude of the spot in which they were. They imagined it was pretty clear they were to the south of Menados, a Dutch plantation, now the city of New York. They therefore began to save some provisions for their journey; but the chief penetrated their design, and endeavored, by every means he possessed in the way of gesture and sign, to dissuade them from attempting it. He showed them that the cold, rain, darkness, and swamps, would prove fatal, unless they were directed by persons acquainted with the route. He pointed to his corn and his fires, and signified that the party was welcome to them. In fact, the goodness of the chief towards them was unbounded. In a little time he made Captain Norwood understand better what he wished to say. He seemed to desire to know whether they wished to go to the south or north. Upon being informed that the south was the direction, the chief was much pleased, and one of his suite made a sort of map on the ground with a stick, and drew the country to the south. The most southerly point he called Achomack, which Captain Norwood believed to be Virginia, and made them understand that it was there he wished to go, at which the chief appeared much gratified.

They began at last to be impatient to go away, which seemed to displease the chief, who again showed them his corn, and in fact forced them to lay aside the thought of departing until he gave the word. On the mention of Achomack he indicated that it was not yet time, and he dispatched a messenger to that place, which after all might not be Virginia. Still everything in the way of attention and kindness, which these Indians could lavish upon the party, was freely yielded. The weather was frosty, and the cold excessive. Captain Norwood had been on a visit to the wife of the chief, conducted by his daughter, and had just returned, when he found that the messenger whom the chief had sent was come back with others, one of whom wore the English dress. He informed Captain Norwood of the ship's arrival, and of the difficulties she encountered before she entered James River, where she ran on shore. This person brought an Indian with him, who served as interpreter. From these it was ascertained that the party were about fifty miles from Virginia. The chief wanted to get up a dance to entertain his guests, but Captain Norwood was too impatient to go away, and would not remain to witness it.

The chief having taken a fancy to Captain Norwood's camlet coat, he presented it to him. A piece of scarlet ribbon was given to the chief's daughter, together with a French tweezer, which delighted her. A few presents from others of the party were tied up with it, to ornament her hair. Captain Norwood, and three or four more who were hale and stout enough for the journey, set out immediately under the guidance of the messengers. Major Morrison, the two women, and some others, were left to wait until the boats, which the governor had ordered to go round to receive them, should arrive. They took a regretful leave of the chief, and set off, passing swamps and creeks without number, and being entertained hospitably on their way by the Indians and their chiefs, when they chanced to fall in with them.

The toil was considerable, and Captain Norwood was nearly overcome by the fatigue, which, from wearing the boots of that age, was very much increased: his shoes he had worn out. At length he became desperate and ready to sink down. When they came within view of a resting place, on the last day but one, he willingly consented to a motion for sleeping out of doors, rather than go a hundred yards farther to a shelter, the next day they ended their toils at Achomack, more properly the county of Northampton, in Virginia. They were treated in the most hospitable manner by the colonists, who would not accept any kind of remuneration for their good offices. At the house of Mr. Yardly, who had been governor of Virginia, and who had married a Dutch lady named Custis, from Rotterdam, whom Captain Norwood had known in Europe from a child, he was treated like a relation, and sojourned ten days, waiting for a passage across the bay to his ultimate destination.

Captain Norwood was well received by the governor, Sir William Berkley, a devoted royalist. He appears to have corresponded with Charles II during his exile, and to have made all appointments in the colony only upon the king's authority. Captain Norwood was his relation, and was sent by him to Holland to solicit of Charles the place of treasurer of Virginia, void by the delinquency of one Claybourne. This place Norwood subsequently obtained, and there it is probable he ended his days. *History of Shipwrecks and Disasters at Sea, From the Most Authentic Sources. V.2.* p. 31-59.

PART 3. THE WRECKS.

This part will share all known shipwrecks that occurred during the reign of James I through Charles I, (1603-1649) located in many different archives.

To be included, the incident must adhere to a basic formula: name of ship (if known), location of wreck around the United Kingdom, (or English ships that wrecked elsewhere whether in the royal navy or belonging to the East India Company), and dates with as much available relevant information as possible. Of course, there are a couple rare exceptions.

During the time researching details of wrecks, I developed an understanding why many sources of modern information are incorrect. One such account from a popular website of information (or misinformation a very close friend Dr. Charlene Berry once said) indicated the *Sea Adventure* had wrecked on the Bermudas in 1609, and the survivors formed a British colony. Great story. It is based upon a letter dated 20 May 1610, describing the plantation of Virginia from the *Calendar of State Papers, Colonial Series, East Indies, China and Japan, 1513-1616, p. 66-67*, "After the *Sea Adventure* was wrecked and with them 100 persons barely provided." From that sentence, several tales were spun of the formation of the English colony on the Bermudas. I am happy to report that the *Sea Adventure* can be tracked until well after 1616, after which time I discontinued my search.

Sometimes the fate of a crew and ship are clearly recorded and a pleasure to include in this volume, but a time consuming and sometimes tedious challenge is to determine from ambiguously worded and or from partial remains of the original document, that these ships either survived or wrecked, blew up, burned, leaked beyond repair, or otherwise sank and were no longer in service; basically ended up under water. If in doubt, I would explain my reasoning.

Have I covered everything? I highly doubt it. But I have reviewed hundreds of electronic and hard cover manuscript collections and travelled to view rare and sometimes wonderful hand illuminated manuscripts that have not been digitized, to attempt to collect and portray all the wrecks included in this part, but as much as I would like to believe I uncovered everything, it would be an understatement.

Some of the ships in this part contain Spanish reales (gold or silver pieces of 8), gold or silver bullion and precious jewels and jewelry that could not be recovered by means at the time and forgotten about as time progressed and those manuscript collections were reviewed by fewer people over the centuries augmented by the destruction of tons of logs and journals by the East India Company.

These are the treasures I located.

1600

The *Guest*.

I overlooked this wreck several times during research including my first volume The Ships and Shipwrecks of the Late Tudor Dynasty. The incident occurred prior to the formation of the East India Company and was not recorded in the Calendars or APC series during the reign of Elizabeth I, though it preceded the reign of King James I and the scope of this volume, I felt it should be mentioned.

"An expedition sailed from Woolwich on the 13 February 1600, with 480 men. The General, James Lancaster, was on board the Dragon. This vessel was bought from the Earl of Cumberland for £3,700, her former name having been the Malice Scourge. She was launched on the 11 December 1599, and rechristened the Red Dragon, being a vessel of 600 tons with a crew of 202 men. John Middleton was on board the vice-admiral, the Hector, of 300 tons, with a crew of 108 men. The Ascension, commanded by William Brand, was a vessel of 260 tons, with a crew of 82 men; and the Susan of 240 tons, under John Heyward, had 88 men. The Guest, of 130 tons, was added as a victualler. The original manuscript journals of this memorable voyage are lost." *The Voyages of Sir James Lancaster, Kt., to the East Indies. Introduction, p. iv.*

"These ships stayed so long in the River of Thames, and in the Downs for want of wind, that it was Easter day before they arrived at Dartmouth, where they spent five or six days in taking in their bread and certain other provisions appointed for them. From thence they departed the eighteenth of April 1601, and road in Tor Bay till the twentieth in the morning." *The Voyages of Sir James Lancaster, Kt., to the East Indies, p. 58-59.*

"The last of June, about midnight we doubled the line and lost sight of the North Star, having the wind at south east, and we held our course south south-west and doubled the Cape of Saint Augustine some six and twenty leagues to the eastwards. The twentieth of July we were shot into nineteen degrees, forty minutes to the southward of the line, the wind enlarging daily to the eastward. Here we discharged the Guest, the ship that went along with us to carry the provisions that our four ships could not take in England. After we had discharged her, we took her masts, sails and yards, and broke down her higher buildings for firewood, and so left her floating in the sea, and followed our course to the southward. The four and twentieth of July we passed the tropic of Capricorn, the wind being north-east by north, we holding our course east south-east. Now, by reason of our long being under the Line (which proceeded of our late coming out of England, for the time of the year was too far spent by six or seven weeks to make a quick navigation) many of our men fell sick. Therefore, the nine and twentieth of July, being in 28 1/2 degrees, he wrote a remembrance to the governor of each ship, either to fetch Saldania or Saint Helena for refreshing." *The Voyages of Sir James Lancaster, Kt., to the East Indies, p. 60-61.*

With the destruction of tons of logs, journals and manuscripts, the precise location where the *Guest* went down is not known at this time. She was allowed to drift with the current stripped of everything to perhaps the main deck and though coordinates were shared in the last letter, it is likely she did not eventually sink in that location.

1604

Mary of Dowglas, (Douglas?)

This wreck was discovered in the *Catalogue of the Harleian Collection of Manuscripts.* Though this wreck was one of a few recorded in that collection, it was the only wreck within the boundaries of this book.

1604. "Part of a certificate touching the wreck of the bark *Mary* of Dowglas, in her voyage from Chester to Barkington in Cumberland, wherein Mr. John Bavand had much corn and grain." *CHC, V. II, #2093, #54.*

This would have been a short voyage from perhaps Liverpool to Cumberland Scotland of about 200 miles. No additional records were found or available. *Mary* of Douglas wrecked along the coast of either England or Scotland with unknown cargo.

1607

The *Union*.

Contained within the introduction of the volume of State Papers referenced: "One of the vessels, the *Ascension*, was wrecked on the coast of India; the other, the *Union*, on the coast of France, purposely by the people of Audierne in bringing her into the haven. The value of the *Union* and her goods was estimated at £70,000." *CSP-C, EI, C&J, 1513-1616, #47, p. xlv.*

3 August 1607. "The *Union*; or the *Unity* to be bought. Some of the company to set down their adventure. Admission of Richard Strongetharm, an adventurer of £275 in the fourth voyage". *CSP-C, EI, C&J, 1513-1616. #375, p. 157.*

5 August 1607. "Authority to buy the *Union*. Carpenters to repair the *Union*, and *Ascension*. Admission of Martin Freeman." *CSP-C, EI, C&J, 1513-1616. #375, p. 157.*

13-28 August 1607. "Authority to buy the *Union*. Carpenters to repair the *Union*, and *Ascension*. Admission of Martin Freeman." *CSP-C, EI, C&J, 1513-1616. #377, p. 157.*

21 August 1607. "The *Union*: thought fit by the governor and Sir James Lancaster to go on the voyage though her repairs will probably be costly. Names added to the committee for buying timber and building a great ship for the fifth voyage." *CSP-C, EI, C&J, 1513-1616. #377, p. 158.*

26 January 1608. "Bread for twenty-four months to be provided; number of men, including generals, factors, mariners, and others, 75 in the *Ascension*, and 65 in the *Union*. The men already hired, with their sureties, to be examined, and those found unfit displaced. Lawrence Pegion hired as surgeon in the *Ascension*, at £338. 4d. per month and £17 to furnish his chest to sea, and Thomas Yonger, surgeon's mate, at 208 per month only. A surgeon to be hired for the *Union*." *CSP-C, EI, C&J, 1513-1616. #393, p. 166.*

19 September 1609. "Account of the voyage of the *Ascension* and the *Union* from the time they set sail on April 1, 1608, to their arrival at Aden on April 8, 1609, where the general [Alex. Sharpey] and myself went a land." *CSP-C, EI, C&J, 1513-1616, #459, p. 193.*

19 August 1611. This is the first mention of her wreck. "Certify to having delivered his letter to Sir Thomas Smith, who took it very kindly that Edmonds should have considered of the [East India Company's] business about the *Union*; and her lading, cast away at Audierne by them of the coast."

CSP-C, EI, C&J, 1513-1616, #577, p. 225. Perhaps she was attempting to make port into the river of Le Goyen. This narrows the wreck area to about 5 miles of coast on Southern France.

Depositions of Pierre de Louarn and Francois le Goff taken on 25 December 1611, while in prison, regarding the "seizure of the goods" from this ship. The main letter mentioned the unjust proceedings of the court of Rennes for compensation for the loss of goods. *CSP-C, EI, C&J, 1513-1616, #602. p. 234.*

End of November 1612. "Mr. Wilson hath been too often in the Indian voyages ever to be good; they might have been a month or six weeks before in Bantam but for him, who said the casting away of the *Union*; was for want of tobacco, for if he had had tobacco, he might have brought her home." *CSP-C, EI, C&J, 1513-1616. #623, p. 243.*

Mid-January 1612. "Hugh Bourman to Sir Thomas Edmonds, ambassador at Kennes, Paris. Represents the unjust proceedings of the court of Rennes in a suit brought by the writer and Mons. De Robinson, on behalf of the society [of East India merchants] for redress of depredations committed upon their ship [the Union, wrecked on the coast,] and as one of the corps to whom the management of the society's affairs has been entrusted, requests his interference at the French Court. Depositions of Pierre De Louarn and Francois Le Goff of Audierne, taken in the prison at Rennes, concerning the seizure of the goods from the English ship above alluded to." *CSP-C, EI, C&J, 1513-1616, #602, p. 234.*

The last known letter on 19 July 1616 mentions that the *Union* was wrecked "among the rocks by the inhabitants of Audierne, who had spoil of the ship and goods to the value of £70,000, and although £7000 has been spent in continually suing for justice, no remedy can be obtained." *CSP-C, EI, C&J, 1513-1616, #1143 p. 471.*

No additional information was located. It would be hard to speculate how much of the ship remained after the valuable cargo was pilfered.

The *Ascension.*

The full account of Captain Alexander Sharpeigh's voyage to India was shared in part two of this book and the *Calendar's* records will be shared in this part. This ship was mentioned in the inventory of 1588 against the Spanish armada as 200 tons with John Chester as captain of 80 mariners.

29 July 1607. "The *Ascension*; sold to the New Company, for £185,178, 6d. A chest to be supplied to keep the money of these two voyages by itself." *CSP-C, EI, C&J, 1513-1616, #374, p. 157.*

1-8 August 1607. Court minutes of the East India Company. "Repair of the *Ascension*. Committee to view three ships and report the price." *CSP-C, EI, C&J, 1513-1616, #375, p. 157*.

12 January 1608. "40 Shillings reward to those who took extraordinary pains with the *Ascension* when in great danger last evening by extremity of ice." *CSP-C, EI, C&J, 1513-1616, #393, p. 165*.

19 January 1608. It was recorded that Thomas Joanes, boatswain of the *Ascension*, was dismissed. *CSP-C, EI, C&J, 1513-1616, #393, p. 165*.

Obscurely classified into a "1608, March, to 1617, June" record #406 of the same volume of State Papers, and over looked a couple times while researching this volume for other material, is a record of a journal kept by John Jourdain during a fourth voyage to the East Indies. "June trading the same in anno 1607 in two good ships, namely, the Ascension and Union, wherein goes general Alexander Sharpey and vice-admiral Captain Richard Rowles; master, Phillip Grove. The which voyage, God bless and prosper, began at the Downs near Sandwich, the 23rd March 1608; with an addition of all my travels after the casting away of the Ascension until 1617 of any worthy the writing; including their travels from the Desert Islands to Socotra; what passed after landing at Aden, as also in Senan [Sana] and Mocha; description of the strength of the city of Aden arrival of the pinnace (Ascension) after the murder of John Luffkin, her master; journey from Aden to Sana, with names of the chief towns passed through; description of Sana, where the Bashaw keeps his court; of their travel from Sana to Mocha." *CSP-C, EI, C&J, 1513-1616. #406, p. 170*.

Those are the rather fragmented bits of information from the copy I reviewed. A footnote of that letter indicates the source document "Two hundred and thirty-five pages. British Museum, Sloane, 858. Narratives of the Fourth Voyage to the East Indies, written by Jones and Henry Morris, are printed in Purchas, I., 228, et seq. A true and almost incredible report of an Englishman that (being cast away in the good ship called the Ascension in Cambaya, the farthest part of the East Indies) travelled by land through many unknown kingdoms and great cities, with a particular description of those kingdoms, cities, and people, by Captain Robert Coverte, is printed in the Harleian Collection of Voyages, II., 237-266." *CSP-C, EI, C&J, 1513-1616, #406, p. 171*.

1 July 1608. It was recorded in the Court Minutes that "Ten Pounds charity given to Sarah, widow of William Brum, captain of the *Ascension* in the first voyage, who was killed by shot from a great piece of ordnance, unadvisedly discharged out of the *Dragon* at the burial of Mr. Winter, near the

coast of East Indies." *CSP-C, EI, C&J, 1513-1616, #417, p. 176*. It is safe to speculate the ship was not damaged and survived.

In a damaged and blemished two and a half page record are bits of additional information. I must admit that this letter was frustrating because of the missing information. Nonetheless, these are the bits and pieces. "(Unknown) to the East India Company. Account of the voyage of the *Ascension* and the *Union* from the time they set sail on 1 April 1608 to their arrival at Aden 8 April 1609. John Lufkin as master who was murdered, but nothing of the captain. They anchored in the bay of Cambaya on 31 August, north side, 30 leagues farther than the master expected. A very brief account of their efforts to save the ship of her wreck in September 1608 and the saving of everyman's life in two boats. Leaving the ship standing almost full of water, to their great griefs." They had apparently narrowly escaped the Portuguese being taken for fishermen of the country. *Calendar of State Papers, Colonial Series, East Indies, China and Japan, 1513-1616. #459, p. 193*.

The last related document located in archives is on 18 March 1611. "Captain Downton to Middleton. Has come to look after him, his men, and provisions. Is not obligated to any Turk, neither will Downton wait his will. Has long forborne to recover what the Turks unjustly detain, having sufficient warning, by the villainy they have committed to the people in the pinnace of the Ascension, that there is no faithful performance to be expected from those truthless Turks. As Middleton is in the tyrant's hands, and dare not right himself, Captain Downton intends to take command of the ships and dispose of them as he thinks fit, to recover Sir Henry, his people, and provisions. Report that they have been taxed by the Turks being women in men's apparel, close they say we should endeavor to make our peace by force." *CSP-C, EI, C&J, 1513-1616, #516, p. 213*.

The only record that shared helpful information was classified into an obscure and broad section which suggests the exact date of the source document was not known by the editors while in collation of the *Calendars*. "...being cast away in the good ship called the Ascension in Cambaya, the farthest part of the East Indies," suggests she sank in Cambaya.

The *Ascension* possibly had a violent encounter with the Portuguese in the Java Sea or Makassar Strait and sank with all crew saved. Cambaya is a location in the region of South Sulawesi in Indonesia. No additional information was found in archives about cargo, ordnance or salvage attempts.

1609

Coast of Kinsayle wreck.

Elements of this wreck led me in many directions seeking additional information and the sum of what was located is a single document contained in a collection of records from 1 July 1609, "certificate of concordatums was granted for extraordinary services to his majesty in three quarter of a year ending June 1609."

This is that document: 1 July 1609. "Henry Crosse, of Barnestable, merchant, in consideration that his ship and goods, to the value of £2,000, was wrecked and cast away upon the coast of Kinsayle, and after service done to her late majesty in landing 400 men at Waterford under the conduct of Sir Anthony Cooke, Knight, in anno 1602, unto which service he was suddenly pressed out of Barnestable, by warrant of certain commissioners in Devonshire, then authorized by commission from the lords of her late majes-ty's council, where he was purposed to have transported his said ship of the burthen of 220 tons, laden with goods, to the islands of Canary, in consider-ation of his service and great loss, having been an humble suitor to the lords of his majesty's Privy Council in England that some favorable respect may be had of him, who, by their letters, have recommended him hither; in consid-eration of all which he is allowed, by concordatum." *CSP-I, James I, 1608-1610, #410, p. 232.*

A search in archives of the year 1602 to 1609 for a first record or mention of the wreck produced no results. I find no additional information or salvage attempts. I almost overlooked this wreck because the document's location is obscure and was not mentioned in the Calendar's index. This 220-ton ship may still contain its cargo and though it would appear she served in a military capacity, she may contain ordnance, small arms, ball and shot and perhaps small amount of pay for soldiers.

Kinsale is a town on the southern coast of Ireland, in County Cork. Two 17th-century fortresses overlook the River Bandon. The vast, star-shaped Charles Fort is to the southeast and the smaller James Fort is on the river's opposite bank.

1610

The *Red Camel.*

18 November 1610. "Some merchants who had a vessel of theirs seized by the Sicilian galleys, failing to recover it, although the viceroy's sentence was quashed in Spain on the ground that the evidence of the sailors was wrung from them by torture under which some of them died, have now put out to the Indian Sea in two good ships, not without permission of the council. They have made reprisals of a Spanish ship which had on board a cargo worth about forty thousand ducats. The Spanish ambassador has lodged a complaint and demands that, in virtue of the capitulations, the ship (the Red Camel) should be given over to him. It was resolved that all should be warehoused till the case could be settled; but both the ambassador and the merchants having sent persons down to the coast to estimate the value of the goods, they, on their own responsibility, put the goods up to auction and knocked them down for a third of their value to creatures of the merchants, and, before the ambassador could be informed, the goods were shipped to Flanders and elsewhere out of the kingdom.

"In the recent bad weather, a Dutch ship which, as I understand, had embarked at Zante certain subjects of your serenity and some currants for Amsterdam, ran upon a shoal off this island, and after losing her rudder was found upon the shore, and without a soul on board. I hoped that they might have been saved by some other ship, but as her boat was found later on it is taken for certain that they have all perished. As soon as I had news of this I appealed to the king for an order sequestrating the ship and directing an inventory to be made; the admiralty had refused to grant this request, as both the lord high admiral and the earl of Arundel, within whose jurisdiction the wreck took place, pretend that it belongs to them in virtue of a law which so rules it in cases where neither human being, dog, nor cat are found on board.

"I urged upon his majesty that this law was not intended to rob the owner, but only to provide for the case where it was impossible to discover the owner; that I now appeared in the name of the unhappy wives and children; that I was sure that if in addition to the sea they should find an enemy in the law of England his majesty's pity would not fail them. I added that on other occasions the law had not been put into effect, and I offered to cite precedents. All I asked now was the sequestration and the inventory, so as not to close the door to those unhappy people for the recovery of the little that the sea had left them. I found the king well informed about the matter; he said that the admiral and earl of Arundel were contending over this wreck;

that as the law was opposed to my request the way of grace must be adopted. I said I accepted the offer either for grace or for justice, and I never doubted but that so piteous a case would meet with his majesty's protection. Later on, lord Salisbury told me to address myself to the admiral and to the earl of Arundel, to both of whom the king had spoken.

"These gentlemen promised to oblige me in so sad a case, but in order not to prejudice their rights, they refused inventory, housing, and examination of marks; they deny that any pool of the cargo has been found. I have written to the governor of Zante for information, nor will I allow the matter to drop, and I will conduct it either by way of justice or of grace; but the distance whence information has to come, and the power of these gentlemen form serious obstacles to the recovery of the goods." *CSPM, V&NI, V.12, 1610-1613. p. 74-75.*

27 November 1610. "His decision will be published later on, probably when no one is expecting it. I have dealt several times with the affairs of the Zante merchants' owners of the currants found on board the *Red Camel*. I am informed that in great part they belonged to Messer Zorzi Balsamo; but as I have no proof, nor marks, nor countersigns, the earl of Arundel, as lord of the manor, has taken possession of the goods and replies to my claims that when I have evidence enough, he will not fail to satisfy my demands out of pure courtesy." *CSPM, V&NI, V.12, 1610-1613, #118, p. 81.*

9 December 1610. "The crew of the *Red Camel*, which loaded in Zante and went ashore on this coast, have all arrived safe on the other side. It does not appear that they were subjects of your serenity, but there were on board her seventy-two barrels and nine sacks of currants belonging to Georgio Balsamo of Zante and a few others belonging to another merchant, whose specification has not yet reached Amsterdam and about which I can get no more information, as the ships books remained in the ship and the master who has come here has no recollection of the subject." *CSPM, V&NI, V.12, 1610-1613, #132, p. 92.*

4 February 1611. "At the same audience I recommended, in the interest of those poor people of Zante, the case of the *Red Camel*, which was cast away on these shores. I said that the earl of Arundel, into whose hands the ship and cargo had fallen, standing with unwonted rigor by his claims, the merchants would consent to a legal settlement of the point provided that the cargo was so safely deposited that the judge could at one and the same time declare ownership and put the owners in possession without further litigation." *CSPM, V&NI, V.12, 1610-1613, #172, p. 113.*

The *Red Camel* was a Dutch ship that had Venetian merchants and their cargo of currants (In the United States, the United Kingdom, and Ireland, "currants" often refer to the Zante currant. These are dried Corinth grapes that are just small raisins. True currants are small berries that grow on shrubs and are more like gooseberries) from Zante that wrecked on the coast of Sussex. The lord high admiral and lord Arundel had both filed a claim on the wreck based on the facts she was "rudderless, neither human, dog nor cat was board."

The Venetian ambassador requested the ship be kept safe and the cargo housed and inventoried "because of Venetian ownership." The ambassador appealed directly to King James who indicated, "the law was against the Venetian claim, but that as an act of grace, he would speak to the two lords." They both were willing to waive their claims, but to avoid prejudice to their rights; they refused to "allow an inventory, warehousing or examination of marks." The estimate of the *Red Camel* was four thousand ducats.

The admiral and Arundel could not arrive at a resolution, even though King James appealed to them. A letter of 18 November 1610 mentioned that her boat (lifeboat in modern terms) was also found without anyone, so all assumed everyone perished at sea.

I was unable to locate a resolve as to who eventually claimed the cargo. It is safe to speculate that it was valuable enough to quarrel over requiring the king to intercede.

The *Red Camel* had wrecked on the shore of Sussex. Inhabitants or other mariners may have striped the ship of tackle, furniture, and cables, leaving only the ship to be consumed by time and the waves.

1614

The *Pearl*, 1614.

On 11 January 1614, a letter to Sir Richard Sands mentions the East India ship the *Pearl* had wrecked on the coast of Ireland and the council issued instructions to search and inventory the goods removed from the ship. *CSP-D, V.33, 1613-1614, p. 324.*

Three subsequent letters only address the cargo (but no inventory) from the ship that was transported by a pinnace and bark to a custom's house in London. The only useful tidbit of information these letters offer is the Spanish ambassador made a claim to some of the cargo. *CSP-D, V.33, 1613-1614, p. 325, 338, 371.*

The *Pearl* possibly departed Spain to encounter a storm or as a result of bad navigation, drove her on the shore of Ireland, possibly between Dingle and Rossiare Harbor. It appears that all or most of the cargo was salvaged so all that would remain would be the ship. I was unable to find additional information on the Spanish claim to some of the cargo.

Carnarvon Wreck.

12 Feb 1614. The council received a letter requesting assistance to search and seize goods belonging to William Cutts, a London merchant, that were cast on the shore near Carnarvon, Northern Wales, in a bark with Robert Lynaker as master. The letter fragment mentioned a Maddox, a factor to Cutts had perished when the ship wrecked. *APC, 1613-1614. p. 345.*

The only possible related record may be in a letter of 26 January 1615 mentioning that Sir Richard Cook and his family are cast away on their journey to Ireland. *CSP-D, James I, 1611-1618, p.270 #10.*

No additional information could be learned. For goods to have washed on shore near Caernarfon, could suggest that the ship wrecked on the rocks in the waterway above Northern Wales. The restrictive waterway entry would most likely prevent wreckage from drifting in from the Irish Sea, so this bark may lie in the waterway.

The *Hector.*

March 1613 "The next voyage was that commanded by Captain Downton, which Purchas calls the 'second joint-stock voyage', but it appears to have been the first. It consisted of the *New Year's Gift*, the *Hector*, the *Merchant Hope*, and the *Solomon*, and sailed from England. This expedition of Downton is famous for a great success gained over the Portuguese fleet." *The Voyages of Sir James Lancaster, Kt., to the East Indies, p. xv.*

28 June 1613. "The general proceeded to court, when the king told him that on that day he could hold no conference, as his army had returned from Joar, bringing back the king of that place as a prisoner, and that many of his nobles were assembled to confer upon matter of state. Thereupon, the general withdrew. The victory was celebrated with great solemnity in both country and city. The fleet consisted of 10 frigates and galleys, some with ordnance, some without, and the army of 20,000 soldiers. A Flemish ship, which had been at Joar, on the approach of the army had put to sea, but her captain, with some twenty of the merchants and mariners, who had been on shore, were taken prisoners, and others of her crew were slain. Captain Best called on the *Fleming* to encourage him, and heard from him of Sir Henry Middleton having been at Bantam, and of the death of most of his merchants

and men; further, he heard of the *Salomon*, that the *Hector* and *Thomas* were bound for England, and Captain Saris in the *James*, which made him uneasy about that vessel's safety." *The Voyages of Sir James Lancaster, Kt., to the East Indies*, p. 255-256. Mr. Markam, editor of *The Voyages of Sir James Lancaster*, mentioned several times about the lost manuscripts of several officers that served on the *Hector*.

23rd January, 1614. This is the last related document to the Hector: "Thomas Elkington to John Oxwicke in Baroche. Laus Deo. Loving friend, your health desired, etc. My last [unto you?] was of the 21st, wherein I wrote you the success [our?] general had with the Portugal's on Friday in the afternoon, which since is confirmed by some of our own people that are come hither about some business. The Hope being the first that began the fight, being at once laid aboard per the three Portugal ships and as many Portugal frigates as could lie about her, having entered their men into her and twice got their forecastle but they very lustily shipped them off again till such time as the other ships came and rescued her, else they would have put her in great danger. The Portugal's came running aboard with great resolution, not so much as shooting a shot, but their courage's were soon quailed. There were in their three ships many cavaliers, the most part whereof were most miserably burned and drowned; so, is the [report?] they lost in all between four and five hundred men. Of our people were slain in the Hope two and hurt some 15 or 16, and her mainmast top and head a little burnt; two killed in the Hector, whereof the coxswain one, killed [?] of a piece which he had not well sponged. God make [us?] thankful for so good a beginning." *Letters Received by the East India Company, V.II, 1613-1615, p. 303-304.*

The *Hector* was not located in any of the *Calendars* relevant to this period of time, but additional information was located in a list of ships of the East India Company, "Hector, (1614), Sunk at Bantam, Careening." from *The Voyages of Sir James Lancaster, Kt, p. 298.*

The last piece of information from *The Voyages of Sir James Lancaster* is from a journal of John Monden, master's mate of the *Hector*, "which sailed from Gravesend on the 28th of February 1614, in the company of the *Hope* and the *Salomon*." With the assistance of the British Library, I was unable to locate that journal. It may have been destroyed with the tons of records the East India Company destroyed.

It is difficult to speculate what the contents of the *Hector* was when it sank at Bantam, former city and ruled by a sultan of Java, Indonesia.

1615

The *Amytie,* 1615.

On 18 June 1615 the council dispatched a letter of assistance to a commission from the high court of the admiralty for restitution of the *Amytie* with a cargo of elephant's teeth (tusks), gold, silver and other goods and merchandise belonging to Francis Monseaux of France, that wrecked in August 1614 upon the sands near Padstow in the county of Cornwall. That is the content of the letter. *APC, V.34 1615-1616, p. 209.*

There are no additional records that any cargo was recovered or attempted to recover. There is a good chance that this ship is perhaps between Trevose Head Lighthouse to Stepper Point along about 4 miles of shore north of Padstow, Cornwall with intact cargo. This is possibly a French ship.

1616

The *Abraham* and the *Jonas.*

As both these ships entered history as a result of running on the Goodwin Sands together, I will include them together.

4 January 1616. A single sentence of memorandum is the first mention that the "*Abraham* and the *Jonas* had wrecked on the Goodwin Sands." *CSP-D, James I, 1611-1618, Volume 2, #2., p. 342.*

The *Abraham:* "Memorandum of the wreck of the Abraham on the Godwin Sands, and the disorderly conduct of the Deal boatmen, in violating their agreement made with the captain touching the salvage, rifling the goods." *CSP-D, James I, 1611-1618, Volume 2, #3., p. 342.*

The *Jonas:* "Memorandum of the wreck of the Jonas on the Godwin Sands, and similar complaint against the Deal boatmen, for bursting open the merchants' packs and rifling them." *CSP-D, James I, 1611-1618, #3, p. 342.*

5 January 1616. "Thomas Fulnetby to Lord Zouch. Two ships ashore on the Godwin Sands. Some of the goods landed." *CSP-D, James I, 1611-1618, Volume 2, #4, p. 342.*

26 February 1616. A letter from John Rand to Lord Zouch "for satisfaction from the owners of the *Jonas* wrecked on the Godwin Sands, for their exertions in saving the ship." *CSP-D, James I, 1611-1618, Volume 2, #71, p. 351.*

No additional information was located about the *Abraham* and *Jonas* after they wrecked on the Goodwin Sands and then stripped of everything.

A Dutch hoy wreck

28 January 1616. "The council dispatched a letter of assistance to the mayor of Lynn Regis, John Atkins, authorized by a commission of the admiralty court to seize all goods that should find their way into any part of their jurisdiction from a Dutch hoy with Hay Edan as master, lately cast away near Lynn Regis. That is the full content of the letter. *APC, V.34, p. 382-383.*

No additional information was found about this Dutch hoy or those involved. It could be submerged within a 6-mile section of coast on either side of Lynn Regis, intact with unknown cargo.

Wreck between Rye and Lydd.

2 February 1617. "Thomas Lord Gerard to the Lord Zouch. In favor of James Linaker, whose bark was cast away in the Downs; many of his goods are cast up at Dover and seized by his Lordship's officers." *CSP-D, James I, 1611-1618, #49, p. 431.*

12 February 1616. A letter from Peter Dibb to Richard Younge. "A small bark, laden with Caen stone, is cast away between Lydd and Rye. Has seized his Lordship's anchor and cable there from. Begs that the Hythe boats may go out to fish a day or two earlier than allowed, there being but little supply of fish." *CSP-D, James I, 1611-1618, #60, p. 349.*

No other information could be learned. Caen stone is a light creamy-yellow limestone quarried near Caen. If a wreck is found in this area, the stone in the cargo hold would assist in identification. This bark would lie along about 9 miles of coastline. I am unsure if it hit the coast or sank just off the shoreline.

Three Dutch shipwrecks.

15 February 1616. "Bond of Samual de Fische, Philip Burlamachi, and others, under a penalty of £10,000 to indemnify Lord Zouch for delivering to them the portion saved of the cargoes of three Dutch vessels wrecked on the Godwin Sands, which they are authorized by the proprietors to receive, and to pay droit and salvage dues." *CSP-D, James I, 1611-1618, #63, p. 350.*

16 February 1616. "Lord Zouch to Thomas Fulnetby. Orders to deliver to Samual Philip Lane de Fische, and others, such portion of the goods of three Dutch vessels, stranded on the Goodwin Sands, as was saved by the inhabitants of the towns adjacent." *CSP-D, James I, 1611-1618, #65, p. 350.*

30 March 1616. Remnants of a letter mention; "Presentments by the jury of Dover, Ringwold, and Kingsdown, upon certain articles given in charge at the admiralty court of Dover, of diverse persons, for maltreating or embez-zling the persons or goods from the Dutch vessels lately wrecked on the Godwin Sands, and other misdemeanors." *CSP-D, James I, 1611-1618, #114, p. 358.*

I was unable to locate additional information in archives. It would appear that the Goodwin Sands claimed three ships. Based on the letters, it is safe to speculate nothing remained in the ships.

The *Golden Wagon*.

Early records in the *Calendar of State Papers, Domestic Series* are only remnants and the National Archives has indicated the originals for many of these letters do not exist. Perhaps lost when the East India Company destroyed journals and logs.

15 February 1616. "Endorsed is a draft of a similar indemnity on bond of James Hugessen, for delivering to Thomas Hoyer the value of an Emden vessel, wrecked." *CSP-D, James I, 1611-1618. #64, p.350*

24 August 1618. A record of an issued bond. "Bond of James Hugessen, jun., of Dover, in £300 to indemnify Lord Zouch for delivering up a ship of Emden called the *Golden Wagon*, wrecked near Dover, to Thomas Hoyes, part owner thereof, on payment of royalties." *CSP-D, James I, 1611-1618. #95, p. 567.*

I was unable to locate additional information. "Wrecked near Dover" helps, but the *Golden Wagon* was from Emden, Germany and perhaps wrecked on the east side of the Goodwin Sands. A storm from the North Sea could have forced her into the sands. Local inhabitants would have pilfered the ship of almost everything.

The *Golden Wagon* was not located in inventories of the Royal Navy or East India Company.

The *Phoenix*.

The first record located is of a *Phoenix* in a 1546 inventory at 40 tons. A few additional records indicated she served through the reign of Edward VI, Jane Grey, Mary I and Elizabeth I with 1587 as the last known record. It is possible this was another *Phoenix*, or she was refitted.

This *Phoenix* was recorded in a 1618 inventory as, "May be made service-able" at 150 tons. It turned up in a 1624 inventory at 250 tons with 20 pieces of ordnance. Two *Phoenix*'s turn up in records of this time including the

Golden Phoenix. Either this ship served for over 80 years, or other ships served before her with this name or variant of.

4 May 1616. "Recognition by Robert Fleming of Dover, master and part owner of the *Phoenix*; wrecked upon the Godwin Sands, that his bark by this casualty doth absolutely belong and appertain as a wreck to Lord Zouch, in right of the royalty due unto him as lord warden of the Cinque Ports." *CSP-D, James I, 1611-1618, #7, p. 365.*

4 May 1616 "[Lord Zouch] to Thomas Fulnetby. Desires that the *Phoenix*; may be repaired at his own charge, and given back to Mr. Fleming, the master." *CSP-D, James I, 1611-1618, #8, p. 365.*

8 May 1616. "John Oliver, under droit-gatherer of Sandwich, to Lord Zouch. A claim was made by an officer of the lord admiral to a ship wrecked on the Godwin Sands, which has been recovered by the men of Sandwich for Lord Zouch". *CSP-D, James I, 1611-1618, #18, p. 366.*

This is possibly related. 21 October 1616. Letter #129. Richard Marsh to Richard Younge. "Particulars of wrecked goods. Dover Castle. Many of them were bought by Hull. Encloses."

Letter #129-I. "List of goods wrecked in the hands of diverse persons who are ordered to restore them to the sergeant of the admiralty, or some other person deputed by the lord warden admiralty court, Sept. 9, 1616. Zouch." *CSP-D, James I, 1611-1618, #129, 129-I, p. 399.*

The Goodwin Sands claimed another ship. It appears that all that could be salvaged was removed. I believe the bark *Phoenix* ran onto the sand bar and did not sink to be rescued and continued in service.

The ship name is carefully spelled with Latin alphabet grapheme in the volume of Calendars, a spelling most word processor word search functions would not reveal. Compounding search difficulties is the Phoenix is not mentioned in the indexes of the Calendars reviewed, only in connection with Goodwin Sands.

The *Samaritan*.

An English ship, which perished far from home.

"About the middle of July 1616, it may please you to understand of the arrival of a Holland ship at Surrat, about the burthen of 350 tons, who having made a voyage from Bantam to Moho and other ports in the Red Sea, laden with pepper and other spices, where having sold the most part thereof to very great benefit, brought their remainders to Surrat and landed the said goods with two factors for making sale thereof, departed thence towards

Bantam about the middle of August following. After whose departure the two factors sometimes frequented our house, reported that an English ship in return from Bantam was cast away upon St. Lorance, her men and goods for the most part saved, and for a certainty thereof they confidently affirmed that they spoke with an English boy of her company at one of their ports in the Red Sea, who had been taken upon the island and sold to the Turks, who reported the same to them, but further did not advise us; which ship we supposed to be the Samaritan, by the time of her departure from Bantam and not arrival at the Cape." *Letters Received by the East India Company, V.6, 1617, p.50.*

Undated in the collection of the fifth volume of the *Letters Received by the East India Company*, "In your Worships' instructions there is mention made of a youth betrayed by them of St. Laurence together with Captain Rowles and others. Of this young man we heard news by the Hollanders at Surat, who being at a place called Casseen in Arabia, the king whereof is father to him of Socatora, they affirm they did see him and learned that he was sold to him of Socatora and presented by him to his father. The boy, being spoken unto by them, answered not, but burst into tears, being presently conveyed away by the Arabians. They also inform us that they had certain news of the casting away of the Samaritan on the island of St. Laurence, but that the people and goods were saved, entrenching themselves on land and have built a pinnace, sent it to Bantam, requiring to send them a ship to take in them and their goods. I dare not to aver this for truth, but it is their certain report." *Letters Received by the East India Company, V.5, 1617, p.150.*

A single letter in the *Calendar's* contained basically the same information but indicated she was Dutch. The letters of the East India Company indicated she is English.

Bantam was a former city of Java Indonesia once ruled by a sultan, near the site of the present day city of Banten. The Samaritan was mentioned as returning from Bantam (Banten) and did not pass the Cape. Plotting several courses, mainly following the 5700-mile journey from Bantam to the Cape, a few islands are near this course, but a St. Lorance, St. Laurence, island of St. Laurence or St. Lawrence, was not located. It is also probable that the Samaritan followed a north then west course through the Bay of Bengal then into the Arabian Sea which correlates with the English boy in a Red Sea port. No islands of that name variant were located along that path.

Christmas Island (about 250 miles south of Banten), was included on English and Dutch navigation charts early in the 17th century, but it was not until 1666 that a map published by a Dutch cartographer included the island. The officers of the Samaritan would not have had that information. The St.

Lawrence Island may have been a label they gave to an unknown island on their charts and has changed several times in 400 years, evading my search. Perhaps I have over thought this incident, but I honestly do not have a wreck site. I look forward to a revision.

Winterton wrecks.

This reference, though from 14 February 1617, mentions the date the wrecks occurred at 12 August 1616. "Wardens and assistants of the Trinity House of Deptford Strand, as appeared by a petition, dated the last of February 1613, and subscribed by 300 persons and upwards, all masters and owners of ships, or fishermen trading upon the north coast, for the raising of lights near to Winterton Ness, for their better and more safe passage, and sailing by the dangerous sands of that place. And where the like instance hath been made again unto the said master and wardens and assistants of the Trinity House, as appeared by a petition of the 20th of October last (upon occasion of the loss of eight ships and goods, to the value of £6000, besides the loss of 60 men, which were there cast away the 12 of August last 1616) for some provision of light to be made for the avoiding the hazard of that channel and sands, which is grown so dangerous, that, without some present help in that kind, they cannot but expect the like hazard and lose hereafter." *APC-1616-1617, p. 141.*

I was unable to locate additional relevant information. Winterton, and Winterton Ness are not the same location. Winterton Ness etymology is correct for the period and helped to identify the location of the wrecks, but variants of the name and location from the year 1200 to 1700 exist. This Winterton Ness is between Horsey and Winterton-on-Sea.

Eight ships wrecked in this location at the same time if the document is to be taken literally. I would assume that would warrant additional information.

Margate Sands wreck.

20 November 1616. "Notice of bond of James Campbell, under penalty of £500 to indemnify Lord Zouch from all claims upon the goods saved from a French bark wrecked on Margate Sands which goods are given up to Campbell, who claims them as owner, on payment of droit rights, and composition to the savers." *CSP-D, James I, 1611-1618, #36, p. 407.*

I believe the following letter may be related to this wreck.

"Proofs that the Downs, Godwin Sands, and other places on that coast are within the lord warden's admiralty jurisdiction." *CSP-D, James I, 1611-1618, #43-II, p. 408.*

Those are the only records located. The French bark may have been blown on land by a November storm from the North Sea.

1617

The *Johanne* of Bourdeaux.

The only surviving records of this ship are in fragmented letters.

10 January 1617. "Bond of Michael Burnley and Jacob Braems of Dover, under penalty of £500, to indemnify Lord Zouch for delivery to them, on behalf of the owner, of the cargo of the bark *Johanne*, belonging to Mondey Beauvois, a French merchant, wrecked upon the Godwin Sands." *CSP-D, James I, 1611-1618, #14, p. 423.*

2 February 1617. "Thomas lord Gerard to Lord Zouch. In favor of James Linaker, whose bark was cast away in the Downs; many of his goods are cast up at Dover, and seized by his lordship's officers." *CSP-D, James I, 1611-1618, #49, p. 431.*

11 February 1617. "Certificate that Mondey Beauvois, French merchant, has received from the officers of the Cinque Ports his bark, the *Johanne* of Bourdeaux, cast away near the Downs, and a portion of the cargo, having paid £6 to Lord Zouch as composition for the best cable and anchor, which belong to him as a royalty." *CSP-D, James I, 1611-1618, #60, p. 433.*

The Downs is a roadstead in the southern North Sea near the English Channel off the east Kent coast, between the North and the South Foreland in southern England that has been the final resting place for many ships over the centuries. It would appear it had claimed another. There are no records of salvage attempts so this ship may have remained intact. If the cables and anchor were recovered, it is probable that other items were recovered and the only item remaining would have been the ship.

Dutch wreck.

3 May 1617. "Richard Marsh to Lord Zouch. A Dutch ship, richly laden at Dover Castle with bullion, specie, &c., ran on shore at Burling-gate, parish of East Dean, beyond Beachey Head; it is claimed by Payne, who holds the manor on lease. Though lately the liberty of the Cinque Ports relative to wrecks has

been limited by Beachey Head, it is said to have anciently extended beyond Seaford to Rednoore, near Newhaven." *CSP-D, James I, 1611-1618, #8, p. 463.*

22 May 1617. "Bond of Andrew Cornellison Bestever, of Medenblick, Holland, and others, under penalty of £800, to indemnify Lord Zouch for restoration to Bestever, the professed owner of the goods of a Dutch ship laden with deals, wrecked on the Godwin Sands, on payment of lord warden's droits, and on composition with the savers." *CSP-D, James I, 1611-1618, #39, p. 468.*

No additional information was located in archives. This Dutch ship could be between Eastbourne and Birling Gap, but unlikely retaining anything of great value including the bullion.

The *Marie*.

23 May 1617. The council sent a letter of assistance from the high court of the admiralty for restitution of the *Marie* of Amsterdam, travelling from St. Lucas Spain toward Amsterdam loaded with Campeche wood, and "with a good quantity of Spanish reales, wedges of silver bullion and other goods, that wrecked upon a rock the 26 April 1616 upon the coast of Sussex," the mariners made it to safety of land. That is the entire letter. *APC, V.35, p. 254.*

29 June 1617. "A letter to the lord treasurer of England. Forasmuch as we are informed that there is certain Spanish money and bullion of silver procured by Phillip Burlamachie, Giles Vandeputt and others out of a wreck upon the coast of Sussex, which they have offered to sell unto the East India Company as conceiving it fit for the said company towards their furnishing of money for the next voyage to the East Indies, now for that the said company have humbly desired to understand the pleasure this board, whether they may have leave to contract for the same and to transport it, as they conceive they may not without special license, for that the same is contrary in some sort to their accustomed course which hath always been to bring it in themselves, or to procure it to be brought in by some of the brethren of the company, we have taken the matter into consideration, and do not find it any way for our part inconvenient, all circumstances consid-ered as the case is, and therefore do pray and require your lordship to give warrant and order by virtue of this our letter for leave unto the East India Company and free liberty as well to buy the said bullion of silver and Spanish money as also to ship it out freely without danger or prejudice to the said company or to any of them. Provided they do not exceed in their whole yearly transportation the sum of £30,000, allowed unto them by his majesty, for which your lordship is to give such direction as you shall think fit. And this

our letter shall be unto your lordship and unto the said company a sufficient warrant and discharge. So, etc." *APC-1616-1617, V.35, p. 282.*

25 July 1617. "A letter to the Lord Zouch, lord warden of the Cinque Ports. Whereas a commission out of the high court of admiralty together with letters of assistance from this board for the due execution thereof were granted forth for restitution of certain bullion and other goods that were saved and brought to shore from a ship lately cast away upon the coast of Sussex, belonging to certain merchants of Amsterdam, as by the said commission and warrant of assistance appears, and forasmuch as information is now made by the said merchants that great store of the said monies and goods are carried and conveyed in to several places within the precincts and liberties of the Cinque Ports, whither the authority of their former commission does not extend for recovery thereof, and have therefore made humble instance unto us for some assistance in that behalf, we have been moved hereby to pray your lordship to give order for the discovery and finding out of all such money and goods as have been conveyed from the foresaid shipwreck into any places within the privileges of the Cinque Ports and for the delivery thereof unto such persons as shall be authorized from the owners to collect and receive the same for their use according to the purport and intent of the foresaid commission of the admiralty." *APC-1616-1617, V.35, p. 321.*

No additional information was located. Based on the record, "travelling from St. Lucas Spain toward Amsterdam... upon the coast of Sussex," the *Marie* of Amsterdam may have wrecked between Selsey and Brighton. It appears that there is a question whether or not the full cargo was recovered; that may never been known. But, it is clear that items were recovered from the ship and though the recovery of all the valuable cargo is rather ambiguously worded, it is safe to speculate no treasure remains with the *Marie* of Amsterdam.

The *John* of Southampton.

Early records in the *Calendar of State Papers, Domestic Series* are only represented by fragments, and the National Archives has indicated some of the original letters no longer exist perhaps in part to the East India Company's disposal of documents. I was only able to locate a single reference to this ship in archives.

19 December 1617. "A bond was issued to three haberdashers of London to indemnify Lord Zouch for the delivery of goods recovered from the *John* of Southampton that wrecked near Hythe." *CSP-D, James I, 1611-1618. p. 508.*

Hythe is a coastal market town on the edge of Romney Marsh, in the district of Folkestone and Hythe on the south coast of Kent. The word "Hythe" or "Hithe" is an Old English word meaning haven or landing place. This ship would perhaps lie within about 8 miles of coastline. I was unable to locate additional information.

1618

The *Hopewell*.

Records of a *Hopewell* indicate she was 200 tons and served in 1588 against the Spanish armada with a crew of 100.

The surviving remnant of the source document was cataloged by the editors of the *Calendars* in a collection of letters assumed to be originally written in 1622. The original document I reviewed of 4 pages was damaged. "An abstract of the evidence of witnesses, whose names and references to their depositions were given in the margin regarding the case of Johnson the owner of the *Hopewell*, against Hurlock the owner of the *Ann Speedwell*, which was run down and sunk in the Thames River by the *Ann Speedwell* on 28 October 1618. The witnesses being on the side of Hurlock, to prove that the *Hopewell* hung out no lights, and that they called aloud to give warning. *CSP-D, Elizabeth and James I, Addenda, 1580-1625, #93, p. 648.*

This or another *Hopewell* turned up in a list of 11 ships bound to fight the Dutch at Batam or Jakarta on 7 April 1620 and in a list of ships belonging to the East India Company.

The *Ann Speedwell* served with Sir Francis Drake with a crew of 14 at 60 tons. There are many versions of the *Speedwell*, but only this record of the *Ann Speedwell*.

9 May 1635. A letter mentions "the *Hopewell* of London, William Wilkinson master, coming from Russia to London loaded with tallow, cable yarn, beaver wood, beaver wombs, and other goods belonging to Richard Swift and other, was lately cast away above the Spits. The admiralty issued a commission of 5 May to take possession of the said goods and merchandise. Parcels of goods being embezzled and carried away into towns which claim to be exempt from the admiralty' are to be recovered." *CSP-D, 1635.* This is a single reference to possibly another ship or the *Hopewell* survived to wreck above the Spits thirteen years later.

A thorough search in the *Calendars*, National Archives and other archives did not yield additional information about this incident or cutting her down or salvage attempts were located. A ship of about 200 tons could block the Thames at certain locations and would warrant additional mention in records.

The *Anne*.

12 March 1618. "Thirteen chests of reales go in the *James Royal* for Bantam, three in the *Gift* for Suinatra, and two in the *Bee* for Masulipatam, besides 500 reales delivered to the *Anne*; for her provision." *CSP-C, EI, C&J, 1617-1621, #295, p. 137.*

15-17 September 1619. Court minutes of the East India Company. "Notice of the arrival of the *Anne*; in the Downs, and the landing of the lord ambassador, whose expenses with his ladies are to be defrayed to Gravesend, where a committee will assemble tomorrow to conduct them to London; a dozen coaches to be ready at Tower Wharf to carry him to his house." *CSP-C, EI, C&J, 1617-1621, #743, p. 296.*

22-25 September 1619. Court minutes from the East India Company reflect a petition from Margery, widow of Peter Bell, accidently killed on the *Anne* and the dishonest conduct of the coroner. *CSP-C, EI, C&J, 1617-1621, #745, p. 297.*

1 October 1619. This is related. "William Baffin, master's mate was awarded a gratuity for his pains and good art in drawing out certain plots of the coast of Persia and the Red Sea. Four Pence would be deducted from the mariners involved. John Brown, carpenter, a very mutinous person, proud and a ringleader, was to be punished." *CSP-C, EI, C&J, 1617-1621, #748, p. 300.*

8 October 1619. Journal of the voyage made by Captain Shilling presented to the company. "The principal mutinous persons in the *Anne*; especially John Browne and Alexander Edward, two of the most notorious offenders, to be punished, for example to others. Notice to be given of the launch at Blackwall of the *Exchange*. Some hard stones brought from Surat by the *Anne* for ballast, given for the use of the city to pave without Moorgate. The stones brought in the *Anne* provided they do not exceed the value of £5 or 20 nobles, to be given to pave by Moorgate for the use of the city." *CSP-C, EI, C&J, 1617-1621, #750, p.302.*

Court minutes from 10 March 1620. "To provide a ship to supply the loss of the *Anne*; Peter Kenton, having one of 350 tons with three decks, fore and aft, to be spoken with." *CSP-C, EI, C&J, 1617-1621, #821, p. 361.*

17 March 1620. "Committee to go down to Gravesend, to be eyewitness of what may be done for recovery of the *Anne*." *CSP-C, EI, C&J, 1617-1621, #825, p. 363.*

20 March 1620. "A ship (the *Anne*) from the East London Indies worth more than £16,000 cast away between London and Gravesend, a thing never heard of in a ship of eight or nine hundred tons. They had had 1000 men about her these eight of ten days at least and are at the charge of £100 a day to recover her, but hear they have little other hope but to cut her up." *CSP-C, EI, C&J, 1617-1621, #825, p. 363.*

Court minutes of 27 March 1620. "Desire of the company to free the *Anne* from her disaster and to have her buoyed up." *CSP-C, EI, C&J, 1617-1621, #829, p. 364.*

The final letter mentioning the *Anne* was 2 December 1620. "The *Anne* was cast away a little beyond Gravesend in the Thames, to the endangering of the river and her own ruin; hears nothing in her can be saved." *CSP-C, EI, C&J, 1617-1621., p. 395.*

Accounts of this ship in the *Calendar's* call this ship the *Anne*, whereas accounts from the East India Company call a ship with similar but not identical circumstances the *Royal Anne* during the same time period. A ship of eight or nine hundred tons would impede shipping along the Thames and there is mention to "cut her up."

The *Speedwell*.

This wreck is slightly problematic due to the name. There is already an *Anne Speedwell* of 28 October 1618 involved in a legal case recorded between the owner of the *Hopewell* which was "struck and sunk in the river Thames" by the *Ann Speedwell*. There is an early entry of the *Speedwell* that served with Sir Francis Drake at 60 tons with a crew of 14.

12 November 1624. This is the first mention of the *Speedwell* wreck. "Captain Chudleigh, of the *Speedwell* to Sir Francis Nethersole, Flushing. Details the disastrous wreck of his ship on November 1; his first care was to preserve Count Mansfeldt. The mischief was occasioned by an ignorant drunken pilot of Flushing, who by Count Mansfeldt's influence, was appointed to conduct the ship." *CSP-D, James I, 1623-1625, #56, p. 377.*

The editors of the *Calendar of State Papers, Domestic* series placed the following letter in November 1624 because the original record is undated. "Petition of Peter Billingham to the commissioners of the navy. Lost all he had by the wreck of the *Speedwell* off Flushing; was left there to see what could be saved from the wreck, and incurred sundry charges thereby. Thanks for their gift of £6; entreats further remuneration, and employment in one of the ships now going out. With reference thereon to Captain Chudleigh, and his report in favor of the petitioner." *CSP-D, James I, 1623-1625, #92, p. 397.*

7 May 1625. "Grant of a pension of 38, per diem to Elizabeth Man, widow of John Man, who lost his life in the king's ship the *Speedwell* for life." *CSP-D, Charles I, 1625, 1626, p. 535.*

17 September 1625. "Petition of Peter Bellingham to Buckingham. Served Queen Elizabeth and his present majesty as 'boteson' (Boatswain) for 47 years, and now in his old age has lost all he had in the *Speedwell*. Prays that he may have the first place of a 'boteson' (Boatswain) that falleth." The words of this petition indicate that it was prepared for presentation during the reign of King James. The date under which it is placed is when it was endorsed as having been received. Seeing as the ship sank in November 1624, the place-ment of this letter is correct, though the wreck date was not known when the editor compiled the *Calendars. CSP-D, Charles I, 1625, 1626, #71, p. 106.*

21 February 1626. "Warrant to pay to the treasurer of the navy and the surveyors of marine victuals, £2,162. 38. 3d., for the ordinary charge of the navy for the present year and £7,137. 13s. 9d., for building two new ships of 350 tons each in place of the *Speedwell* which was cast away; also for length-ening the graving-dock at Chatham." *CSP-D, Charles I, 1625, 1626, p. 562.*

I was unable to determine the cargo or what, if anything, was recovered from the *Speedwell*. Mr. Billingham had indicated he had lost everything, so it may be safe to assume she sunk in deep water off the coast of Flushing, Corn-wall and could still contain personal artifacts and perhaps other valuables.

The *Blind Fortune*.

Late November 1618, "Warrant [from Lord Zouch] to Thomas Fulnetby, to deliver the goods saved from the Dutch bark, the *Blind Fortune* lately wrecked on the Godwin Sands, to Josias Ente and Willam Horne, on payment of customary dues." *CSP-D, James I, 1611-1618. #113, p. 599.*

I was unable to locate additional information in archives. The Fortune of London appears in archival documents from about 1627. The Goodwin Sands claimed another ship.

1619

The *Sampson*, of Horn

18 January 1619. "Warrant from Lord Zouch to Thomas Fulnetby, to deliver up to Philip Lane, Michael Castell and Daniel Van Haringhook, of London, procurators for the owners, the portion saved of the cargo of the

ship Sampson, of Horne, wrecked on the Godwin Sands, on their paying the Cinque Port droits, and then compounding with the savers." *CSP-D, James 1619-1623, #48, p.5.*

Although about a full year until the next related document, odds are unlikely that two separate incidents of ship(s) of Horne wrecking on the Goodwin Sands, so this record is included.

2 December 1619. "William Ward to Lord Zouch. The Ramsgate men saved a ship stranded on the Godwin Sands, and had £90 for their trouble. Captain Turner has gone along the coast, bidding the people retain all things saved for the lord admiral; wishes to commit him to the Castle. Begs instructions about some horses belonging to a gentleman of the French ambassador, stayed at Dover by the agent of the Farmers [of Customs]. Encloses." *CSP-D, James 1619-1623, #57, p.100.*

Enclosed: "Thomas Fulnet to Lord Zouch. Two ships of Horne, in Holland, were cast away upon the Godwin Sands, one of which was saved by the Ramsgate boatmen, and the best anchor and cable claimed for the lord Warden, when the lord Admiral sent Captain Turner to seize all wrecks upon the Sands. Recommends that Captain Turner be confined in Dover Castle, for meddling in his Lordship's jurisdiction." *CSP-D, James 1619-1623, #57-1, p..100.*

I am unable to determine whether one or two ships perished on the Goodwin Sands with only a portion of the cargo recovered.

The *Sun*.

1 March 1619. From Jakarta describing "a cruel bloody fight" between the English and Dutch fleet. "On 15 November 1619, they arrived at an island called Engano about 3 of the clock and at about 6 of the clock, the *Sun* was cast away, wherein I lost all that I had in that ship to my shirt, myself being in a smaller ship with the president." From the preface of the *Calendar of State Papers-Colonial Series, East Indies, China and Japan, 1617-1621* volume.

31 January 1619. Additional information, "the loss of the *Sun* partly caused by want of judgment." *CSP-C, EI, C&J, 1617-1621, p. 242.*

23 February 1619. John Perry received news of the loss of the *Sun* then who wrote to the East India Company informing them of the loss of most of her company. There is mention of encountering foul weather, but I am unable to determine if that affected the *Sun*. *CSP-C, EI, C&J, 1617-1621, p. 250.*

23 March 1619. Contained in a long letter is mention that the *Sun* "struck upon the rocks of Engano...and that Sir Thomas Dale began the fight with the *Sun*. When within sight of the Dutch fleet, Sir Thomas Dale began the

fight with the *Sun* of Holland. It continued about three hours, in which time the English shot above 1,200 great shot from six ships. Chased the Dutch the next day through the Bay of Jakarta, in sight of their castle." *CSP-C, EI, C&J*, *1617-1621, p. 265.*

21 May 1619. "Record of a consultation held aboard the *Moon* to go to Engano with the *Moon, Clove, Globe, Peppercorn, Advice*, and the *Dragon's Claw* to try to recover the money cast away in the *Sun*." *CSP-C, EI, C&J, 1617-1621, p. 275.*

On 13 July 1619. "The Peppercorn has Masulipatam arrived, one of Sir Thomas Dale's fleet, forced by extremity of weather from the rest, which were riding at Engano in quest of what was lost in the Sun. She brought a letter from the Cape from Thomas Barwick, with news of the death of the queen of England and Sir Walter Raleigh, and the overthrow of his project; also that the two companies of Holland and England were united, and that he had letters for the two Presidents." *CSP-C, EI, C&J, 1617-1621, p. 284.*

26 August 1619. Additional information is shared, "the loss of the *Sun*, with the saving of Sir Thomas Dale and others; the rest, swimming ashore, were slain by the Indians of that country." *CSP-C, EI, C&J, 1617-1621, p. 292.*

21 October 1619. "Sir Thomas Dale with the Moon, Clove, Globe, Peppercorn, Advice, and Dragon's Claw went to Engano to see what they could recover from the Sun, but got nothing but a little of his own plate; he found not one Englishman alive, but some 16 or 18 of their skulls lying in a heap together. Sir Thomas killed two of their people, burnt and cut down part of their houses and trees, and so left the place, but the diseases our people took there and aboard the China junks left not them until many ended this life." *CSP-C, EI, C&J, 1617-1621, #775, p. 324-325.*

26 January 1620. Court minutes of the East India Company, "letter read from Nathaniel Martin from Scilly, endeavoring to excuse himself for the casting away of the *Sun*, and to lay the imputation upon Sir Thomas Dale, leaving his ship." *CSP-C, EI, C&J, 1617-1621, p. 346.*

The total loss of the *Sun* and cargo is expressed in a couple letters in February and March. "With the loss of 60 men, not a pennyworth of goods saved." *CSP-C, EI, C&J, 1617-1621, p. 362.*

May 1620. "The fleet set sail from the straits of Sunda the next day; some with Sir Thomas Dale to Engano, to recover, if possible, the money lost in the Sun, and relieve the men left there, if any were alive; the others, with Captain Pring for the coast, to join strength at Priaman, there to meet with the ships from England and Captain Bonner's, and all go to Bantam." *CSP-C, EI, C&J, 1617-1621, #856, p. 374.*

21 October 1621. First mention of the loss of 2000 Spanish reales "of the company's money" in the *Sun. CSP-C, EI, C&J, 1617-1621, p. 474.*

25 October 1621. "Sir Thomas Dale, upon Ball's knowledge, lost all his estate when the *Sun* was lost, and yet he had by him when he died near 2,000 reales, besides silks sent home to Lady Dale." *CSP-C, EI, C&J, 1617-1621, #1136, p. 477.*

Cape Engaño is a cape located at the northern point of Palaui Island, off the northeastern most point of the island of Luzon in the Philippines. Based on the records, the Sun of Holland struck rocks at Engano and sank with at least 2000 Spanish reales and whatever else that were not recovered. The fact that numerous attempts were made to recover the valuables, suggest she sank in more than 100' of water off the northern point of Palaui Island.

The *Expedition*.

The choice to include this wreck was difficult. Though she was an English ship, I was unable to locate her final resting place.

Early records indicate the *Expedition* was out of Dartmouth and a bark of 30 tons. The only early record located was of 17 March 1579. Perhaps another *Expedition* or this ship was refitted and or overhauled.

12 March 1619. "The *Expedition* landed all she had at Jask. Their endeavors to improve the prices prevented by the customer. Half the tin has been sent for Persia, and the rest landed and sold; larger quantities, 60 chests, may be sent for the supply of Surat and Persia. Employment of the *Royal Ann* in the Red Sea; her return the *Expedition* was sent to Persia. Amount of bullion, specie, and English and Indian commodities taken by the *Expedition*, expecting her with seventy-one bales of silk provided last year." *CSP-C, EI, C&J, 1617-1621, #624, p. 258.*

12 March 1619. "The other series had been there in her way the *Expedition*; surprised two Portugal ships laden with commodities from Goa to Ormuz, estimated, besides the vessels, which are very useful for your occasions, to be worth some £2,000 or £3,000. Find encouragement for the sale of sundry English commodities in Persia, but hope further conditions will be proposed for the company's trade before a large supply is furnished. The *Royal Ann*, from which much more was expected, had not such success as the *Expedition*, the captain, and factors of different opinions as to the construction of Sir Thomas Roe's orders and intent." *CSP-C, EI, C&J, 1617-1621, #624, p. 259.*

13 November 1619. "Two of the Holland ships of great force, one with 38 and one 32 pieces of ordnance. The *Bear*, *Expedition*, and *Rose* yielded without any fight at all; the *Expedition*; had but ten men, the *Rose* fourteen, all the rest fighting in the *Dragon*. Barwicke, either out of cowardliness or sincerity of

religion, yielded his ship *Bear* without firing a shot, though better able to maintain fight than the *Dragon*." *CSP-C, EI, C&J, 1617-1621, #767, p. 321.*

13 December 1620. A letter to the East India Company includes: "knows not what has become of the *Unicorn* and *Hope*, except they be returned to Patani or Jakarta. List of Dutch ships arrived. Also, the *Swan*, Howdane captain; and the *Expedition*; cast away in this port at anchor in a great storm, and not to be recovered. How all this shipping was disposed of. Commodities received from the ships, and what have been sold." *CSP-C, EI, C&J, 1617-1621, #930, p. 397.*

15 May 1622. The *Expedition* "Lost on the cable of the *Great James*." *CSP-C, EI, C&J, 1617-1621., #64, p. 29.*

7 June 1622. "Captain Pring indicated that Captain Speck, a Dutchman, caused the loss of the *Expedition* by taking out ballast in order to stow goods, and being thereby over-lightened, she overset in a perry of wind, riding at anchor. The Dutch tried to blame the incident on the *James*, twart the *James* hawse, but could not find a man to make that statement." *CSP-C, EI, C&J, 1617-1621. #98, p. 47.*

September-January 1622-1623. "The *Expedition*; taken by the Hollanders; overthrown by the cable of an Englishman; by the right of the sea to be borne half and half, but if the law of the sea bear it not, they will render the whole." *CSP-C, EI, C&J, 1617-1621, #205, p. 81.*

Following the *James Royal*, she was expected to arrive from Jakarta about 6 March 1622, then expected from Sumatra about 16 March 1622. "Lost on the cable" could suggest the *Expedition* was either in tow, or tied to the *James Royal* during a storm, but there is mention of being at anchor. The only clue that may assist in the location of her wreck is in the 13 December 1620 letter; "cast away in this port" that was written in Firando, Hirado Island, (Hiradoshima) (also previously named Hiranoshima and Firando Island) is the fourth largest island in Nagasaki Prefecture. Its coasts are washed by East China Sea. The *Expedition* could lie along the north or south side of the island or about 22 miles of shore. An index reference in the *Calendar of State Papers, Colonial Series, China and Persia, 1625-1629* mentions the names of ships of the East India Company taken by the Dutch with a reference to the *Expedition*.

Yarmouth wreck.

17 September 1619. A single mention of "the wreck of Yarmouth of one of the Greenland ships appertaining to the account of the Unites Companies." *CSP-C, EI, C&J, 1617-1621. #743, p. 296.*

No additional information could be located. A wreck lies off the coast of Yarmouth, England perhaps between Winterton-on-sea to Lowestoft.

Goodwin Sands wreck.

2 December 1619. "The Ramsgate men saved a ship stranded on the Godwin Sands, and had £90 for their trouble. Captain Turner has gone along the coast, bidding the people retain all things saved for the lord admiral; wishes to commit him to the castle. Begs instructions about some horses belonging to a gentleman of the French ambassador, stayed at Dover by the agent of the farmers [of Customs]. Encloses."

Enclosed in the above letter. "Thomas Fulnetby to Lord Zouch. Two ships of Horne, in Holland, were cast away upon the Godwin Sands, one of which was saved by the Ramsgate boatmen, and the best anchor and cable claimed for the lord warden, when the lord admiral sent Captain Turner to seize all wrecks upon the Sands. Recommends that Captain Turner be confined in Dover Castle, for meddling in his lordship's jurisdiction." *CSP-D, James I, 1618-1623, #57, p. 100.*

No additional information was located. No records of goods washing on shore were located. Two ships hit the Goodwin Sands and it appears one ship was recovered.

Holyhead wreck.

24 December 1619. The council sent a letter, "to the high sheriff of the county of Anglesey, Wales, regarding Sir Thomas Roper, knight and captain of a company of foot soldiers, perished in a ship that wrecked near Holyhead, Wales loaded with goods belonging to Roper that was cast on shore. The council requested that a diligent search and inquiry be made and inventory made then placed in safe custody. A note indicated the letter was sent by post the same day at 12 o'clock at noon." *APC, V.37, p. 96.*

10 January 1620. The council was informed that Roper did not perish in the wreck and was in Ireland, but others had. "Had with them in goods and money to a good value together likewise with diverse writings and evidence of importance." The council was led to believe that much of the important cargo was recovered, but required proof. *APC, V.37, p. 103.*

11 February 1620. The last letter adds that there was a small amount of money not recovered or was possibly sent out of Ireland and that the inhabitants near the coast where the ship had wrecked recovered many dead bodies,

stripped them, and then took anything they could then threw the bodies in the sea. The council was sure there was little chance to recover anything and requested that all opportunity should be taken to recover anything possible, including money and goods. *APC, V.37, p. 128.*

Without knowing where the ship departed, it is difficult to determine whether the ship had wrecked on the north or south side of Holy Island, but it is more probable on the south side. It appears that this ship may have retained most of its cargo and some small quantity of valuables.

1620

North Wales wreck.

11 February 1620. "A letter to Sir Richard Treavor, knight, vice admiral of North Wales. You shall understand that since our late address unto you for the finding out and preserving of such moneys and writings as were got to share and saved upon the late unfortunate accident of a ship that was cast away upon that coast, wherein the lord viscount Thurles and a second son of the lord Dunboyne, with many others perished, information hath been given unto us, as well by the earl of Ormond, father to the said lord viscount Thurles, as by Terrence Bryen, gentleman, a scholar at Eaton School, to whom (as is informed) there was some moneys to the value of £60 or there about sent out of Ireland, which was likewise lost in the foresaid ship, that the inhabitants near unto that coast where the said ship was cast away have taken up many of the dead bodies, stripped them, took away what they had about them, and after threw them into the sea, whereby there is little hope to recover any thing that is fallen into the hands of such people but by a stricter course of proceeding then hitherto hath been taken and therefore we have been moved hereby to pray and require you to take notice of the information this bearer shall give unto you in this behalf, and, calling before you such persons as he shall nominate or shall be otherwise thought meet to be examined, to employ your best diligence and care in finding out any of the moneys, goods, evidences, or writings so lost as aforesaid, and the same to put in safe custody, according to our former directions, until you have certified us thereof and received further order, wherein we assure ourselves of your best endeavors. And so, etc." *APC, 1619-1621, p. 128.*

There is not enough information to place the wreck within a tighter distance other than the north coast of Wales. If bodies had washed on shore, then it is possible that little was removed from the ship and may had retained the small amount of valuables that sank with the ship. Considering the length of the letter and the possible links associated, there was no other information located.

Romney wreck.

[6?] April 1620. "Thomas Fulnetby to Lord Zouch. Will not surrender without permission the goods which were saved from a Flemish pink cast away near Romney. Begs leave to kill a hare on Good Friday, as huntsmen say that those who have not a hare against Easter must eat a red herring." *CSP-D, 1619-1623, #67. p. 137.*

No additional information was found. New Romney is a market town in Kent England, on the edge of Romney Marsh, an area of flat, agricultural land reclaimed from the sea after the harbor began to silt up. New Romney, one of the original Cinque Ports, was once a seaport, with the harbor adjacent to the church, but is now more than a mile from the sea. This ship may have been salvaged of all that was valuable, but the ship, ordnance, tackle may have remained.

The *Unicorn*.

Though this is an English ship, it did not wreck around the United Kingdom and does deserve mention as it possibly met with a violent end, "The *Unicorn* cast away in the most wild hurricane ever felt, and all the sailors blown away."

The *Unicorn* is mentioned in a 1546 inventory at 240 tons with a crew of 130 and 16 gunners. It also served against the 1588 Spanish armada with a crew of 66. It is not mentioned beyond that in the royal navy so perhaps it was transferred or sold to the East India Company or another merchant about the time King James I ascended the throne. This *Unicorn* is mentioned in an inventory of 1617-1621.

In the manuscript of Mr. Phineas Pett, he mentioned the *Unicorn*. "In February 1634, the *Unicorn* built at Woolwich, by Mr. Boat, was launched; his majesty was present, as he was likewise the next day at Deptford, at the launching of the *James*."

12 July 1620. "Captain Pring departed for Japan with the *Royal James* and the *Unicorn* to careen (to turn the ship on its side for cleaning, caulking, or repair) there, expected to be in Jakarta in December." *CSP-C, EI, C&J, 1617-1621, #878, p. 381.*

25 October 1620. The first mention that the *Unicorn* sank. "The Unicorn cast away on the coast of China; the men saved, and, through the favor of the Chinese, allowed to buy some small junks in which they were shipped." *CSP-C, EI, C&J, 1617-1621, #917, p. 393.*

31 December 1620. "*Unicorn* left the *Royal James* in a cruel storm, cast away on the coast of China." *CSP-C, EI, C&J, 1617-1621, #947, p. 404.*

29 May 1621. "Had we not been within twelve leagues of the coast of China, we had not had escaped drowning, every man of us was an account for a crew member." *CSP-C, EI, C&J, 1617-1621, #1014, p. 429.*

30 September 1621. "All men saved with a chest of money." *CSP-C, EI, C&J, 1617-1621, #1112, p. 462.*

25 October 1621. Court minutes of the East India Company mentioned that George Bell had confessed he might have laden home the *Unicorn* "which if he had done he had save the ship and so many men's lives as perished in her, which was to the state." *CSP-C, EI, C&J, 1617-1621, #1136, p. 477.*

The *Unicorn* was lost within 36 miles of the China coast. Cargo unknown. If the *Unicorn* departed Japan after repairs, it could rest somewhere perhaps within 100 miles north or south of Shanghai, a major port. There is not enough information to narrow the wreck site down.

The *White Bear*

Contained within *The Voyages of Sir James Lancaster, of the East Indies* under a list of ships of the East India Company, p. 295, mentions that the *Merchant Royal's* name was altered to the *Bear* in 1619 and had sailed, then changed to the *White Bear* that was burnt by the Dutch in 1620.

6 November 1619. "Concerning the loss of the *Bear*, with which he may be maliciously taxed, there was such odds that there was no hope of escaping. The danger of landing her treasure; fears of the factory being robbed three nights before; one John Tucker killed." *CSP-C, EI, C&J, 1617-1621, #761, p. 371.*

13 November 1619. "Two of the Holland ships of great force, one with 38 and one 32 pieces of ordnance. The *Bear*, *Expedition*, and *Rose* yielded without any fight at all; the *Expedition;* had but ten men, the *Rose* fourteen, all the rest fighting in the *Dragon*. Barwicke, either out of cowardliness or sincerity of religion, yielded his ship *Bear* without firing a shot, though better able to maintain fight than the *Dragon*." *CSP-C, EI, C&J, 1617-1621, #767, p. 321.*

20 November 1619. "The Flemings had fourteen chests of money in the *Bear*; Barwick might very well have saved all the company's money by sending it ashore." *CSP-C, EI, C&J, 1617-1621, #764, p. 320.*

10 July 1620. "Petition of the East India Company to the council, for punishment of Thomas Berwick, appointed by them master of the Bear, who betrayed that ship and others to the Hollanders."

Enclosed with the above letter: "19. I. Statement of the conduct of Thomas Berwick, that meeting Sir Thomas Roe off the Cape, Sir Thomas gave him letters to English factors, and Houltman, the Dutch commander, gave him letters to their people at Bantam, persuading a truce, on the ground that peace was negotiating in England; relying upon which Berwick acted as though all danger was over, and several vessels were taken in consequence. Grounds on which he is suspected of treachery and of secret intelligence with the Dutch." *CSP-D, James I, 1619-1623, p. 163.*

20 July 1620. "Saying, their own safeties enforced them to give such liberty to their sailors, to encourage them to fight. Have demanded restitution of the 100,000 reales taken in the *Bear*; and *Star*, but they were not ashamed impudently to equalize their losses with ours, and refused to make demand thereof until we likewise brought in what our demands were on our part, till when they utterly refuse to restore any goods or money whatsoever." *CSP-C, EI, C&J, 1617-1621, #883, p. 385.*

15 October 1620. "Our people refuse to accept the *Dragon*, because the Dutch had lamed her by misusage; the *Bear* burnt in satisfaction of their galley." *CSP-C, EI, C&J, 1617-1621, #914, p. 392.*

The *Bear* is mentioned in the inventory of 1604 at the ascension of James I at 900 tons with 340 mariners, 40 gunners, 120 soldiers with a total crew of 340. In the 1607 inventory, it was the *Bear*, but in the 1618 inventory, it was called the *White Bear*. In the 1622-1624 inventory, the *Bear* and White Bear are mentioned as two separate ships.

Dover wreck

The records for this wreck are fragmented.

27 November 1620. "A fishing boat of the town, driven to sea by a storm, ran on shore near Calais, and the governor claims two thirds of its value as a forfeit." *CSP-D, James I, 1619-1623, #92, p. 194.*

27 November 1620. "Petition of Henry Sergeant, William Earl, and Thomas, Perkins, Dover, owners of the above-named fishing boat (reference to above letter and no name located), for his influence for restitution of their boat, the loss of which would undo them." *CSP-D, James I, 1619-1623, #93, p. 194.*

No additional information located in archives. This appears to be a rather small incident barely worth mentioning in records. Nevertheless, a small

English fishing boat wrecked near Calais with a great chance of a few items of value.

1621

The *Ark Noah*, Hamburg.

12 March 1621. "James Hugessen, to Lord Zouch. Wreck of the *Ark Noah*, Dover, a large Hamburg ship, laden with sugar, spices, coin, &c., on the Godwin Sands. Can do nothing with the goods, having incurred his lordship's displeasure." *CSP-D, James I. 1619-1623, #17, p. 234.*

15 March 1621. "Sir Henry Mainwaring to Lord Zouch. The money from the wreck is about £4,000. Mr. Fulnetby keeps it safely in Deal Castle, and will not allow him to take it to Dover, without his lordship's special warrant. Begs that Fulnetby may be ordered to obey him, as a sergeant should a lieutenant. Forty casks of cinnamon and four bags of pepper were saved." *CSP-D, James I, 1619-1623, #22-1, p. 234.*

22 March 1621. "Bond of Samual de Fische, Phil. Burlamachi, and others, in £20,000, to indemnify Lord Zouch for restoring the cargo of a ship of Hamburg, wrecked upon the Godwin Sands." *CSP-D, James I. 1619-1623, #33, p. 237.*

June 1621. "Petition of Claes Stavele, mariner, to Lord Zouch, for restoration of what has been saved from his ship *Ark Noah*, wrecked on the Godwin Sands, one third of which belongs to the savers, and the rest to his lordship. With report thereon." *CSP-D, James I. 1619-1623, #142, p. 270.*

I was unable to locate additional information in archives. It is easy to assume that the full amount of money was not recovered from Ark Noah, but impossible to determine how much money may have remained with the ship when the sands claimed another ship.

Bay of Galway wreck.

6 June 1621. "St. John (Lord Grandison) to the Privy Council. Received their letters of the 18th of April, of a French ship not arrested but wrecked in the Bay of Galway. It appears that a ship of Newhaven (one Andrew the captain) had made a voyage towards the Indies by a commission of the admiral of France; in his return home, came weather beaten with loss of masts and sails into the Bay of Galway, and for want of knowledge of the place and sufficient pilots was thrown upon the rocks and splitted. The captain and company were received into the town, and the goods and merchandize

(as much as could be saved) brought and laid up in safety, where they still remain without diminution, the captain having a key with himself of the cellar where they are laid. The mayor, finding the company to be composed of several nations, and likely to be a man-of-war, and that the merchants of that town had of late endured sundry depredations at sea by French men-of-war, advertised him of it, and had a commission to him and others to examine the company, and found by [Unreadable] that the commission of the admiral of France, authorizing [Unreadable] to make war upon the Spaniards beyond the line, which they understood to be the equinoctial line, they had taken prizes about Cape Verd, and the isles about Cape Verd and Sierra Leon, and in the Bay of Mexico, being north of the line, and that some of the merchants of Galway deposed besides, that the lieutenant of this ship had not long since been in a French man-of-war, and robbed a ship freighted by them to the value of £800. Upon this, he (St. John) gave order for the dismissing all but the captain and lieutenant and one or two of the principal men of the ship, and to preserve the goods in safety till further notice might be taken thereof. Sends copies of examinations, that as well the ambassador of France as the ambassador of Spain (whom this affair may concern) may receive satisfaction of what has been done. In behalf of the town is a suitor, that having gratis lodged and relieved most of the company, they may out of the goods be satisfied of such money as they disbursed for removing the ship out of the channel.—Dublin, 6 June 1621." *CSP-I, 1615-1625, #748, p. 326-327.*

"Examination of Edyen Framon, of Diporte, France, and others. Details the voyage of the ship and the prizes captured. 30 January 1620 (1) Signed: Andrew Linch, mayor, Da. Peck, Valentine Blake." *CSP-I, 1615-1625, #749, p. 327.*

"Examination of Morirlagh O'Connor, of Gallwaie, sailor, and of Peires de Salla Novaesq, Senior de Rocabin, lieutenant under Captain Andrews. In relation to the same matter." 21 Feb. 1620. *CSP-I, 1615-1625, #751, p. 327.*

"Examination of William Austen, of Southampton, England, pilot, in relation to the same matter. 4 April 1621." *CSP-I, 1615-1625, #752, p. 328.*

18 April 1623. "Lord Deputy Falkland to Sir George Calvert, S.P., Ireland, had received a letter from the lords concerning one captain Andreas Niennart, a Frenchman, to restore him wrecked goods at Galway, and leave to carry men for the Indies. Had been informed that he was a companion and very conversant with a most noted pirate that lurked in this kingdom, whom he had tried to trace. Thinks that this captain was as guilty of piracy as the other, and prays him to acquaint the lords therewith that he may know their further pleasure how far he shall proceed. Dublin Castle, 18 April 1623." *CSP-I, 1615-1625, #1014, p. 407.*

No additional records could be located. The inventory of what was removed from the ship would have been a great indicator of what may remain on the ship, but is unattainable. There is an excellent chance some of the prizes would remain on this ship.

Galway Bay is on the west coast of Ireland, between County Galway in the province of Connacht to the north and the Burren in County Clare in the province of Munster to the south. Galway city is located on the northeast side of the bay. The bay is about 12 miles wide at the opening to the North Atlantic Ocean and about 15 miles deep.

1622

The *Whale*.

Though this was an English ship, it did not wreck near homeport. Nevertheless, it deserves a place here.

First mention of this wreck and the single reference to the value of the lost cargo is in the preface of *The Calendar of State Papers, Colonial Series, East Indies, China and Japan 1622-1624*. She was loaded with silk and other goods to the value of £150,000, (about 18 million today). "The loss of which was severely felt by the company and affected to some extent, as may be imagined, the dividend of their stock."

11 January 1622. "The long stay of the Whale and Trial put them in fear that they are fallen on the back side of Java; unless they arrive soon the pepper expected from Jambi cannot be shipped to England, nor their lack of provisions supplied." *CSP-C, EI, C&J, 1622-1624, #9, p. 5.*

6 March 1622. Within a long letter to the East India Company is mentioned, "the Whale and Trial not yet arrived." *CSP-C, EI, C&J, 1622-1624, #43, p. 20.*

There is almost a full year of information that I am unable to fill.

10 March 1623. "Entreats Christopher Rosons to see five bales, marked with the writer's name, sent aboard the Whale." *CSP-C, EI, C&J, 1622-1624, #28, p. 117.*

16 December 1623. "Emmanuel Butta to the East India Company. Account of the passages and navigation of the Blessing in company with the Discovery and Reformation left the Lizard, in Cornwall, 3 April 1622, and anchored in Swally road 3rd October, and met there the London, Jonas, Whale, Dolphin, Lion, Rose and for Flemings. On January 9, the *Whale*; and *Dolphin* set sail for Surat with 250 bales of silk, we finding the coast to be clear of Portugal's.

Met the *Dolphin* who told us the unlooked-for news that great misfortune to the *Whale*". *CSP-C, EI, C&J, 1622-1624, #373, p. 212.*

17 December 1623. "Have ill tidings that the *Whale*, with a rich cargo from Persia and Surat, sunk right down in the sea 10 leagues off the road of Surat, 36 men drowned, and nothing saved of her goods, by reason of a plank that sprung in her." That information traveled overland to Masculipatam (Machilipatham, India) about 625 miles. *CSP-C, EI, C&J, 1622-1624, #375, p. 214.*

21 March 1624. "Are resolved to send three ships for England this year, which will partly recompense the loss of the *Whale*; last year, which with her full lading sunk in the sea and drowned most part of her men." *CSP-C, EI, C&J, 1622-1624, #432, p. 260.*

28 May 1624. Additional information is shared in a letter, "he relates that a rich English ship, the *Whale*; laden with silk and indigo, from Surat, is perished upon the homeward voyage, and that there has been a treason of the inhabitants with some English against the fort of Amboyna." *CSP-C, EI, C&J, 1622-1624, #460, p.283.*

19 June 1624. "The *Elizabeth* and *Exchange, London,* newly arrived from the East Indies with tidings of the loss of the *Whale*; with three or four hundred bales of silk and other rich commodities not far from Surat; they bring a fresh cry against the tyranny and injustice of the Hollanders towards our men lately murdered or executed by them there." *CSP-C, EI, C&J, 1622-1624, #447, p. 293.*

8 September 1624. Court minutes of the East India Company. "Wages to be paid to those of the *Whale's* men that died before the ship was cast away, or that were before then transported to other ships, but not to the others, because the loss of the ship is imputed to the negligence of those in her. The master of the *Whale*; attending to justify himself was told that she was merely lost by his negligence, that she overset by being overladen in her upper works, carrying 40 pieces of ordnance, whereof four brass cannon of 4,000 weight a piece, besides great store of goods for private trade; the way in which she was lost is described, and he said that no care had been wanting in him, only the visiting hand of God brought it to pass; it was held fit to have the matter examined in the admiralty." *CSP-C, EI, C&J, 1622-1624, #594, p. 389.*

Records of the court minutes from the East India Company between these two dates only summarize with a notation of mariners seeking lost wages.

19 November 1624. Court minutes of the East India Company. "Monnox's journal it appeared that Woodcock had gotten an unknown booty at Ormuz, whereof no account is come to the company, besides the loss of the *Whale*, of which he had charge; Woodcock endeavored to wash off these accusa-

tions with bare denials, but the court was altogether unsatisfied with his answers." *CSP-C, EI, C&J, 1622-1624, #682, p. 445.*

The gap in records of 6 March 1622 to 10 March 1623 may be explained simply as nothing to report. No issues with the ship.

Based on records, the *Whale* sank within the harbor 10 leagues or about 30 miles off the road of Surat India. If she was top heavy and rolled over, then it is safe to speculate that the only items to survive were those that could float when the *Whale* sank with 40 pieces of ordnance and 4 brass canons (4000 pounds each). If a ship was located in this area, then that information would help to identify her.

It is probable she may contain other valuables including pay for soldiers.

The *St. Anthony*.

The wrecking of this ship does not follow within the guidelines as the others in this edition as it is a Spanish ship and wrecked in the Bermudas, nevertheless there is interesting information to be shared.

In March 1818, the East India Company began to destroy many volumes of books of journals and logs prior to 1800. These included the chief, second mate's, boatswain's, and surveyor's books. Some of those that survived only recorded in the Calendars series and other similar collections. It is a great loss to maritime history and most certainly would have given additional information to incidents like the St. Anthony.

The next three letters are included together under the date of 6 February 1622. Letters #2-2-I and 2-2-II are undated.

#2. "Gondomar, the Spanish ambassador in England, to the company of merchants of the Bermudas. The St. Anthony of 300 tons was wrecked near those islands, and her freight, which consisted of, gold, silver, and merchandise, to the value of more than 6,000 crowns, was seized by the English there, who also took possession of the cock boat, and even of the clothes belonging to the passengers, Spaniards. Requests immediate satisfaction for those losses, and security for the freedom of five Spaniards, captives in the Bermudas." *CSP-C, 1574-1660, p. 27-28.*

6 February 1622. #2-2-I. The company's answer to Gondomar. "Are surprised at the ambassador's allegation, which they believe is grounded upon misinformation. Thanks rather than accusations are deserved, and have been given by the better sort of the unfortunate Spaniards who were wrecked. All Gondomar's charges are entirely refuted. The vessel was suddenly beaten all to shivers ten miles from land; no treasure could be recovered, and every

means was taken to assist and provide for the comfort of the shipwrecked passengers. *CSP-C, 1574-1660, p. 28.*

6 February 1622. #2-2-II, Gondomar's reply to the company. "Desires exceedingly that this business of the Spanish wreck might be accommodated and ended without further process, but seeing by their answer that there cannot be agreement made, he must, therefore, refer it to the king his master, that his subjects may receive satisfaction for losses and injuries received." *CSP-C, 1574-1660, Volume 2, #1, p. 28.*

January-September 1622. "A small book in which are fourteen letters and a proclamation from Captain Nathaniel Butler, governor of the Somers Islands, to my sergeant-major, relating to the wreck of the Spanish vessel (the *St. Anthony*). Copies, certified by Edward Collingwood, Sec." *CSP-C, 1574-1660, Volume 2, #11, p. 33.*

22 February 1622. A record was entered that "interrogatories to be administered to the masters, mariners, and passengers of the *Joseph* and the *James* lately returned from the Somers Island and others touching the complaint of certain Spaniards wrecked upon the rocks near that coast." *CSP-C, 1574-1660, p. 27-28.*

An undated note of between September and October 1622 was included in the *Calendars* regarding several voyages made by William Seymour regarding the Spanish wreck. *CSP-C, 1574-1660, p. 33.*

No additional information was located in archives. The *St. Anthony* could perhaps have wrecked on the north side of the Bermuda Island "beaten all to shivers ten miles from land." If the company of merchant's rebuke is correct, then there is gold, silver, and other valuable merchandise on this ship of a value at that time of more than 6,000 Crowns. This is the only reason I chose to include her in this book.

In 1609, about 150 English travelers aboard the Virginia Company ship Sea Venture, enroute to the colony of Jamestown, Virginia, were blown off course by a hurricane and shipwrecked at Bermuda, which they named the Somers Isles for their leader, Sir George Somers. Several wonderful tales have emerged on websites that the survivors from that wreck founded the British occupation of those islands.

An average ship of 300 tons would have a crew of perhaps 150-123 with about 30-40 iron and 2-4 brass ordnance. These pieces of ordnance would help to locate this ship off the coast and to identify her in addition to other items of interest.

The *Angel Rachel.*

21 February 1622. "Thomas Elfick to Lord Zouch. Wreck of a ship of Hamburg on a rock near Seaford; has saved her best anchor and cable for his lordship." *CSP-D, James I, 1619-1623, #118, p. 349.*

23 February 1622. "Petition of Joachim Sleur and Hendrick Bras, merchants of Hamburg to Lord Zouch. Their ship, the *Angel Rachel*, laden with wines, raisins, and oil, from Malaga, was cast away at Seaford; they saved part of the cargo, but it was taken from them by the inhabitants, who, like savage people, took the very clothes from their backs, ransacked the vessel, cut the wine pipes, and carried away the wine in buckets. Mr. Elfick, a chief man there, pretending to help them, and buy their wine, was extortionate and fraudulent in his dealings with them. Entreat redress." *CSP-D, James I, 1619-1623, #125, p. 349.*

No additional records located in archives. There is not enough information to suggest a possible wreck site location within several miles along Seaford. It is safe to speculate that anything that could be removed was removed.

Seaford is a town in East Sussex, England, and east of Newhaven and west of Eastbourne. In the Middle Ages, Seaford was one of the main ports serving Southern England.

Sheringham Wreck.

March 1622. "[Unknown] to Lord (Buckingham?). A ship of Amsterdam, bound for Hamburg, was cast away at Sheringham, Norfolk, in October 1621; many of the rich wares on board were saved, but stolen by the people of the country, and, in spite of a commission issued for their recovery, at suit of Sir Noel de Caron, many are still detained. Begs him to assist John Braddock, procurator for the owners, in recovering them." *CSP-D, James I, 1619-1623, #104, 370.*

The fragmented and damaged letter is the only reference to this wreck and no additional information was located. The wares mentioned were not all recovered, and the ship may still contain pieces of Dutch Delftware in addition to other items of value. It is safe to speculate that if the local inhabitants had access to the cargo of wares, then anything else that could be removed was removed where she sank perhaps between Weybourne Beach and Cromer Beach.

The *Unity*.

Another English ship that was lost far from home port. The *Unity* is first mentioned as having served with Sir Francis Drake at 80 tons with a crew of 70, then in the 1588 inventory against the Spanish armada at 80 tons with Humphrey Sidman as captain of 70 mariners. The *Unity* is not mentioned in the inventories of the East India Company, but the following entries show that she served with the company.

6 March 1622. "The *Unity* would depart Acheen at Jakarta to Pulicat and Mascilipatam, (saltwater lagoon on the Coromandel Coast of Andhra Pradesh state, southern India.) Harris, the mate of this ship, sent home as drunken, vicious villain." *CSP-C-EI, C&J, 1622-1624, p. 21.*

12 May 1622. The *Unity* was ready to depart with 20,000 Spanish reales of eight. *CSP-C-EI, C&J, 1622-1624, p.38.*

6 September 1622. It was reported that the *Unity* while travelling from Banda to Amboyna, "split in pieces on the cliffs of Amboyna, with a loss of 43 souls; 43 persons were saved and there is hope of recovering the ordnance." *CSP-C-EI, C&J, 1622-1624, #145, p.65.*

It was reported on 9 February 1623 that a chest sent to Pulicat on this ship was stolen. *CSP-C-EI, C&J, 1622-1624, #264, p.108.*

There are approximately a dozen additional records following the 6 September 1622. Two placed the *Unity* in another location at a much later date while the remainder described her as wrecked and removed from the books. The *Unity* was not located in other editions of the *Calendars* series or other resources in archives.

Ambon Island has about 27 miles of coastline facing Banda Islands, with an out crop about 16 miles long that a storm could have driven the *Unity* on to. There would still be approximately 70 pieces of ordnance remaining if she retained her ordnance. Though a chest was described as stolen, whether it was the chest containing the 20,000 Spanish reales is unknown. There are no records of the salvage of any items from the *Unity* or of the 20,000 Spanish reales.

Ireland Wreck.

A single letter is the source of this information for this wreck. A letter was sent on 3 April 1622 concerning "a restraint and stop of a license formerly granted to for transporting pipe staves and other cloven ware cut out of woods into foreign parts." *APC, V.38, p. 181.*

John Chapman petitioned the council on 11 April 1622, regarding a ship that in November 1621 was loaded with 33,000 pipe staves at the port of Wexford Ireland. The ship was wrecked, but the staves were saved and brought back into the port of Wexford and another ship was hired to transport the staves to Spain. *APC, V.38, 191-192.*

No additional information is available. It is hard to determine where the ship was headed, but Wexford is at a location along the coast that does help to narrow the wreck site to perhaps 20 miles from what is now Rossiare Harbor to Ballgarrent from Wexford. The pipe staves being made of wood perhaps floated leaving a ship of perhaps 50-80 tons. No records are known about salvage attempts or plundering by inhabitants.

The *Defence.*

The editor of these *Calendars* determined that the following letter was written in February 1622. "Inventory of our known losses to our best estimation. Endorsed. Invoice of ships and goods hereunder written, besides such shipping as are to be restored, as also the goods returned into Europe, and so much as yet no advertisement of. In the Star, Bear, Dragon, and Expedition, Sampson and Hound, Solomon and Attendance, Swan and Defence, amounting to 211,840 reales." *CSP-C, EI, C&J, 1622-1624, #40, p. 18.*

15 May 1622. "This day spent in examination of proofs showed by the English in demanding the Bear, Dragon, Sampson, and Attendance. The lords think them sufficient, and give their reasons. The Dutch cannot admit the publication of the treaty to have been a sufficient demand; the Defence, Solomon, and Attendance were abandoned, the Star and Swan restored in the Indies, the Expedition lost on the cable of the Great James, the Dragon refused because spoiled, but the Bear, Sampson, and Hound it is equitable should be restored." *CSP-C, EI, C&J, 1622-1624, p. 29.*

14 December 1622. Contained in a very long letter, "The Solomon and Defence were laid up for wrecks at Banda." *CSP-C, EI, C&J, 1622-1624, p. 202.*

Banta is in the region of Rajasthan (a state in Northern India). Rajasthan's capital Jaipur is approximately 267 km / 166 miles away from Banta. The distance from Banta to India's capital New Delhi is approximately 496 km / 308 miles.

No additional records were located for this ship with a search up to 1630 to provide possible evidence whether it was a wreck or not. Though not definitive proof, this remains unresolved.

Bude Bay Wreck.

Officials in Ireland informed the council on 13 June 1622 that a petition was filed by James Nugent and Adam Talbot, merchants in Dublin regarding a bark that they loaded about 1 February 1621 of diverse' goods and merchandise of a great value to be transported to Calais France. About 15 days later, a storm drove the ship into the beach sand of what is now called Bude Bay, Cornwall. The bark perished and all but the goods and crew were saved, apparently by local inhabitants. The account mentions "they did in great numbers run down the cliffs and places near the sea." *APC-D, V.38, p. 251.*

There is no additional information available. The section of Bude's coastline contains sandstone cliffs. History has recorded wrecks along this section of coastline, but nothing this early. Based on the location of the inhabitants, there is about a 3-mile stretch of coastline in which this bark wrecked.

The *Trial*.

Though the *Trial* is an English ship, it did not wreck in or around the United Kingdom.

This ship does not appear in the inventory *State of the navy of 1618 of 39 ships and vessels.*

(#1) 10 July 1622. "The long hoped for *Trial*, laden with provisions, was lost upon a hedge of rocks 300 leagues (1035 miles) from hence (Batavia) {Jakarta} in 22 degrees latitude on 25 May. The master and 43 crew were saved in the skiff and long boat all the rest, nearly 100 men, with letters perished. She had but 500 reales in her, but is a great loss, and we shall be plunged in our business if speedy supply come not from England, for both our meat and money is all spent." *CSP-C, EI, C&J, 1622-1624, #110, p. 48-49.*

(#2) 22 August 1622. "Account of the voyage of the *Trial* after leaving the Cape the 19th of March. On 25 May, through carelessness, they struck upon the rocks, 300 miles from the Straits of Sunda; the hold was full of water in an instant; Broock, the master, got out the skiff, provisioned it, chose his crew, to the number of nine, out of his fellows and consorts, promised to take him and Jackson on board, but like a Judas, slipped away privately without them, leaving 128 souls to God's mercy, whereof 36 got off in the long boat, and the ship suddenly broke up before they had got a quarter of a mile. Details their adventures and privations, discovery of certain islands, and safe arrival two days after Broock. Serious charges against Broock; he has given no account of the company's money's, spangles, and letters, which the writer saw put into the skiff, but admits that he threw overboard some of the letters, after having read them, because they were wet, but as the writer thinks, because they would have done him no good if he had honestly delivered them. He made plots against Jackson and Ellam, which were supported by the false swearing of his consorts and many more gross villainies. The death of so many witnesses renders it difficult to prove anything. Hopes he may never go to sea with him or the like. He and Jackson were much persecuted and injured for opposing his dishonesty. Kempe and Danby have proved very dishonest in assisting Broock, begs for assistance in recovering his debt from Jackson's adventure in the second joint stock, to help him in his poor and distressed state." *CSP-C, EI, C&J, 1622-1624, #134, p. 56.*

(#3) 25 August 1622. "John Broock, late master of the Trial, to the East India Company, at Crosby House, London. Met at the Cape of Good Hope with the Charles, Captain John Bickell, and would fain have had one of his master's mates, as neither himself, nor any of his mates had ever been the dangerous course from the Cape to Jakarta, but not one would go without increase of wages. Describes the ship's course until the 25th of May, when, at 11 p.m., she struck upon some sharp sunken rocks, for the most part two fathoms under water. The men were struck in a maze, for they could see neither breach, land, rocks, nor sign of danger. Before she struck a second time, the wind began suddenly to fresh and blow; by two o'clock he had got out the long boat and skiff, and seeing the ship full of water, and the wind to increase, he made all the means he could to save his life, and as many of his companions as he could. He put the company's money, gold, spangles, and letters, with his own money and commission and letters, in the long boat, and sent them by John Norden, William Hicca, and John Willoughby, but the men being in dissension would not suffer the boat to be lowered into the water, nor the things to be put into the boat, but what one put in, the other threw overboard, so that none were saved. His people crying out of the skiff to come in and save his life, the ship beginning to open, he ran down by a rope over the people into the skiff, which he had near broken, and they put off at four in the morning. Half an hour after the ship fell in pieces; 10 men were saved in the skiff, and 36 in the long boat, in all 46 men and boys out of 139 were saved, whose names are all given. He came away with his boat for the Straits, and fell in with the east end of Java, 8th of June, at Bantam the 21st, and Jakarta the 25th. They had so much rain and sea that their boat was always half full of water, and their distress was great, as the president and his council, having examined himself and all his people that were saved, were truly informed. This island lieth false in longitude 200 leagues, as he has found by woeful experience, as also these sunken rocks, as by his draught will appear. Narrow escape of a Dutch ship in the same place, which rode three days at the mercy of God. Captain Fitzherbert missed this danger narrowly. Always in that course experience of variation is the greatest help to any man." *CSP-C, EI, C&J, 1622-1624, #138, p. 58.*

(#4) 27 August 1622. The last relevant letter shares additional information. "On 25 May last the long expected ship, the Trial, was cast away upon an unknown shoal of rocks lying in latitude 22, some 238 leagues, about 820 miles, from Java, with an easy gale and lair weather; she bilged and was instantly full of water, whereupon the master, John Broock, got into the skiff with eight men and a boy, his son, and left the ship; the long boat some two hours after, with 30 men, got also from the ship, and both arrived here, the skiff the 25 June, the long boat on 28 June; the rest of the men, near 100, perished with the ship and all that was in her, including the company's letters." *CSP-C, EI, C&J, 1622-1624, #143, p. 60-61.*

I spent many hours reviewing Java nautical charts and how the four records fit in, arriving at the same conclusion each time, motivated by the strong desire to determine a wreck site, but that simply was not the case. Records #1 and #4 mention the *Trial* wrecked at 22 degrees latitude. Record #2 mentions her course from Cape Town to the wreck site 300 miles from the Straits. Record #3 suggests she wrecked east of Java on the south side, and they rowed west to Jakarta in the skiff and long boat.

My hypothesis: Christmas Island. Though not as far south as 22 degrees latitude, the reference "this island lieth false in longitude 200 leagues," may refer to this island that is 300 miles south of the Straits of Sundra with 3000-6500 meters of deep water and no visible obstructions between the two points. An English East India Company ship named the island after passing it on Christmas 1643 but was not published until 1666 by a Dutch cartographer; so, it may not have been on their charts in 1622 and not seen by the watch when they struck rocks at about 11:00 p.m. The prevailing currents could have pushed the skiff and long boat to the east end of Java when the crew saw land and corrected their course to Jakarta. Referenced nautical map of Java prepared and published by the Defense Mapping Agency, copyrighted in 1996.

There are no records of salvage or recovery of items from the *Trial*, so is very possible that other items may have sunk with the ship. Depending on how quickly they abandoned their ship, some of the reales may still be with her.

This wreck was intriguing and I sincerely hope I interpreted the facts correctly. I will admit I look forward to a revision and the possibility that someone has a better idea or to share a bit of obscure information leading to a revision. I have met many wonderful people resulting in stimulating conver-sations that way.

Norfolk Wreck.

25 October 1622. "The council received information of a petition by merchants of Amsterdam Holland regarding a ship of that town, that departed in November 1621 with goods of several sorts to great value besides 13 passengers of worth had in their trunks, packs and otherwise, to Hamburg and wrecked near Sheringham Norfolk. Goods that floated to shore were recovered by local inhabitants. Local authorities were ordered to recover what they could and returned to merchants." That is the content of the letter. *CSP-D, V.38, p. 344-345.*

It must have been a very powerful storm to push this ship almost 180 degrees off its course from Amsterdam to Hamburg for it to end up on the coast of Norfolk. The North Sea has a long reputation for fierce storms during that time of year, or perhaps it was a result of very poor navigation.

Nevertheless, a ship wrecked off the English coast perhaps 5 miles west of Sheringham to about Sea Palling or along about 20 miles of coastline. "13 passengers of worth" suggests they had gold and or silver coin or bullion, and perhaps a quantity of Spanish reales and fine jewelry with fine precious stones still in the trunks of their owners. No records are known that anything was recovered or attempts to salvage were made.

Galloway wreck.

14 December 1622. "The council addressed a complaint from Captain Nieuart, a Frenchman, regarding a complaint against Andrew Linch of diverse parcels of goods that Linch recovered out of a French ship that wrecked at Galloway Scotland. A letter to the lord deputy. You will perceive by the enclosed petition of captain Niewart, a Frenchman, what his complaint and pretenses are against Andrew Linch, of Galloway; in that kingdom, touching diverse parcels of goods recovered by the said Linch out of a French ship wrecked there, which he now concealed and unjustly detained from the said captain, as he offered to prove; the examination of which business we have thought good to referee unto your lordship and hereby to recommend the cause unto your lordship, that as we doubt not but you will do him justice so he may receive it with as much expedition as may be." *APC, 1621-1623. p. 367.*

Nieuart claimed Linch was hiding the stolen goods and offered to prove it and desired the council to take appropriate action. That is all the information regarding this wreck.

Galloway is about 65 miles south of Edinburgh. The ship may have been travelling from Calais to Glasgow and a storm blew her into the 25 miles of coast of Galloway.

1623

The *Anne Lyon*.

28 November 1623. "Statement by the same, that Sir Henry Mainwaring refused to assist certain merchants of Sandwich in recovering the goods of a wrecked vessel, which had been embezzled by the inhabitants of the town." *CSP-D, James I, 1623-1625, #94, p. 121.*

1 December 1623. "Bond of Derrick Hoston to Ruytinck of London, and Peter Mace of Sandwich, in £1100, to indemnify Lord Zouch for restoring to Hoston a quantity of Brazil wood, recovered from the wreck of the *Anne Lyon* at Sandwich." *CSP-D, James I, 1623-1625, v. clv, #2, p. 122.*

1 December 1623. "Bond of Samuel Vischer and Robert de la Bar, of London, in £2000, to indemnify Lord Zouch for restoration to them of sugar, cinnamon, and other goods recovered from the above wreck." *CSP-D, James I, 1623-1625, v. clv, #3, 122.*

Sandwich is a town and civil parish in the Dover District of Kent, Southeast England. I was unable to locate additional information and it would appear anything of value was salvaged.

1624

Ramsgate wreck.

12 July (?) 1624. "Petition of John Hudson of Dover, to Lord Zouch, for favor concerning the duties belonging to his lordship from the goods saved from his vessel, wrecked near Ramsgate." *CSP-D, Charles I, 1623-1625, #82, p. 14.*

29 October 1624. Written at Ramsgate. "Thomas Fulnetby to Nicholas. A cable and anchor have been demanded and seized by Sir Richard Bingley, as belonging to his ship, though they had no mark; he takes up goods, and holds a market on board, and sells them to strangers." *CSP-D, Charles I, 1623-1625, #115, p. 365.*

16 November 1624. I believe this is related correspondence. "Written at Ramsgate. The little bark from Calais in Sandwich harbor; she sprung a leak at sea, but is repaired, and ready to sail. Some of the merchants have taken out their goods to go by land, as they were injured by the wet, but as all are entered at the custom house, entreats that they may have a discharge and go forward." *CSP-D, Charles I, 1623-1625, #67, p. 379.*

18 November 1624. I believe this is related correspondence. "Richard Fishborn to Nicholas. Mr. Fulnetby pleads Nicholas' order for staying certain goods, which, being injured by water in a Calais bark, were put into a wagon, to be forwarded by land, and being perishable, are much spoiled by delay. Desires to know upon what authority he has detained them, as he will have to answer for it to the owners." *CSP-D, Charles I, 1623-1625, #81, p. 381.*

30 November 1624. "Peter Mace to Nicholas. Has told the owners of the goods in a small vessel of Dartmouth, that nothing can be done about them without Nicholas's order." Enclosed, *CSP-D, Charles I, 1623-1625, #88, p. 397.*

30 November 1624. The enclosed note to the previous letter. "Thomas Fulnetby to the Same. A Dartmouth bark ran aground [near Ramsgate], laden with hides, aqua vita, and yarns." *CSP-D, Charles I, 1623-1625, #88-1, p. 397.*

A French bark from Calais either ran aground near Ramsgate or sprung a leak which was repaired and sailed away. No additional information could be located. The cargo appears to have been recovered.

The *White Swan.*

15 July 1624. A record of a bond issued to James Hugessen of Dover and three mariners from Hamburg "to indemnify Lord Zouch to deliver the furniture, tackle and goods salvaged from the ship of Hamburg." *CSP-D, 1623-1625, 303, #8, p. 303.*

I was unable to locate additional information. Perhaps the ship had wrecked on the Goodwin Sands given the proximity to Dover. This ship name was not located in archives.

1625

The *Lion.*

Information on the or a *Lion* indicated it launched in 1536 at 160 tons. It fell into the category of 'Fourth Rate', but the type is unknown. From 1539 to about 1547, it had an armament of 34 to 36 iron cannons, 4 brass guns, and

8-14 handguns. Between 1544 and 1547, it saw service in Scotland. Records indicate it was condemned in 1559. It was suggested that it captured a Portuguese merchant ship near the Isle of Wright on 1 January 1560. I am unsure if it is the same *Lion*, but for it to be in service for 89 years is not impossible, but a little unlikely. It is very probable that it was refitted which is often the case and placed back in service to be used by the East India Company, or it is a new ship of 300 tons. So, for the purpose of this entry, I will begin with the first entry of January 1625.

21-24 January 1625. Four ships were prepared to sail from Erith London. The *Lion* of 300 tons had a crew of 100. *CSP-C, EI, C&P, 1625-1629. #21, p. 14.*

21-23 February 1625. Court minutes of the East India Company indicated the *Lion* would carry 3 chests of money. *CSP-C, EI, C&P, 1625-1629. #65, p. 34.*

Details of the next events are vague, and the original documents have been damaged making them difficult to decipher. It appears the *Lion* fought with the Portuguese for 2-3 days with several other English ships and escaped to Gombroon, where the Portuguese admiral attacked her, and the crew defended her the best they could in their "weakened state" but the gunner resolved to blow her up instead of surrendering her to the Portuguese. The Portuguese hung 26 of the crew but sent one man to Kerridge with letters. Two of the English ships forsook the *Lion* to pursue the five galleons to eventually return to Bombay battered and lost masts and yards.

10 June 1626. "The *Lion* encountered by five galleons defended herself bravely yet with much difficulty escaped to Gombroon, landed her money, coral, and cloth, but was the next day assailed by Rufrero's fleet of frigates; defended herself the second time valiantly to Rufrero's great disadvantage, yet at last was with multitudes so oppressed that she fired herself; her poor remainder of men, 26, leapt into the sea, were taken by the Portuguese, and put all but one to death. The *Palsgrave* and *Dolphin* forsook the *Lion*; in her chief distress in her first conflict, were pursued by the five galleons and diverse frigates and when overtaken made two day's fight, but the event not known, or what has become of them, only the galleons have returned to Bombay with loss of masts and yards, therefore some hope still remains that the two ships may be in safety. But well might both Dutch and English have been intercepted by the Portuguese, had not a storm first put them from their anchors in Swally Road, in which two of them perished and the rest were so dispersed that the *Jonas*, *Ann*, *Falcon*, and three Dutch ships, though straggling, yet arrived in safety without resistance. And although those three English ships fell into their laps, yet the *Lion*; saved the best of her goods and sold her cargo dearly." *CSP-C, EI, C&P, 1625-1629. #328, p. 207-208.*

26 July 1626. A letter to the council of Batavia mentioned "it is some comfort that she sold her hull to its value and that our countrymen there lost confirmed." I was unable to learn more from the damaged document. *CSP-C, EI, C&P, 1625-1629, #346, p. 228.*

25 August 1626. "There is disastrous news, for the Palsgrave and Dolphin are fled no man knows where. The manner was thus: there were four great galleons came from Lisbon and challenged the English and Dutch ships in Swally roads ship to ship or all together, but they refused; in the meantime the fleet from England arrived on the coast, and the galleons encountered them and fought with them three days; they boarded the Lion thrice, the master, Rd. Swanly, being slain, and she valiantly freed herself; the Palsgrave and Dolphin fled and left the Lion in this distress, while the Jonas and Anne and three Dutch ships in the road most basely lay still, yet heard their ordnance and were urged by president Kerridge to succor them. The Lion escaped to Gombroon and there her goods were landed, which Rufrero perceived, being there with a fleet of frigates, and resolutely assaulted her; the men made such resistance as their weak ability could perform, but being unable to defend her, blew her up and fired her; the Portuguese saved the men, whom they presently hanged, but one they saved and sent with letters to Kerridge. By this occasion they are all idle at Surat, having neither goods nor money; they sent a pinnace to look for the Palsgrave and Dolphin and to advise the fleets of Europe to join six Dutch ships which are in the Red Sea. The Great James and Jonas are gone richly laden for England." Many of these letters are damaged and mutilated. *CSP-C, EI, C&P, 1625-1629, #358, p. 239.*

20-22 September 1626. Court minutes of the East India Company ordered that all women whose husbands were killed on the *Moon* were to receive a full month of their pay. *CSP-C, EI, C&P, 1625-1629. #361, p. 243.*

20-24 November 1626. "Request of Thomas Winterborn late quartermaster of the *Lion*; for maintenance and employment; he had served 24 years and lost all he had in the *Lion*; and had both his hands maimed in the fight, the court remembered he had been suspected to have aided Ruy Friero in his escape out of the *Lion*; before Surat, and in the fight at Gombroon when the gunner resolved to blow up the ship, had given warning to the frigates to stand off, for which Ruy Friero had given him his liberty, which he utterly denied; where upon the court ordered payment of his wages, but deferred his employment." *CSP-C, EI, C&P, 1625-1629, #375, p. 265.*

The *Lion* was sunk off the coast of Damaun, about 54 miles south of Surat India. The money and most of her furniture was removed. Ordnance and perhaps some cargo would have remained. "She sold her hull" could mean that the hull was disassembled or sold to be salvaged.

Three Downs wrecks.

15 February 1625. "Sir Richard Bingley to Buckingham. Has been prevented Garland, by the foul weather from staying in Calais road, to escort the Downs. French troops: three of their vessels were cast away. Three ships are wrecked in the Downs. Has delayed to obey a command of council for release of the Hamburg vessels, because it was not signed by his Grace." *CSP-D, Charles I, 1623-1625, #63, p. 476.* Though this is the source letter, it is a fragment of the original that I was not able to obtain.

21 February 1625. "William Leonard to Nicholas. Particulars of anchors and cables found in the Downs; and in Dover Road, and taken for the lord warden. Peter Dibb forbids his meddling in these matters. Asks directions." *CSP-D, Charles I, 1623-1625, #18, p. 480.*

2 March 1625. "Nicholas to Sir John Hippisley. Requests him to send all Savoy records bearing upon the extent of the admiralty jurisdiction of the Cinque Ports; believes it to be from the Shoe-beacon in Essex to Rednore in Sussex, but the admiralty court in London wish to judge on matters of wrecks in the Downs, and deny the lord warden's right to floating wrecks, unless they are near enough to land to be reached on horseback. The cause is now to be finally determined. Hopes to prove the lord warden rights." *CSP-D, Charles I, 1623-1625, p. 489.*

No additional information was located. The Downs is a roadstead in the southern North Sea near the English Channel off the east Kent coast, between the North and the South Foreland in southern England that is the final resting place for many ships over the centuries. It would appear it has claimed three more. There are no records of salvage attempts or cargo washing on shore. These may remain intact but deteriorated through time.

The Little Anne.

29 March 1625. "Another letter of the like tenor directed as this before written on the behalf of Thomas Barnard and the owners of the ship called the Little Anne, of London, which was negligently sunk in the Downs by one Moy Lambert, admiral of the Holland ships." *APC, V.40, p. 9.*

The fragment of the original letter does not share more. The British Library indicated this document was possibly destroyed by fire in 1731. No additional information was located. The Downs mentioned in this letter is most likely in the Southern North Sea off the coast of Kent England, between North and South Foreland in Southern England and history mentions that storms would often drive ships on the sands or shore there. It is safe to speculate this ship rests between Dover Bay and Deal with an unknown cargo.

Anglesey wreck.

6 April 1625. A letter to the mayor of West Chester. "Whereas it appears by a letter from the mayor of Beaumaris to our good lord, the Lord Conway, that two hundred or thereabout of the men who had been levied and embarked for the kingdom of Ireland were cast by tempest upon the coast of Anglesey, where they escaped to land with much danger and difficulty, and do still remain there for want of shipping; we do therefore hereby require and charge you, presently upon receipt of these our letters, to provide and send to Beaumaris, a sufficient number of good ships or barques, for the transporting of those men to such parts of Ireland as are appointed and assigned for their landing. And for as much as there is a new levy to be made of three hundred men to supply the like number which hath perished at sea, through the extremity of foul weather in their passage towards the aforesaid kingdom of Ireland, we do likewise require and charge you to prepare and have in readiness a sufficient number of good ships or Barques, for the transporting of them also, according to farther directions which shall be given." *APC, 1625, 1626, p. 20.*

30 May 1625. It was reported that 190 men departed to Dublin to replace those lost in the wreck to include 54 soldiers. *APC, 1625, 1626, p. 84.*

No additional information was located in archives. It is possible the ship departed the port of Liverpool on a west course toward Dublin when a violent tempest blew the ship into Beaumaris, next to the Meanai Sea, on the Isle of Anglesey and Wales, or as far as what is now Pennon Point.

The ship would have most certainly contained weapons, shot, powder, ordnance, and other provisions that soldiers would have required. There is a slight possibility that the ship contained small amounts of money to buy supplies and pay for the soldiers.

The *St. Remy.*

6 June 1625. It was reported that the Dutch chased a ship of Dunkirk, the *St. Remy*, onto the Goodwin Sands off Margate where it perished in the quicksand. Most of the crew with the captain had made it safely to land. The Dutch recovered 20 guns from the ship, though they did belong to the admiralty. *CSPM, V, NI, 1625-1626. #96, p. 71*

12 June 1625. "The Dutch chased a Dunkirk ship (*) to the Goodwin Sands, off Margate, where it perished in the quicksand. Most of the crew with the captain escaped to this kingdom. The Dutch recovered 20 guns from the ship, although they may pertain to the admiralty here. The captain

and men of the Dunkirker have been made prisoners by his majesty's order, and Buckingham gave instructions en route that all Dunkirk ships which come to these ports shall be detained."

(*) "The St. Remy, see Bruneau's letter of the 12th June. State Papers, Foreign, Spain." CSPM, V, NI, 1625-1626. #96, p. 71.

13 June 1625. "The men of the Dunkirk ship; remain prisoners, the matter being referred to the admiralty, to judge whether they are pirates." CSPM, V, NI, 1625-1626. #104, p. 76.

20 June 1625. "The prisoners from the Dunkirk ship number sixty. They propose through them to recover the goods taken from the king's subjects. The order to detain all ships of Flanders and Spain is announced as being because of merchants and not of the Catholic king or the Infanta. They would like, through pinpricks to induce the other side to break and put them doubly in the right, but the Spaniards will put up with them or else will respond with similar injuries." CSPM, V, NI, 1625-1626, #114, p. 83.

30 October 1625. "A large Dunkirk ship carrying upwards of forty guns, was stranded lately on the Lincolnshire coast. The men were all brought prisoners to London, the ship and guns being recovered, but the Dunkirkers still continue in force at sea." CSPM, V, NI, 1625-1626, #788, p. 596.

The Goodwin Sands had claimed another ship. It is not clear what was recovered, but it is safe to assume that the ship was stripped of everything by the Dutch and or English.

The Moon.

The recovery efforts of the cargo from this ship are well recorded. Pepper was the most important spice of this era and was followed in popularity by cinnamon, ginger, and cloves. Certainly, a prize cargo worthy of debate, and certainly worth fighting over.

16 September 1625. This is the first mention of the wreck of the Moon. "Sir John Hippesley to the Duke of Buckingham. Arrival at Dover of four ships from the East Indies, but one, the Moon of 800 tons laden with pepper, was cast away near the castle, and there will be little saved, because it was all loose. The other three in the Downs, and what to do with them he knows not because they are of so great a value." CSP-C, EI, C&P, 1625-1629, p. 92.

27 September 1625. In their ship the Moon, "lately cast away at Dover, arrived as passenger a Dutchman, who by his own confession was one of the judges that gave sentence of death on their innocent servants at Amboyna, upon which he is detained prisoner in Dover Castle, and certain papers were

taken about him which they make no doubt may produce good effect in the discovery of that bloody massacre." *CSP-C, EI, C&P, 1625-1629, p. 93.*

9 November 1625. Court minutes of the East India Company. "Information of Thomas Sanderson, purser of the Diamond, that he heard Captain Brookes say at the Cape concerning the Moon, that he would turn the nose of the ship the wrong way, and that he wished the ship were at Leghorn. That the several committees for every particular employment were appointed. Complaint by Leatt of negligence in the warehouse at the exchange in allowing porters and others to carry away privately pepper and other spices. Mr. Abdi requested to treat with Mr. Vandeputt about a parcel of quicksilver." *CSP-C, EI, C&P, 1625-1629, #203, p. 109.*

16-19 November 1625. "Mr. Grove attending was told by Mr. governor that if the pepper wrecked in the Moon, which his servant obtained by breaking open a lock in the night, were not brought in speedily, they would arrest him on an action of £1,000, and charge his servant with felony: he said he was altogether ignorant of the breaking open of the lock, and that all the pepper he had should be brought in." *CSP-C, EI, C&P, 1625-1629, #211, p. 115.*

30 November 1625. "That by reason of the loss of three ships, the last whereof, being the Moon, was not so little worth as £60,000, their debts and the payment of mariners, the coffers were much exhausted, and the committees had thought fit to raise money by sale of pepper, by taking out one half capital on stock and another with sureties payable at five-six months." *CSP-C, EI, C&P, 1625-1629, #288, p. 121.*

1-7 December 1625. "Request of Brook, now in Dover Castle for the willful casting away of the Moon, for a trial; a committee appointed to consult civil lawyers how to proceed against him." *CSP-C, EI, C&P, 1625-1629, #229, p. 122.*

23-25 January 1626. "Court minutes of the East India Company. Concerning the seizure of pepper from the Moon brought to London by Rawlins and Mason; the court would give no compensation fearing to make a precedent, and because some of it was seized for his majesty it might be lost to the company. The trial of Brookes and the rest to be prosecuted as speedily as possible. £100 given to Sir John Hippisley in recompense for the best anchor and cable of the Moon, and for his pains in obliging the company, over and above £20 already given to his lady. Chauncey to be released from his bond for goods recovered from the Moon. Two months' pay yearly of husband's wages allowed to every mariner's wife; question if the same allowance shall be made to mothers and other friends of bachelors, referred to Styles and Leatt." *CSP-C, EI, C&P, 1625-1629, #245, p. 141.*

3 March 1626. "Letter read from Bartholomew Churchman, late master of the Moon, prisoner in Dover Castle, praying for his release and complaining

against John Hunter, Oliver Straught, and others, referred for consideration." *CSP-C, EI, C&P, 1625-1629, #277, p. 175.*

19 April 1626. "Answer of John Brookes, late master of the Moon, to calumnies and false accusations imposed upon him as the chief and only cause in casting away the said ship, and that this unfortunate accident had murdered him in his reputation and robbed him of his means; he related particularly, by way of journal, his journey to the Indies in 1622; how the Trial, whereof he then was master, was cast away, through no fault of his, but by such a disaster as might have befallen the most skillful mariner; how he had advised the company to make their plantation at Champore or Bessee and not at Lagundy, in regard of the badness of the harbor and want of water, and how Gonninge, who approved rather of Lagundy, threatened therefore to stay him in the country three years longer. He further alleged that being pressed to take his voyage home in the Moon he absolutely refused, knowing her weakness and how extremely she was eaten with the worms, but at the encouragement of Brockenden he altered his resolution. He accused Saunders as the ground and main of this scandal raised against him, adding Scudamore and Hunter as confederates in giving out that he would run away with the ship; that he was driven by tempest into the Nests, and then prepared himself to come into the Downs. That when the ship struck aground he was not present at the opening of Mr. Brockenden's chest, nor had any of the diamonds and jewels, but confessed that his boy had them; he inveighed against Yonge for causing him to be committed, and complained of the company for keeping him in prison seven months, there having been 14 courts of admiralty in that time. The deputy then demanded what he did further desire, for whatsoever he had delivered was rather a repetition of his life than any manifestation or clearing of his innocence; his request was for a speedy trial, which the deputy answered was reasonable and the court would willingly incline thereto, and as they have begun with him in a legal course so they would proceed with all expedition." *CSP-C, EI, C&P, 1625-1629, #300, p. 187.*

16 May 1626. "Minuets of the general court recorded a cargo value of £55,000, but only 4-5000 recovered." *CSP-C, EI, C&P, 1625-1629, #318, p. 199.*

24 May 1626. "Bartholonew Churchman, late master of the *Moon*, demanded to know what wickedness or villainy he committed to occasion his long imprisonment in Dover Castle, protesting his innocence. John Brook was also charged with maliciously cast away the *Moon* on the rocks near Dover." *CSP-C, EI, C&P, 1625-1629, #321, p. 203.*

24 July 1626. "Request of Jacob Johnson, a diver of Dover, who had contracted to recover all the Moon's 59 ordnance, for payment on account, he having taken up 43, resolved not to pay any more until his bargain be

performed; those that have taken out pepper to transport and have sold it in town to be warned to court according to former order." *CSP-C, EI, C&P, 1625-1629, #343, p. 226.*

4 August 1626. "The surgeon from the *Moon* was discovered to have pawned 4 silver spoons and the top of a casting bottle and ordered to return them because they were not lost." *CSP-C, EI, C&P, 1625-1629, #350, p. 229.*

Dover Castle is a medieval castle in Dover, Kent, England. It was founded in the 11th century and has been described as the "Key to England" due to its defensive significance throughout history. The *Moon* wrecked along the coast of the castle.

The cargo was valued at £55,000, but only 4-5000 was recovered. Sixteen pieces of ordnance were not recovered and though what remained of the pepper would have long since perished, their containers and other less valuable cargo would remain. It would be safe to speculate that any money or other valuables could have been recovered. There are no additional records of ship's furniture recovered except cordage and anchors.

Dover wreck.

22 September 1625. "Sir Maurice Abbot, governor of the East India Company to Secretary Woodford Coke. 5 ships had returned from the East Indies, laden with indigo, pepper, and calicoes; one had been cast away near Dover. Sends Mr. Sherburne, their secretary, to solicit a warrant from the duke of Buckingham, for the seizure and recovery of the pepper and other goods saved by the inhabitants thereabouts. Congratulates Sir John Coke on the honor lately conferred upon him, i.e., his appointment as secretary of state." *CSP-D, Charles I, 1625, 1626, #93, p. 109.*

It would appear this was one of several ships affected by a tempest of 13 October 1625, but this was the only reported total loss of a ship. There are a few records of additional losses, but none provided enough information to determine if they were related to this shipwreck or warrant separate mention. It is safe to speculate that the ship was loaded with cargo from the East Indies, but no cargo inventories were available. No additional information was located in archives. This ship possibly hit the Goodwin Sands.

The *Rose.*

This ship was problematic because of her name. *Rose*, in addition to several variants encountered during research such as the *Mary Rose* and the

Rose of Amsterdam is common before and after this period. Furthermore, it was time consuming separating the ship from an inn called the Rose at Knightsbridge in Middlesex and another inn at Pudding Lane in London.

13 October 1625. The *Rose* was dispatched to Masulipatam India on 23 August with coral from London, cloves, sandalwood, alum, and money to the amount of 34,333 reales. *CSP-C, EI, C&P, 1625-1629, p. 96.*

6 February 1626. "Court minutes of the East India Company mentioned in a letter that the *Rose* was manned with a weak crew. Furthermore, the *Rose* was dispatched with 21 English and 12 blacks, loaded with money, cloves, sandalwood, alum and polished coral, 14 days after she was met in the straits of Malacca. The *Rose* was to be newly rigged with new cordage and cables." *CSP-C, EI, C&P, 1625-1629, p. 150.*

8 February 1626. Fragment of a letter mentions "they sent a pinnace after the *Rose*, and intercepted all boats that came off from the shore to her." The letter mentioned the abuses of the Dutch in Jakarta. *CSP-C, EI, C&P, 1625-1629, #44, p. 24.*

26 May 1626. A report was recorded at Whitehall that "John Wolton master of a ship called the *Rose* and *Katherine* of Dover, was contracted with by one Lodovick Deling, a merchant of Bruges in Flanders, for the fetching of wines from Nates in France." *APC, 1625-1626, p. 488.*

12 April 1626. The court minutes of the East India Company recorded that 7 English and 5 Portuguese were sick on board the *Rose*." *CSP-C, EI, C&P, 1625-1629, #255, p. 146*

10 June 1626. Letters from Masulipatam indicated the *Rose* wrecked in Bejarone, 31 leagues from Masulipatam, "her goods saved by Danish ships and delivered to Masulipatam, but her leak found incurable, and her hull therefore fired, losing 12 blacks and 5 English, the rest weak." *CSP-C, EI, C&P, 1625-1629, #328, p. 208.*

26 September 1626. "A petition was filed by William Hope, gunner of the *Rose* of Woodbridge, against Captain Hagthrope for the sale of stores." *CSP-D, Charles I, 1625, 1626, p. 438.*

21 July 1627. News of the loss was sent to the East India Company and that her ordnance was saved. *CSP-C, EI, C&P, 1625-1629, #466, p. 384.*

20 May 1628. This is the last mention of this *Rose* in minutes of a general court. "The *Abigail* also and *Rose* employed for the coast of Coromandel with cargazoons to the value of 89,512 reales of 8 (pieces of 8) miscarried, but the goods saved, with 10,167 reales remaining there might produce at Jakarta 300,000 reales." *CSP-C, EI, C&P, 1625-1629, #656, p.501.*

It is difficult to pinpoint the precise location the *Rose* sank based on records. Perhaps she sank about 93 miles off the coast of India between

Masulipatam and Kakinada. If the leak in the *Rose* was slow, that may have allowed the Dutch time to recover some or all the cargo before it sank. If she sank quickly, then she may contain the 10,167 reales and other cargo.

Calais wreck.

18 October 1625. "Robert Earl of Warwick, to Secretary Conway. On Friday last, a man-of-war, supposed of Dunkirk, came into Colne water and sounded the channel. The late storm had caused 18 of the Holland men-of-war to cut their masts by the board; 4 are sunk in the road, and one Scottish ship lost, and 2 English; a third English ship is ashore at Calais. The ships of Dunkirk may now go out at their pleasure. The duke is hourly expected." *CSP-D, 1625, 1626. #90, p. 126.*

19 October 1625. "Joshua Downing to the commissioners of the navy. Further report of the losses of the Hollanders and English in the storm of the 13th. Of the four English men-of-war, three were cast away at Calais with above 240 men; the 4th came into Dover dismasted. Three ships now in the Downs; two without captains, masters, or gunners on board, and the third without victuals. Seven ships prepared at Dover to fire the Dunkirk ships, and the morning of the storm Sir John Hippisley and the writer went out to view the manner of the Dunkirk ships riding, but were obliged to put back, the Dover men through grief and fear will by no means undertake any further." *CSP-D, 1625, 1626, #5, p. 127.*

26 November 1625. "Secretary Coke to Secretary Conway. The owners of the ships lately cast away in Calais Road desire letters to enable them to recover their goods. The French are bad restorers, but the demand may be reasonable. Rumors at Calais of the good and bad success of our fleet. Encloses." *CSP-D, 1625, 1626, #34, p. 160.*

Enclosed: "Commissioners of the navy to Secretary Coke. Sir John Hippisley having certified the great loss sustained by the owners of four ships wrecked before Calais in the late great storm, Secretary Coke is requested to procure letters from the council to M. La Force in Calais, that the owners might have their goods saved from the wreck." *CSP-D, 1625, 1626, #34-1, p. 160.*

No additional information was located in archives. Based on records, it is safe to speculate that three ships wrecked off the coast of Calais France. If these were men-of-war ships, then they wrecked with full ordnance and possibly pay for soldiers. Though there were no records located of English or French salvage attempts, it may have occurred nevertheless. Furthermore, these ships may have been beaten severally by the storm scattering debris for miles along the shore.

The English ship may still lie off the coast of Calais with full ordnance.

Isle of Wight wreck.

23 October 1625. The only relation of this letter is mention of the storm that possibly caused the wreck of this ship: "Captain John Pennington to Buckingham. Losses in the storm of the 13th. On Monday last 12 of the Dunkirkers came out, and Garland in the Downs, on Friday 10 more. On the morrow he purposes to sail in pursuit with 5 ships. Want of stores and provisions, arising from want of money. If the Duke holds his resolution in going for the Low Countries, he ought to have a very good guard of ships." *CSP-D, Domestic, Charles I, 1625, #28, p. 131.*

18 November 1625. "Lord Conway to Captain Anthony Ersfield, deputy vice-admiral of the Isle of Wight. To the same effect as the preceding, but instead of the last paragraph about the prize ship this clause was added: I have received yours of the eighth concerning the shipwreck at Chale bay, and thank you for upholding the privileges belonging to my office of vice-admiral which I will not quit in any part, you are therefore to keep safe those things you have seized for me, and either take the usual course against those who presumed to buy the goods without warrant and disobeyed your deputy, or else certify me what accept it is meet to call them unto and in what way." *CSP-D, Charles I, 1625-1649, v. 23, #45, p. 68.*

18 January 1626. "Sir John Leigh to Secretary Conway. In October last there was cast away and split in pieces on the coast of the Isle of Wight a ship of Lisbon taken by Hollanders. That certain of his neighbors, Robert Urrey, John Horden, William Orchard, and Edward Blieth, dwelling near the place, having assisted the crew and helped to save such goods as would have been carried away by the sea, were invited by the captain and master of the ship to purchase the same as by their bills of sale appeared. I understand these parties are now arrested by order of your deputy vice-admiral, Captain Ersfield, and are to appear in the high court of admiralty to answer the premises. They have requested me to write to you in their behalf; and I can say that they are men of very good and honest repute in the country, and being ignorant in these causes would not have dealt in this had not the poor sailors in their necessity cast it on them." *CSP-D, Domestic, Charles I, 1625-1649, #16, p. 97.*

The Isle of Wight claimed another ship. It is safe to speculate that anything worth recovering was taken from the ship. How much was recovered depends on how bad it was "split in pieces" or the amount of time they had before the sea claimed her. Chale Bay is a bay on the south-west coast of the Isle of Wight, England and west of the village of Chale from which it takes its name.

The *Long Robert.*

2 November 1625. "Sir Thomas Love to Nicholas. In the storm of the 12th October they lost the Long Robert, with 175 men, 1 ketch, and all their long boats. Account of the capture of fort Puntal, and of the defenses whereby the enemy prevented the ships from attacking Cadiz. They have put out to sea to look for the West India fleet. The army not fitted to stay out a winter journey. Ships leaky. Capture of three ships which come out of St. Lucar; they say they belong to Hamburg and France. The ketches so old and leaky they must be sunk. Present order should be taken to dispose of such soldiers as come home." *CSP-D, Charles I, 1625-1626, #9, p. 140-141.*

(?) August 1626. "Petition of owners and masters of ships belonging to Ipswich to the council. Twenty-four ships of Ipswich were taken up for the expedition to Cadiz, on each of which their owners expended from £80 to £100, of which they cannot yet receive any part; many servants of the petitioners, who were pressed into the service, served for thirteen months, and received only 9s. 4d. per month; the Long Robert, one of the twenty-four ships, was lost with all hands, to the utter undoing of many poor mariners' wives and loss to the owners of £1,200, for which they have not received any recompense; hoped by the employment of their returned ships to have got some maintenance, but they dare not go to sea for fear of the Dunkirkers, who have taken two of their ships; for thirty years past twelve ships were built every year at Ipswich, but the trade has been stopped since Michaelmas last; pray for redress and the guarding of the coasts." *CSP-D, Charles I, 1625-1626, #85, p. 415.*

Despite the unique name of this ship, no additional information was located in archives. Sir Thomas Love was a captain and wrote the letter of 2 November 1625 while aboard the Anne Royal and in a letter of 6 October 1625, the Anne Royal was reported to have been forced into Catwater (Plymouth) because of bad storms. It is possible the Long Robert attempted to make Plymouth seeking refuge from the storm. November storms can be deadly.

The *Morris.*

This entry is part of the motivation to research shipwrecks for the rare treasure ship. The treasure lost in the Morris may be small in size, but would certainly look big on display in a museum.

The *Morris* first entered into records on 18 November 1625. "Court minutes from the East India Company. Ordered that Stevens make ready the

William and *Blessing* with all speed, launch their new ship the *Morris.*" *CSP-C, EI, C&P, 1625-1629. #211, p. 116.*

November 10-12 1628. "Court minutes of the East India Company. That preparations cannot be made for launching the *Charles* this spring, because Boatswain Ingram is sent in quest of the *Morris.*. No tidings having been received of the *Morris* since she was driven from her anchor in the late great storm, resolved to dispend forthwith the *Reformation* in quest of her, with cables, anchors, and other necessaries." *CSP-C, EI, C&P, 1625-1629, #745, p. 571.*

19 November 1628. "Court minutes of the East India Company. On the sad news received this morning of the wreck of the Morris on the coast of Holland, ordered that the Reformation be unladen and the men discharged, and that a caveat be entered to detain the wages of the Morris's men till further order." *CSP-C, EI, C&P, 1625-1629, p. 572-573.*

24 November 1628. "Letters to be written to Mr. Poynett, the younger, to go down forthwith to the Downs and endeavor the recovery of the anchors and cables let slip out of the Palsgrave, Dolphin, Discovery, and Morris in the late great storm." *CSP-C, EI, C&P, 1625-1629, #752, p. 575.*

26 November 1628. "Court minutes of the East India Company. Factor's letter to be read to that purpose, wherewith his majesty seemed well pleased; he also let his majesty know of the present sent to him by the king of Bantam in the ship Morris, which was unfortunately cast away on the fly land near the Texel on the coast of Holland, which his majesty seemed very sorry for." *CSP-C, EI, C&P, 1625-1629, #752, p. 575.*

28 November 1628. "Court minutes of the East India Company indicated that all their four ships were in extreme danger, during the late great storm, but that the *Palsgrave, Dolphin,* and *Discovery* were now in the river in safety, but the *Morris;* was cast away and lost; that for her preservation a skillful pilot and 70 fresh men with all things necessary were put aboard since her coming into the Downs, and other measures taken for relief of the other ships, that the *Morris;* was driven on the coast of Holland and could not be found, but beating up and down unhappily met with a Holland man-of-war, which put a pilot aboard to conduct her into the Texel, but the storm continuing he missed his course and was driven upon the sands of the Fly Island, where the ship was cast away with the loss of 80 men and all her goods except some small matter." *CSP-C, EI, C&P, 1625-1629, #753, p. 578.*

5-10 December 1628. This may be a related record because of the date. "Court minutes of the East India Company. Books of account recovered and to sell at Amsterdam some small parcels of her goods recovered out of the sea." *CSP-C, EI, C&P, 1625-1629, #758, p. 851.*

8 December 1628. "Court minutes of the East India Company, recorded a statement of Mr. governor in answer to idle and vain rumors which he desired might be blown over and washed away that the disaster to the *Morris* had happened through the improvidence of the committees in not supplying her with cables and anchors." *CSP-C, EI, C&P, 1625-1629, #759, p.581.*

16 February 1629. "Court minutes of the East India Company. Ordered that notice be taken in the letters for Bantam by the London of their king's present to his majesty, and of his 500 pecul of pepper cast away in the Morris, and that his majesty be supplicated to write a letter to satisfy that king of the truth thereof; but the present to be returned to that king, as he cannot have the powder and shot he desired, left to further consideration." *CSP-C, EI, C&P, 1625-1629, #798, p. 627.*

2 March 1629. "Court minutes of the East India Company. Ordered that Mr. Sherburne procure a letter from his majesty to the king of Bantam, to take notice of the loss of the *Morris*; and all her lading, with the king of Bantam's present, but the present to be sent to that king was left to further consideration." *CSP-C, EI, C&P, 1625-1629, #804, p. 635.*

6 March 1629. "Court minutes of the East India Company. Ordered to provide 20 muskets and 20 pistols for a present to the king of Bantam, notwithstanding the loss of his pepper in the *Morris*." *CSP-C, EI, C&P, 1625-1629, #806, p. 639.*

20 March 1629. "Gratitude's of 10 Shillings were paid to several widows of men lost on the *Morris*." *CSP-C, EI, C&P, 1625-1629, p. 644.*

March (?) "Particular of the presents sent by the king of Bantam to his majesty. One crest on dagger with a gold handle, one fair lance part plated with gold. The king has put aboard the Morris 500 pecull of pepper (piquillo pepper is a variety of sweet tasting chili pepper), consigning it to his majesty, with desire to have returned to him 40 snaphance pieces (Snaphaunce is a type of musket rifle) from 5 to 7 feet long, with powder and shot for great ordnance; conceive that if he be returned to the value of his pepper or with some small advantage he will be content; have required him to send the height of the great shot and the bore of the pieces. These particulars being sent in the Morris which was cast away, his majesty's letters to the king of Bantam are desired, taking notice of the wreck of said ship and of his intended present to his majesty, that he may receive satisfaction in that return is not made of the things desired for his pepper, together with some intimation of his majesty's thanks for his kind reception of the English and of the privileges and extraordinary respect they receive, which his majesty desires may be continued and enlarged." *CSP-C, EI, C&P, 1625-1629, #815, p. 645-646.*

If located, "one crest on dagger with a gold handle, one fair lance part plated with gold" would certainly be a well viewed artifact in a museum in addition to a few valuables such as jewelry and small amounts of money, silver and or gold that sank with the ship.

I am unsure "except some small matter" is indiscreetly referring to the gifts. The record of 5-10 December 1628, "Books of account recovered and to sell at Amsterdam some small parcels of her goods recovered out of the sea," does not supply enough information to definitively indicate it is related.

The *Morris* was caught in a storm and driven northeast out of the channel to wreck on about 10 miles of coast of Fly Island, or what is now Oost Vlieland or East Flyland. Taking into consideration the importance of the gifts from the king of Bantam Indonesia, no additional information was located in archives related to the *Morris* or the gifts. If the gifts or other valuables were recovered then it was not recorded.

The *Gift of God*.

This ship and wreck location presented a challenge as there is also a *Gift of God* from Dieppe France. The sum of these records allows me to place this in with the English ships. A *Gift of God* is mentioned in the 1588 English ship inventory against the Spanish armada at 180 tons with Thomas Luntlowe as captain of 80 mariners and fitted in London. Furthermore, several records survive of her service to her majesty's navy.

24 December 1625. "Certificate of corn, beans, and malt, belonging to Joshua Gogar on board the *Gift of God* of Sandwich, William Jewett, master." *CSP-D, Charles I, March 1625-January 1649, #73, p. 77.*

23 August 1626. "Letter to the earl of Totnes, master of the ordinance. Whereas Archibald Douglas, captain of the good ship called the *Gift of God*, had his said ship pressed in his majesty's service and employed unto Dunkirk, where it was cast away, and did furnish by direction for the setting forth of the said ship diverse necessary provisions of war for the advancement of his majesty's service which were likewise cast away; these are therefore to pray and require your lordship to cause to be issued and delivered unto the said Archibald Douglas out of his majesty's stores remaining in your custody twenty seven barrels of powder, thirty six muskets with bandoliers unto them, four dozen of pikes and eighteen cutting swords, which he did advance for his majesty's service, as by certificate of Sir John Hipsley, lieutenant of Dover, does appear for which this shall be your sufficient warrant. And so etc." *APC, 1626, June – December, p. 215.*

There are no additional related English ship records found in archives. If a shipwreck of about 180 tons is located along the 15 to 20 miles of Dunkirk coast and if she contains a fair quantity (perhaps the quantity of replacements is a good indication) of ordnance, weapons, powder and shot then that would help to identify it as the *Morris*. It is only speculation to presume she contained pay for soldiers.

1626

The *Spy*.

The *Spy* is first mentioned as having served in the English fleet against the Spanish armada at 50 tons and a crew of 40. It next appears in a 1603 ship inventory at the death of Queen Elizabeth I at 50 tons with 30 mariners, 5 gunners and 5 soldiers. It had 4 sakers, 2 minions and 3 falcons for ordnance.

6 February 1626. "On 6th August, the *Royal James* with the *Spy*, reloaded with cloves and 100,000 reales of 8, sailed for Surat, in company with three Dutch ships, to encounter enemies at Ormuz. It was reported the *Spy* was sighted from Surat and on 31 January had anchored off Hector Island loaded with 100,000 reales of 8." *CSP-C, EI, C&P, 1625-1629, #255, p. 148.*

4 March 1626. "Directions and instructions from the president and council of Surat to John Phelps, master in the Spy. His present employment is to meet with this year's expected feet from England. To sail with Captain Weddell and his fleet, and to keep them company until licensed by him and his council to depart, then to bend his course about the north end of St. Lawrence Island and thence to the Bay of Augustine, where, if he find any English ships, he shall deliver to the commander our advices; but as their touching at that place is uncertain, not to stay longer than to refresh his people and fit his vessel, and leave letters with two men of that place. Next to address himself to the four Comoro Islands, and visit each successively, and leave letters to advertise his purpose of residence at Mohilla. Being joined with our other friends from England, to surrender himself to the commander of that fleet, and with that fleet apply himself for Surat and attend our further order. To entertain aboard his vessel two Dutchmen who have advice for their ships likewise expected out of Europe." *CSP-C, EI, C&P, 1625-1629, #267, p. 168.*

29 November 1626. "The *Spy* arrived in June at Augustine's Bay, on St. Lawrence Island. The *Spy*; not returned; conceive she is either harboring at

Socotra or cast away; do not believe she is taken by the enemy." *CSP-C, EI, C&P, 1625-1629, #378, p. 271.*

If this is the same ship, tracking each of the recorded locations, given variances in translations and cartography of the period, this ship spent a great deal of time in the Indian Ocean. The next record shares the information needed to most.

October 1629. Contained within a letter to the East India Company; "Amongst them was one from Surat with letters from the president, ordering them to make inquiry after the *Spy*, sent the former year to the Islands of Comorro, but they could never hear any tidings of her." *CSP-C, EI, C&P, 1625-1629, #866, p. 685.*

Unfortunately, there is approximately two million square miles of ocean to search based on the single record. There is no mention if the 100,000 pieces of 8 were unloaded at any port or of recovery attempts or additional relevant records.

Records indicate the *Spy* was built in June and launched in October 1620 at 300 tons. The *Mercury* was her sister. The *Spy* may still contain this money and or other valuables.

Holderness wreck.

8 April 1626. "Henry Viscount Dunbar to Buckingham. A ship which received diverse shot under water, whereby she had been sunk, had come ashore within his liberty of Holderness with a cargo of wine much damaged. He has a grant of wreck which has been allowed by former lord high admirals. Many ships taken daily by Dunkirker's on that coast." *CSP-D, 1625-1626, #54, p. 306.*

5 (?) September 1626. "Richard Wyan to Nicholas. The ships on shore at Bramston in Holderness are no wreck, because their companies came ashore. No man can have any right in the suspected Dunkirker but the king or the duke." *CSP-D, Charles I, 1625-1626, #31, p. 421.*

No additional information could be located about this wreck. No records are known of recovery or salvage attempts.

"...because their companies came ashore" suggests it either anchored or sank off shore. It is safe to assume that only the containers of wine, depending on the material they were made of, ordnance, tackle, and furniture and possible valuables such as small amount of coin or bullion remained when the crew abandoned their ship out of desperation.

Holderness is an area of the East Riding of Yorkshire, on the north-east coast of England.

The *Globe*.

The *Globe* does not appear in ship inventories prior to King James I, but does in the ship inventories of the East India Company. To exacerbate search problems is the Globe theatre in London. That required a review of every related record in the archives to differentiate the *Globe* of London, the Globe theatre or other ships with the name *Globe* in different variants such as the *Globe* of Pool wreck of 1627.

31 March 1626. "Six chests of coral come home in the *Globe* to be dispersed in other ships for Surat." *CSP-C, EI, C&P, 1625-1629, V.4, #285, p. 180.*

8 December 1626. "Whereas a petition was this day presented to the Board by 8 December Sydruch Williams, of London, merchant, showing that the petitioner hath lately bought of the commissioners for the sale of prize goods a parcel of commodities to the value of £500, which the petitioner by order of this board was commanded to pay unto the register of the admiralty court, and further showing that the petitioner was part owner of a ship called the Globe of London, about the burthen of 350 tons, with 22 cast pieces of ordinance, which ship being pressed for his majesty's service for the late voyage of Calais, was in her return cast away upon coast of Ireland and utterly lost, to the petitioner's great hindrance, which is likewise certified by the commissioners of the navy, and therefore humbly besought the board to give order that the hire of the said ship (being cast up by the commissioners of the navy) might be allowed and defaulted out of the said sum of £500, so to be paid into the admiralty as aforesaid; their lordships taking the same into their considerations and the finding the petitioner's case to be very commensurable in regard of his great hindrance sustained by loss of the said ship in his majesty's service, and being satisfied by a certificate in writing under the hands of the said commissioners, that there was due for the freight of the said ship the sum of £432. 28. 3d. Have thought fit to recommend it to the lord treasurer to give order for the petitioner's satisfaction, either in such sort as is by him humbly desired, or by some other speedy course such as his lordship shall think fit." *APC-June-December 1626, p. 405-406.*

28 January 1627. "Whereas in the ships which were set forth by the city of London there have been diverse mutinies against the captains and commanders of them and practices to drown the captains, whereby (as it is informed) the coxswain of the Globe was cast away, his majesty, considering in his princely wisdom the greatness of the crime, and the dangerous consequence thereof if it should pass unpunished." *APC-June-December 1626, p. 37.*

It is easy to assume she was returning to Ireland from Calias to be over-taken by a tempest often notoriously dangerous in December and wrecked along about 160 miles of Irish southern coast. A wreck found with 22 cast iron cannons and about 350 tons in size would no longer be anonymous.

No additional information was discovered in archives. From that point on, there are many references to the Globe theatre in London.

1627

Swansea wreck.

January (?) 1627. "Petition of Cornelis Pietersen to Buckingham. His ship having been cast away near Swansea, his only effects are the goods saved from the wreck. On reaching London he is told that goods saved from ships wrecked are forfeited to the crown. Prays that at any rate he may be paid his freight." *CSP-D, 1627-1628, #45, p. 40.*

Can we imagine how Mr. Pietersen felt after losing his ship and salvaging a few personal belongings to have them taken by the crown when he returned home because it was salvaged goods?

No additional records located in archives. I was unable to locate an inventory of the goods confiscated by the crown. It is hard to speculate what, if anything, was recovered from this ship. There is about 45 miles of coast west of Swansea Wales that would be the logical location of her running ashore if the ship was traveling north from the channel.

The *Globe* of Pool.

There were several records encountered during research for the previous *Globe* that differentiated them into a separate incident. This is that collection.

15 January 1627. Letter from "Captain Robert Orme to Nicholas. Had sent his purser to give Portsmouth, intimation of a mutiny on board his ship, the *Benediction*, and also in the *Globe*. Solicits instructions." *CSP-D, Charles I, V2, 1627-1628, #43, p. 20.*

29 January 1627. "All the city ships had Portsmouth, been discharged, except the *Globe*; the *Benediction*, and the *Primrose*. Examinations respecting the mutinies are being taken." *CSP-D, Charles I, V2, 1627-1628, #65, p. 35.*

2 April 1627. "Examination of James Brooke and William Aschough [Ayscough], respecting 20 chests of treasure alleged to have been put

aboard the *Globe*; at the Hope by servants of the Duke of Buckingham." *CSP-D, Charles I, V2, 1627-1628, #12-1, p. 122.*

18 April 1627. "The grand jury for the admiralty have presented four seamen of the *Globe*; and three of the *Benediction* for mutiny. The lords desire to have them capitally punished, but Sir Henry Marten says that can only be done by martial law." *CSP-D, Charles I, V2, 1627-1628, #56, p. 141.*

29 May 1627. A Letter from Buckingham to Captain John Pennington. "He is to order the Whitehall captains of the *Globe*; the *Benediction*, and the *Primrose* to repair to Portsmouth, where they are to bring their ships aground to be washed and tallowed, and to take in a further supply of victuals." *CSP-D, Charles I, V2, 1627-1628, #13, p. 195.*

6 February 1628. "Commissioners of the navy to Nicholas. The *Globe*; cannot be brought into Woolwich Dock this spring tide, they therefore beg him to procure the duke's warrant for letting into the dock in the meantime the *London* and the *Reformation*, two ships of the East India Company selected for his Majesty's service." *CSP-D, Charles I, V2, 1627-1628, #51, p. 547.*

19 December 1628. "And in the late expedition to the Isle of Retz another ship of the petitioners called the *Globe* of Poole being about 500 tons was taken and employed in his majesty's service and after the return was unfortunately cast away in the River of Thames by the negligence of his majesty's officers, for the loss whereof as also for the freight of her the petitioner had received no satisfaction by reason whereof the petitioner was brought to great distress and destitute of all means to satisfy his creditors but likewise in daily danger of arrest, and therefore humbly besought his majesty's royal protection for one whole year." *APC, July 1626-April 1629, V.42, #818, p. 268.*

Bryard petitioned the council requesting additional leniency, as he was unable to pay his creditors for another year. *APC, 1629-1630, p. 228.*

The *Globe* of Pool lies within the 29 miles of the Thames River prior to the London Bridge which is about 65' deep and she rests with many other ships in the river Thames. There are no records of salvage attempts or goods recovered. It is safe to assume that the masts were cut because they presented a hazard, if so, then it is not hard to speculate that additional items were salvaged.

The *Green Dragon* and *Champen.*

The *Green Dragon* is mentioned in a 1579 record with a complaint of being plundered. That is the earliest record located in archives.

9 July 1627. "Inventories of the duke's tenths (share) taken out of the following prizes: Our Lady's Prayers; the *Green Dragon*; the *Pearl of Poole*;

the Lewes of Nantes; the St. Peter of Schiedam; a ship captured by Captain Lux, and the Bartholomew, all brought into Bristol; also out of the Nostra Seniora and another ship, brought into Lyme Regis." *CSP-C, EI, C&P, 1625-1629, #52-1, p. 247.* This letter mentions that the *Green Dragon* was a prize suggesting this *Green Dragon* was not English.

5 February 1628 Written at London. "The duke of Buckingham to Sir Fulke Greville and Edward London. Deputy vice admirals of the Isle of Wight, and to Robert Newland, merchant. Order of the high court of admiralty to restore to the East India Company goods saved from the Green Dragon and the Champen two East India vessels wrecked on the coast of the said island." *CSP-C, EI, C&P, 1625-1629, #36, p. 545.*

Despite the rather unique name, the *Green Dragon* has very few related documents. The duke's one tenth of a cargo could be an indication of the valuable cargo not recovered enhanced with orders of the high court of admiralty to restore the recovered goods to the East India Company. Without a departure location, it is difficult to determine what side of the island she wrecked on. It would be a safe to speculate that the ship was stripped of everything removable.

Needles wrecks.

These wrecks could possibly fit under the term treasure ship.

17 October 1627. "William Towerson to Secretary Conway. The servants of the East India Company finding aboard one of the Dutch ships, one Forbishe, [Forbes] a Scotsman, who acted as interpreter at the torture of Amboyna, he had been brought before the earl of Holland, and, on confession, giving a material relation, had been sent up to the council. That instant had received information that two Dutch East Indiamen outward-bound had been cast away near the Needles, or on the shore of the main." *CSP-D, 1627-1628, #6, p. 392.*

18 October 1627. "Edward Reed to Secretary Conway. The next day, after Mr. Wyan, Sir Fulke Greville, and the writer came to Yarmouth (Isle of Wight) in the night, the English ship, that was the subject of their commission, stole from under the castle, carrying away the man the writer left aboard, into Southampton river, where she remains. The merchant pretends it was to fulfill a warrant sent to the customer there from the lord treasurer. Three Dutch East India ships have miscarried in coming in at the Needles, one of them, men and all, laden with provisions. The tonnage of the three ships is estimated at 1,600 tons. Their voyage was for a plantation, and they carry with them many women and children." *CSP-D, 1627-1628, #18, p. 395.*

18 October 1627. "Henry Earl of Holland to Nicholas. A fleet of Dutch East Indiamen had been driven into the Needles, and two of them are wrecked. They have in them chests of silver and other things of value, which may possibly be recovered. Advertises him thereof that he may take care of the rights of the king and the lord admiral. Had sent Captain Towerson to examine the state of the wreck." *CSP-D, 1627-1628, #22, p. 397.*

No additional information was learned. The letter of 18 October 1627 contains interesting information regarding chests of silver, perhaps Spanish reales that two of the outward bound Dutch East Indiamen were transporting when they wrecked. No known records that salvage occurred or of anything regarding the chests of silver were discovered in archives. It is safe to speculate that if any of the chests of silver could be recovered, they would have recovered as many as possible. But, on the other hand, there may still be several or many "chests of silver and other things of value" waiting to be discovered then placed on display in a museum for future generations to learn from and enjoy.

The Needles is a row of three stacks of chalk that ascend from the sea off the western coast of the Isle of Wight in the English Channel, close to Alum Bay, and part of Totland, the westernmost civil parish of the Isle of Wight.

1628

The *St. Peter.*

There is a *St. Peter* of Calais France that impeded research progress. Furthermore, in a record of 9 July 1627, "Inventories of the duke's tenths (share) taken out of the following prizes," mention a St. Peter of Schiedam (Rotterdam/Hague). This St. Peter is Gottenburgh, Sweden.

(?) March 1628. This may suggest the *St. Peter* was either captured or sunk. "Statement, addressed [to the Council?], of circumstances which go to prove that the *Hunter*, the *St. Peter* and three other Hamburgers, are all lawful prizes." *CSP-D, Charles I, 1628-1629, #121, p. 52.*

9 April 1628. "Petition of John Briggs, master and owner of the St. Peter, of Gottenburgh, Sweden, to the king. His ship was burnt by the French in the Isle of Rhé, being then in the king's service. There is owing to him £300, for freight. Has been sixteen months from his wife and children, is 70 years of age, and has no means left to carry him home. Prays for immediate payment of the £300, and subsequent satisfaction for the loss of his ship and goods,

to the value of £1,500. [Underwritten is a reference to the Duke of Buck-ingham.]." *CSP-D, Charles I, 1628-1629, #63, p. 68.*

23 June 1628. "Order of council. Sir John Wentworth, by order of June 8, 1627, obtained the loan of the French prize, the *Notre Dame*, and the pinnace the *St. Peter*, for one year. The ships needing repair, and he not having taken any prize, the loan is renewed for another year." *CSP-D, Charles I, 1628-1629, #3, p. 174.*

18 July 1628. "Officers of the navy to Buckingham. Report on the case of John Brigges, master of the St. Peter, of Gottenburgh. He was pressed by Sir Ralph Bingley to transport soldiers from Ireland to the Isle of Rhé, where his ship was burned by the French. Report the amount due to him for freight and victual. For satisfaction of the goods and ship burnt, they find no precedent that his majesty was ever charged with those hazards, or paid the ships freighted longer than they had being." *CSP-D, Charles I, 1628-1629, #27, p. 217-218.*

12 August 1628. "Captain William Jewell to Nicholas. If he will bestead him to the prevailing for the *St. Peter*; he will bestow on Mrs. Nicholas a basin and ewer of £40." *CSP-D, Charles I, 1628-1629, #70, p. 253.*

19 September 1628. "The affirmation of Richard Beele, master's mate of the *Francis*, of Colchester, and four others of the company of the same ship, respecting the violent rescue of persons impressed by them at Stonehouse, under a warrant from the officers of the navy, out of the *St. Peter* belonging to William Rowe, constable of the same town with various speeches of William Rowe on that occasion." *CSP-D, Charles I, 1628-1629, #37, p. 333.*

14 November 1628. "Prays for a gift of the old prize ship, the *St. Peter* of Calais, appraised at £247." *CSP-D, Charles I, 1628-1629, #59, p. 379.*

1 December 1628. "Grant to Isabel, widow of Lieutenant Francis Musgrave, slain at the assault of the citadel in the Isle of Rhé, of the prize ship, the *St. Peter* with all tackle and furniture." *CSP-D, Charles I, 1628-1629, p. 401.*

19 December 1628. "Commissioners for sale of prize goods to the lord's commissioners of the admiralty. On October 25 last received directions not to sell the *St. Peter* of Calais, a Dutch pram. They have now received a privy seal, dated 2nd December instructions for delivery of the same to Isabel Musgrave, widow, as a gift from the king." *CSP-D, Charles I, 1628-1629, #56, p. 410.*

13 March 1629. #68. "Humphrey Haggett to Nicholas. By his lord's command [the earl of Arundel] sends papers concerning a vessel ashore near Arundel, and requests his opinion whether she is either wreck or prize." *CSP-D, Charles I, 1628-1629, #68, p. 492.*

#68-1. "Petition of John le Rowla, and company, owners of the long ship, the St. Peter, to Thomas earl of Arundel, for the restoration of the goods aboard their vessel, which had been run ashore near Arundel after a severe engagement with a Dunkirker." *CSP-D, Charles I, 1628-1629, #68-1, p. 493.*

#68-3. "Declaration of Jacob Johnson and another, two of the crew of the St. Peter, relating the circumstances of their engagement with the Dunkirker, and their being forced to run their ship ashore near Arundel; with a statement of the goods brought ashore from the same ship, and November 21, what became of them. December 1, 1628." *CSP-D, Charles I, 1628-1629, #68-3, p. 492-493.*

The captain of the St. Peter of Gottenburgh Sweden, chose to beach the ship preventing her capture on the shore near Arundel. "A statement of the goods brought ashore" is a safe indication that she sank off shore and that not all cargo was recovered.

The *Phoenix* of Hamburg.

This wreck is problematic because of the English ship the *Phoenix* mentioned in a 1546 inventory at 40 tons with 46 mariners and 4 gunners. There is a single record of this ship, but the documents were lumped together in an undated collection possibly from 1633 edited by John Bruce under the direction of the master of the rolls.

10 April 1628. "It is a pity the *Phoenix* should lie and consume in harbor at the king's charge." *CSP-D, Charles I, 1628-1629, #77, p. 70.* This may a reference to the *Phoenix* of London.

1633(?) There is a single document in which the *Phoenix* of Hamburg is mentioned. "Petition of Edward Ayscough to the king. Has spent nineteen years and much money in the service of the king and his father, and has brought about £60,000 to the king, but has never received any reward. The Phoenix of Hamburg was about two or three years ago cast away upon Brixton Bay near the Isle of Wight, having in her some small quantities of bullion. Prays a grant of the same." *CSP-D, 1633-1634, #34, p. 368.*

The editors of the *Calendars* may have made the decision to place the record in 1633 based documents I was not able to review.

This ship could have wrecked perhaps between Brighstone and Atherfield along about 2 miles of coast. There are no records of salvage attempts or if the "small quantity of bullion" was recovered. It may be easy to surmise that based on the quantity of (or lack of) records regarding the "small quantities of bullion," the incident was forgotten about in history and just a grain of sand on the beach of correspondence.

The Phoenix of Hamburg may still contain the bullion and was not recovered. I would assume the bullion would warrant additional correspondence, but none was located. I would like to believe this incident could also fit under the term treasure ship.

Isle of Wight wreck.

12 June 1628. "The council addressed the lord treasurer regarding a petition by Jacob Johnson master of a Dutch ship returning from Bordeaux France to Holland loaded with French wines and prunes when a man-of-war chased and forced the ship in the Isle of Wight. There it sprung a leak and requested to unload the cargo on shore." *APC, 1627-1628, p. 491.*

It may be safe to assume that permission was granted to unload the cargo. I was unable to locate additional information. Based on their course, it is logical the ship rests on the west side of the Isle of Wight about 12 miles of coastline.

1629

The *James* of London.

It was in the best opinion of the editors of the *Calendar Series* to place the next letter in the year 1629 category

1629(?). "Petition of James Duppa, Nathan Wright, and the rest of the owners of the James of London, to the king. On 30th May 1629, since peace proclaimed, Captain Bontemps took the James, at anchor on the coast of Barbary, and brought her to Dieppe where she lies sunk and spoiled. Pray that a course may be taken for the ship to be speedily restored to them." *CSP-D, Charles I, 1629-1631. #18, p. 133.*

20 January 1629. A chart of warrants for "issuing letter of marquee, granted by the lords of commissioners of the admiralty during the year 1629, include mention of the *James* with Captain James Duppa, Captain William Harman and others as owners, at 250 tons with Captain Harman as captain." *CSP-D, Charles I, 1629-1631. (VCLVII-1625-1637), p. 151.*

April 22 1629. "Trinity House certificates for the year 1629 share additional information about the *James* of London, where built; Flemish bottom at 300 tons." *CSP-D, Charles I, 1629-1631. (VCLVII-1625-1637), p. 157.*

18 March 1631. "George Rookes, Robert Grove, Robert Tockley, Elias Jurdan, and Robert Woodroffe to the council. Complain of the capture of

the *James* of London, and the *Bride*, taken by Captain Bontemps after the peace with France, and carried into Dieppe. Solicit restitution." *CSP-D, Charles I, 1629-1631. #113, p. 542.*

It was in the best opinion of the editors of the *Calendar Series* to place the next four letters in the year 1631 category.

1631(?) 1 December 1629. "Petition of Ralph Freeman, Alderman of London, to the having in December 1629, laden in the James of London, Richard Edmunds, master, bound for Newhaven in France, goods worth £500, the ship was chased by Dunkirkers, and to avoid capture was run ashore at Iport (Yport), on the coast of Normandy. Ship and cargo were seized by Mons. de Mesmont, the lord of the soil, and after long suit in the admiralty of France order was made for sale of the goods, and sequestering the proceeds. John Granger, an Englishman, petitioner's attorney, going to Iport to execute this order with certain other persons, Mons. de Mesmont caused them to be set upon with great knotted cords and cudgels, and to save their lives they signed a consent that the goods might be sold by the officers of Fecamp, a town not far from the wreck, who there upon sold them to Mons. de Mesmont, at a third part of their value. Prays redress for this horrible outrage." *CSP-D, Charles I, 1631-1633, #24, p. 218.*

1631(?) "Particular of the carriage of the sale of the goods of the James of London, at Dieppe. Order was obtained by the English ambassador suspending the sale, whereupon Captain Bontemps took post for Paris, and procured an order contradicting the former, and on his return proceeded to sell the next morning." *CSP-D, Charles I, 1631-1633, #41, p. 236.*

1631 (?) "Petition of Walter Coventry, Nicholas Crisp, and others, merchants' adventurers, and proprietors of the James of London, to the council. Some of their goods being in the hands of Mr. Burlamachi, the petitioners pray a reference to Sir Henry Marten, to do them justice, so far as such goods extend, and for the rest that they may have letters of marquee." *CSP-D, Charles I, 1631-1633, #42, p. 27.*

1632 (?) "Petition of Captain James Duppa, Nathaniel Wright, George Rookes, Augustine Phillips, and others, owners of the James of London, to the same. By the treaty between Sir Isaac Wake, and others appointed by the French king, it was agreed that the said ship, with all her provisions as she came in at Dieppe, should be delivered to petitioners, and satisfaction be given for what was wanting. The ship is utterly spoiled, so that although at her setting to sea she cost £3,100 she will not now yield £500. Pray that they may receive the benefit of the said treaty." *CSP-D, Charles I, 1631-1633, #49, p. 481.*

It is safe to assume that after Mons. de Mesmont used cudgels and knotted rope to beat John Granger, the petitioner's attorney, until he signed away the goods, that all the cargo was removed from the James of London and sold away.

No additional information was located in archives. The letter of 1 December 1629 placed under the 1631 category, gives the approximate date of wreck at December 1629 and location at Yport, about 2.5 miles west of Fecamp. The waves would have eventually broken the ship up after it was stripped of everything. No follow-up on the interrogation techniques used by Mons. de Mesmont.

The St. Anne Maria.

17 January 1629. "Inventory of the goods taken and brought into the hands of me, James Salmon, out of the Spanish ship St. Anne Maria, brought into Castlehaven by Captain Peter Fransey of Amsterdam, and there cast away and broken up. The wreck and all that could be saved were sold to me. [Here follows a list of dying stuff called silvester, anchors, sails, rigging, arms, gingerbread, Spanish bedsteads, &c., and an estimate of what their purchase and salvage have cost]." CSP-I, 1625-1632, #1302-1, p. 429. I was informed the document mentioned within brackets was not available.

5 February 1629. "Sir William St. Leger to the lord deputy. Reports that a galleon lately cast away near Castlehaven was a Spaniard surprised by the Dutch. A Dutch officer was put on board to carry her to Holland, but this gives him no right to sell her. 43 cannons have fallen overboard, but can be recovered." CSP-I, 1625-1632, #1302, p. 429.

12 July 1630. "Sir William St. Ledger to the English Privy Council. [Mallow]. I have got your letters ordering me to assist Jacob Johnson, the diver, in diving for bullion, &c., in the ports of this province, also your letter supporting the Dutch West India merchants in their search for the goods of the Spanish ship lately overwhelmed in the sea near Castlehaven in Ireland, which belongs to them, as the warrant says, by right of war. They have got up some of the goods of the Spanish ship and will get the rest if they are not disturbed by Johnson, who is now upon weighing the remainder. I think your letter for Johnson transcends that for the Dutch West India Company, but I have told Johnson not to take away anything that he picks up until I hear from you." CSP-I, 1625-1632, #1738, p. 557.

"Assist Jacob Johnson, the diver, in diving for bullion, &c., in the ports of this province" could be interpreted a couple ways including this ship was carrying bullion and a diver was employed to recover some or all treasure in addition to the items mentioned in the letter. Further in the letter, "they have got up some of the goods" could refer to diving. Diving bells were in use at the time which would certainly aid in any recovery effort.

No additional information was located. Based on the sum of the documents, the diver only recovered "some" of the cargo. Not enough information to label as a treasure ship, but very close. A ship that lost 43 cannons could be about 800 to 1000 tons with 120 to 150 guns. The St. Anne Maria does not turn up in a list of Spanish ships involved in the Battle of the Down in 1639. A war ship is a good choice for transporting bullion.

The St. Anne Maria wrecked along perhaps a 5 mile stretch of uneven coast in Castlehaven, a civil parish in County Cork, Ireland, located approximately 75 km southwest of Cork City on the coast.

Milford Haven wreck.

17 February 1629. "Sir James Perrott to John Thorowgood, secretary to William earl of Pembroke. Sent of late to the earl for directions for a ship at Llanelly, which will be lost if not looked to. Now sends a letter respecting a Spanish carvel arrived at Milford Haven, laden with wheat, whereof some perished with storm, and the rest will be spoiled by the country people, if present order be not given to save and sell it. Enclosed." *CSP-D, Charles I, 1628-1629, #10, p. 474.*

Enclosed note: "Note of the contents of the Spanish carvel above mentioned, with the names of the principal country people who had plundered the wreck." *CSP-D, Charles I, 1628-1629, #10-1, p. 474.*

18 April 1629. "Sir James Perrott to Nicholas. Returns the commission for the Spanish carvel which came into Milford Haven laden with corn." *CSP-D, Charles I, 1628-1629, #9, p. 523.*

No additional information could be learned from archives. It is difficult to determine what else was plundered then salvaged from the ship when it wrecked in Milford Haven. A Spanish carvel is about 50 or 60 tons with three masts; it is likely the ship was stripped of everything as a prize. Ballast pile, larger brass or iron cannons that were not recovered, would have survived to present times somewhere along about two miles of coast of Milford Haven, a very old town and a community in Pembrokeshire, Wales. The Milford Haven Waterway is an estuary forming a natural harbor that has been used as a port since the middle Ages.

French man-of-war

19 February 1629. "Petition of Sir William Irving to the same. On September 27 last, in the parish of St. Kevern, near Falmouth, a French man-of-war was cast away, and forsaken by her crew. Four men, at the hazard of their lives, took possession of her in the king's name, but were expelled by a company of disordered people, who spoiled the ship and embezzled her ordnance and appurtenances. Prays for a grant of the ship and her accoutrements, and a commission to Sir John Killigrew and Richard Erisey to seize all articles which belonged to her. Underwritten is a minute, that the king granted the petitioner, his servant, his humble suit. Whitehall." *CSP-D, Charles I, 1628-1629, #17, 476.*

No additional records were found in archives. Some French war ships could contain 120 guns on three decks. Because these were intimidating ships, of which few other ships could possibly over take them by force, made them the safest for transporting bullion or coin.

St. Keverne is often noted as being odd because it clusters around a central square overlooked by the 15th century church of St. Akeveranus. This ship may have wrecked about a mile on either side of Porthoustock. No additional information or records of salvage attempts or goods floating to shore were located. It is difficult to speculate if all the ordnance was recovered, that would help to supply additional information about this shipwreck.

Severn wreck.

21 March 1629. "Sir Edward Rodney to Nicholas. The city will not give way to his deputies mustering their ships and mariners, pretending that the admiral has no jurisdiction there. In January last a small bark was wrecked in the Severn, and the goods cast ashore at Weston super-Mare and Breane, where they are claimed by the lords of the manors. Prays the lords' commissioners to call in question such claim, as other lords of manors follow the example." *CSP-D, Charles I, 1628-1629. #28, p. 501*

No additional records were located in archives. Weston-super-Mare, also known as Weston, is a seaside town in North Somerset, England. It lies by the Bristol Channel 20 miles southwest of Bristol between Worlebury Hill and Bleadon Hill. The wreck area described is about 7 miles of coastline. Based on that letter, most of the ship sank and some items were recovered.

Castlehaven wreck.

7 November 1629. "The King to Sir Thomas Crooke and others. Commission out of London of the court of admiralty to inquire for, and take into their custody, a Spanish galleon; captured by ships of the East Indies, and lately cast away at Castlehaven, in Ireland, with all goods on board the same, and to make a return thereof to the court of admiralty of England sitting at the Guildhall in Southwark." *CSP-D, Charles I, 1629-1631, #27, p. 90.*

1 August 1630. "Petition of the West India Company of the United Provinces to the council. A Spanish galleon, captured by a ship of the petitioners, was about December 1628 cast away at Castlehaven in Ireland. By an order of council of 5 September 1628, free passage was granted to all ships of the petitioners, with right to all wreck of their vessels cast away in his majesty's dominions. They have ever since labored for recovery of their wrecked goods at Castlehaven, but Jacob Johnson has lately come thither, and has taken away wrecked goods, made ready for removal by the petitioner's workmen. Pray that he may be restrained from interfering." *CSP-D, Charles I, 1629-1631, #1, p. 319.*

A Spanish galleon of perhaps 500-800 tons with 20 to 40 guns, wrecked in Castlehaven, Ireland, after being captured by East India ships. It is safe to assume that everything but the ship was taken, and no records were located regarding of the fate of this Spanish galleon. As with some Spanish ships, this may have had some quantity of coin in it, but there are no records or hints of that. There are no known records of salvage attempts.

The three mile section of Southern Irish coast with Castlehaven in the center is a collection of small coves with sometimes submerged sharp rocks. A storm would most surely pulverize the ship in a short period of time. Anything not removed prior to that, may still be in the area.

1630

The *Samuel*.

20 February 1630. "Edward Heynes to the East India Company. Since his Gombroon departure with the fleet 19th April from Torbay, passed the Cape 18th July with an unexpected speedy passage, and gained the Island of Molalia 14th August without accident, except that the small ship Samuel, Willam Taylor, surprised a small Portugal junk trading from St. Lawrence to Mozambique with 3,280 sticks sandal wood of mean value, paddy, or rice,

and 126 slaves, of which they divided to each ship its proportion, whereof the pursers are to be accountable. Departed thence 25th August and arrived in Swally Road 10th October, with the loss of some men, and many by the badness of the air of Molalia languishing without hope of recovery, where they found only the Jonas, Captain Swanley, and six Dutch ships. During their abode in this road by the importunity or rather force of the governor and merchants of Surat, the president was compelled to command the Samuel laden with Moors goods intended for Persia to ride at Surat Bar in company with a small Dutch ship to secure certain junks of the Moors lading for Mocha and Persia from the Portugal's; whose caphila of frigates passing by for Cambaya, emboldened by the small force of these two ships, desperately laid the Dutch aboard with eight frigates and the Samuel with four, who as valiantly defended themselves to the destruction of three or four frigates and many of the enemy, until a train laid in the Samuel doubting to be entered by the enemy took fire to her utter ruin, loss of 14 men, and extreme hurt to the master and as many more, who were taken up by the Dutch." *CSP-C, EI &P, 1630-1634, #10, p. 4-5.*

13 April 1630. "It is said the enemy brought out 3,000 soldiers with all needful provisions of war, intending this summer to beleaguer Ormuz, expecting nine ships yearly from the king of Spain, with a resolution to expel the English and Dutch out of these seas. At return of the ships from Persia they expected an encounter upon this coast, but the enemy attends a greater strength, not daring to meet upon equal terms, yet on 6th December past, 12 frigates attempted the burning of the Dutch Wesopp of 24 guns, and the Samuel, riding at the river's mouth; eight fell upon the Dutch, who burnt two and sunk another, and four upon the Samuel, whose master improvidently laying a train, expecting they would have boarded her, fired and blew himself and all his people over-board; lamentably burnt himself, 15 were saved by the Dutch, and as many more perished or were taken prisoners, the vessel and one of the frigates burnt, and 100 bags of rice, besides provisions, lost; she was full laden with Moors' goods for Persia." *CSP-C, EI &P, 1630-1634, #32, p. 22.*

6 May 1630. "Mr. Taylor, late master of the Samuel, ordered to deliver in a relation of the fight with the Portugal frigates, and how said ship was burned. Mr. Sambrooke to clear accounts with poor men (? not) private traders, but to forbear to pay any offending in that kind, and all officers who are most blamable for same." *CSP-C, EI &P, 1630-1634, p. 155.*

It was a difficult decision for the master to blow the ship up instead of allowing the enemy to have her. The *Samuel* is known to have burnt then sank with full cargo "riding at the river's mouth" could place her in the Gulf of

Khambhat at the mouth of the Mahi River, perhaps within a few miles each side of city of Khambhat, also known as Cambay, India.

Moorish arts and crafts were in high demand throughout most of Europe and the lost cargo may have included fine hand-woven cloth and rugs often embellished with many colors and designs, enameled jewelry and or pottery. Furthermore, the Samuel may contain some of the prize from a small Portugal junk.

There are no records of salvage attempts. If the ship had burned to the water line before sinking, then any cargo stored below deck at or above the ballast pile may have survived.

Brighthelmstone wreck.

22 February 1630. "Sir Walter Covert to Thomas Earl of Arundel and Surrey, and Slaugham, Edward Earl of Dorset, lord lieutenants of Sussex. On Sunday last there was chased on shore at Brighthelmstone a Dunkirker of 160 tons with 78 men and 10 pieces of ordnance. The ship was bulged, but the inhabitants saved the masts, ordnance, and other things. They pray that the pieces may be kept in the town for their safeguard." *CSP-D, Charles I, 1629-1631, #46, p. 195-196.*

22 February 1630. "Paul Greensmith to Abraham Dawes. Reports the wreck of the Dunkirker at Brighthelmstone mentioned above, which he conceived belonged to the king. When he came thither he found the ship pulled all to pieces, and the goods distributed among the people in the town. Gave the ordnance into the hands of the constable and requests directions." *CSP-D, Charles I, 1629-1631, #47, p. 196.*

No related additional information was located in archives.

It is safe to say that the ship was picked clean after it wrecked on the coast at Brighthelmstone. Brighthelmstone was shortened to Brighton in about 1660. Nothing would remain of this ship worth any value but pieces of timber and ballast.

Nevertheless, this ship deserves mention in tribute to a vessel that men loved and trusted for many years, not to mention the possible thousands of miles it had sailed.

The *Seventh Whelp.*

This is a memorial for the *Seventh Whelp* because she was sacrificed preventing the enemy from owning her. The decision the master made to blow the ship up resulted in the death of about 60 crewmembers, but the enemy did not take possession. A short, but rare account from a survivor described the death of members of his family when the ship exploded and burned, and then of his further peril while floating in the ocean.

This ship is mentioned in a 1633 inventory of the king's ships at 186 tons, a crew of 70 and carried 14 pieces of ordnance. Also in the inventory is mention of ten different *Whelps*.

28 July 1630. "Sir Henry Mervyn to Nicholas. Junction of his whole fleet in the Downs, except the ship under command of Captain Gibbon. Has placed Captain Cooper in his command. Has appointed the Convertive and the Tenth Whelp to ply to the westward of the Isle of Wight, and has sent with them the Miniken. The Mary Rose and the Second Whelp are to ride betwixt the Downs and the Isle of Wight. Himself, the Seventh Whelp, and the Niver, having put over my lord duke for the coast of France, purpose to follow after the Convertive, and to employ himself to and again as occasion shall serve. Begs allowance of men and victuals for the Niver." *CSP-D, Charles I, 1629-1631#50, p. 314-315.*

19 September 1630. "Sir Henry Mervyn to the lords of the admiralty. Has ordered the *Mary Rose, Seventh Whelp*, and *Miniken* to range the northern coast between Newcastle and Orfordness, so that colliers and fishermen may follow their employments." *CSP-D, Charles I, 1629-1631, #45, p. 343.*

25 September 1630. "Captain Francis Sydenham to the lords of the admiralty. Gives account of the capture of a Dunkirker, which had been very unfairly endeavored to be taken from him by a Dutch man-of-war, road, the *Rue Basse* of Enckhuysen, Captain John Bleker. During the contest the *Seventh Whelp* was accidentally blown up and lost, only ten of her crew being saved, of whom the captain was one. Aboard the Dunkirker Sydenham had captured 23 men belonging to the Dutch vessel, whom he had sent ashore until he had order for their release." *CSP-D, Charles I, 1629-1631, #64, p. 347.*

30 September 1630. "Captain Francis Sydenham to Nicholas. Recapitulates the circumstances of the capture of a Dunkirker and misconduct of a Dutch vessel, as detailed in his letter to the lords of the admiralty road. He entreats Nicholas to procure him an order what to do with the 23 Dutchmen, and that he may keep his prize out for the time his ship is victualed, he not having any other ship with him, in consequence of the loss of the Seventh Whelp." *CSP-D, Charles I, 1629-1631, #87, p. 351.*

12 February 1631. "Petition of John Potter, late cook of the *Seventh Whelp*, to the lords of the admiralty. Petitioner served in the *Seven Stars*, and when the *Seventh Whelp* was blown up lost all he had, and escaped with great peril of his life, being taken up swimming in the sea. Prays to be admitted cook of the *Third Whelp*." *CSP-D, Charles I, 1631-1633. #70, p. 505.*

26 February 1631. "Petition of Dawtry Cooper, captain of the late pinnace, the Seventh Whelp, to the lords of the admiralty. Having been at above £250 charge in this last years' service, besides the loss of his son, his nephew, several loving friends, and all his goods, and understanding that they intend to send out the St. Claude, he prays for the command of her." *CSP-D, Charles I, 1631-1633. #62, p. 518.*

3 July 1632. "Petition of the same to the lords of the admiralty. About two years ago they gave their warrant for petitioner to take charge of the Ninth Whelp, but by the importunity of Sir Thomas Button they called petitioner back, to his loss of 80£, besides the loss of his son, his nephew, and all that he had, in the Seventh Whelp, and his expenditure in 18 months attendance. Prays for the employment in Ireland, which Captain Fogg would be glad to get rid of." *CSP-D, Charles I, 1631-1633, #6, p. 371.*

The last known position of the *Seventh Whelp* was recorded in 19 September 1630 to patrol about 250 miles along the coast between Newcastle and Orfordness. There is no indication of a location in the 25 September 1630 record of the small battle, so perhaps it occurred between Newcastle and Orfordness. A single clue that may be helpful is the location Captain Francis Sydenham wrote from was on the *Mary Rose* in North Yarmouth Road, about 22 miles east of Norwich, after the loss of the ship. Perhaps the closest town to the wreck.

The brief but horrific events the cook shared and the loss of a "son, nephew, and all that he had" by another survivor, help to paint a portrait of the horror man can inflict on man during the events of the small battle and the decision one man made and the death of about 60 crew members.

In the event the inventory of 14 pieces of ordnance is correct, that would help to identify a wreck if discovered. It is safe to speculate that the *Seventh Whelp* sank with full cargo and other items perhaps of some value.

North Foreland wreck.

25 October 1630. "Sir Thomas Walsingham to Nicholas. Is glad to hear the lords' resolution. Hereafter, let things go which way they will, he will not meddle. The 3rd of this month there was a great wreck of a Rotterdam ship, bound for Venice, on the coast of Kent, near the North Foreland, two miles from shore. Goods from this wreck, taken up by men that dwell in the writer's jurisdiction and presented in his courts, have been claimed by the court of admiralty, by which means the duchess and himself shall lose their shares and the right of his place. Wishes advice thereon. All wrecks are granted to him in his patent." *CSP-D, Charles I, 1629-1631, #84, p. 366.*

No additional information was located in archives. This ship wrecked close to North Foreland between Margate and Ramsgate. North Foreland is a chalk headland on the Kent coast of southeast England where a light was first exhibited in 1499, but the first real lighthouse was built by Sir John Meldrum in 1636, that consisted of a two-story octagonal tower made of timber, lath, and plaster with an iron coal-burning grate on top; this tower was destroyed by fire in 1683.

This ship sank about two miles from shore, perhaps within sight of the lighthouse. There are no records of anything recovered, so it is likely she sank with cargo, tackle, and furniture and possibly some valuables.

The *Leopard.*

The *Leopard* is mentioned in a 1633 inventory of the king's ships with a keel of 103' at 698 tons with a crew of 250 and 36 pieces of ordnance.

22 November 1630. "Certificate of Thomas Smedmor, mayor of Poole, and Thomas Robarts, justice of the peace there, that Ellery Addisse and John Mills appeared before them and affirmed that when their ship, the *Leopard* of Poole, was wrecked at Castlehaven, they and others of the crew labored to save for Sir Thomas Freke, their owner, such goods as they could, and that they drew to shore seven pieces of ordnance, and could have saved more, but were put from their labor by Thomas Salmon." *CSP-D, Charles I, 1629-1631, #86, p. 388.*

18 December 1630. "Lords of the admiralty to Jacob Johnson, the diver. About two years ago Sir Thomas Freke's ship, the *Leopard*, of Weymouth, was cast away near Castlehaven in Ireland, with 18 pieces of ordnance, and soon after most of the ordnance were taken up by Sir Thomas's own servants, since which time Johnson has recovered three or more for his majesty's use. Sir Thomas Freke's ship having been used as a man-of-war, Johnson is authorized to deliver to Sir Thomas all such ordnance, he first giving Johnson reasonable content for his pains." *CSP-D, 1629-1631, #18, p. 413.*

Though the ship's name is unique, only two related documents were located. No information was located to help determine if the Leopard was from Weymouth or Poole. Records mentioned the Leopard wrecked about two years prior to the 1630, but I was unable to locate information about the Leopard from 1628 or 1629. It would be safe to speculate that if most of the ordnance was recovered, then anything of value may have been as well. If the ordnance was hard to recover, then perhaps some other items remain with the ship that the diver was unable to retrieve.

The Swallow and Charles.

Though these wrecks did not occur within the United Kingdom, they are English treasure ships whose fates were the same.

Records indicate the *Swallow* was acquired in 1544 as a third-rate galleon at 300 tons. It is first mentioned in an inventory of 1546 at 240 tons with a crew of 130 and 30 gunners. In 1560, Admiral Winter wrote in his log it was one of 12 ships believed to have been lost in a fierce storm, but it is mentioned in inventories against the Spanish armada of 1588 then mentioned in an inventory of 1603 at 330 tons with a crew of 160. The *Swallow* does not appear in inventories of the royal navy beyond 1603 and perhaps was acquired by The East India Company and does appear in the E.I.C. inventory of 1622-1624.

The large gaps may be explained a couple ways. The ship served for over 80 years with possible multiple refits and one or two overhauls, or there is more than one *Swallow* in the 80-year span.

6 December 1630. "Have laden for England with pepper, cloves, &c. as per invoice, enclosed, the Swallow newly careened and sheathed, assisted by the Dutch, chiefly to give notice of the state of their affairs. Doubt to lade home besides the Swallow and Star, the Exchange or Speedwell this year, for they will have near 400 tons pepper remaining and will make hard shift to compass the rest from store of Bantam. Have filled the Swallow with pepper out of the Christopher to bring her leaks above water, the pepper of one room swimming with water, which they will bring ashore and dry." *CSP-C, EI &P, 1630-1634, #103, p. 91.*

7 January 1633. At Swally Road. In a letter to the East India Company. "The Charles and Swallow burnt by accident, with all the circumstances. 7,638 reales of 8 saved in the Swallow, and hope to save the remains of her money. The Charles sunk in deep water; she had cloth and lead in her. Some few men burnt, some drowned, some hurt." *CSP-C, EI &P, 1630-1634, #374, p. 342.*

25 January 1633. "The master and officers of the *Swallow* sent home in irons. Two months' pay was delivered to the sailors whose apparel was burnt in the *Swallow* and *Charles.*" *CSP-C, EI &P, 1630-1634, p. 358.*

9 February 1633. More details emerged. "The *Swallow* having fired the *Charles* a few days past by shooting off ordnance in her gun room, by which accident both ships perished in a few hours to the great danger of the whole fleet." The record indicated that it happened on 1 January 1633. *CSP-C, EI &P, 1630-1634, #399, p. 365.*

2 August 1633. It is mentioned in a very long letter to the East India Company of 1st January 1633 "happened the unfortunate accident of fire on the Swallow, and thereby the Charles, caused by the great commanders not observing the company's orders. It seems the sea commanders urged the president and council to try their cause, for 7th January they were called to Surat and examined with frivolous questions concerning Henry Sill and Christopher Reade, &c, and told that in regard Rastell, who sent for them, was deceased, they should be sent for England, and so dismissed." *CSP-C, EI &P, 1630-1634, #477, p. 445.*

27 August 1633. A letter written from St. Sebastian while on board the Charles of London, mentions a bag containing 2,000 reales in addition to a sealed up box sent by Prestwick Eaton to George Wellingham in London. *CSP-D, Charles, 1633-1634, #29, p. 193.*

25-28 September 1633. "Court minutes of the East India Company. Petition of Giles Waterman, late Master of the Swallow, that though the firing of the ships Charles and Swallow was laid upon him by some of the company's officers in India, he desired he might be heard in his defense, not doubting that the edge of their fury will be taken from him and laid upon the authors of this great loss; resolved, howbeit persuaded they have matter sufficient to proceed against him by a legal way, to suspend his commitment till he be heard, and appointed Friday next to take an examination of this business, when Waterman and the other prisoners returned home are to attend." *CSP-C, EI &P, 1630-1634, #492, p. 461.*

4 October 1633. "Court minutes of the East India Company. Giles Waterman, late master, John Headland, and John Carter, mates, and Miles White, gunner of the Swallow; questioned as to the burning of the Swallow and Charles; Waterman blamed the gunner for having his fireworks and loose powder in the gun room, which occasioned the firing of the ship when the guns were shot often to salute the ships in the road, and utterly denied he had given the two first cuts to the cable, by means whereof the Swallow; fell fowl of the Charles and fired her, and seemed to recriminate Captain Weddell who was not aboard, otherwise the ship might have been saved, and for his further justification produced an apology in writing; the gunner answered that the shooting of the piece was done by the master's command, notwithstanding he had represented the danger of firing the ship if two guns were shot off, and that he brought up the fireworks by order from Captain Weddell, to be ready in case she should meet the enemy, the Swallow; being then bound southward with the Dutch ships; he also delivered an apology in writing, and the court having also heard the mates, conceived the master

blameworthy, and the rest had offended little or nothing, yet deferred the business to further." *CSP-C, EI &P, 1630-1634, #496, p. 470.*

4-15 November 1633. "Court minutes of the East India Company. Petition of Miles White, gunner in the *Swallow*; clearing himself and laying the fault of the fire on Giles Waterman, the master, annexing diverse reasons, which are ordered to be carefully preserved as a testimony against Waterman at his trial and Mountney and Cappur directed, according to the course of the admiralty to enter bond for the prosecution of the suit, the court promising to save them harmless." *CSP-C, EI &P, 1630-1634, #511, p. 483.*

25-27 November 1633. "Court minutes of the East India Company. Petition of James Bamford, mate in the Charles for his wages, but on information that he was the chief cause of the disaster to the Charles, by resisting such as would have cut her cable, whereby she would have escaped the fire of the Swallow, the court thought fit first to take a further examination of the business at next court." *CSP-C, EI &P, 1630-1634, #515, p. 493.*

4 December 1633. "Consideration of petition of Giles Waterman, prisoner in the Marshalsea, for his willful firing of the *Swallow*; resolved after the same had been disputed at large, that Cappur attend Sir Henry Marten who had referred petitioner to this court, not to accept of petitioner's own bail for his appearance at the trial, the rather that he being of a weak estate, it is conceived they shall have no other recompense for him than corporal punishment, which was held very requisite even for example sake." *CSP-C, EI &P, 1630-1634, p. 496.*

There are condensed records in various manuscript collections, but they all share the same information. Regardless of who was at fault for setting the *Swallow* on fire, it would be safe to speculate the *Swallow* and *Charles* rest off the coast of Suvali, (Swally Hole) west of Surat India and perhaps within a five-mile stretch of what is now Hazira beach.

The *Swallow* may contain an unknown quantity of the Spanish reales not recovered, "7,638 reales of 8 saved" leads to the obvious question; out of how many?

The *Charles* was only known to have a bag containing Spanish 2,000 reales and a sealed box in addition to cloth and lead, but was never located. It is safe to speculate nothing was recovered from this ship.

The fire would have destroyed the ships, but the cargo below the water line had a better chance of surviving. The ordnance these ships contain could assist in the identification of a discovered wreck. Finding a quantity of Spanish reales from either ship (or both!) would certainly add luster to any museum exhibit.

1631

The *John.*

Though the *John* was an English ship, she was lost far from home and deserves a mention here.

3 January 1631. "William Hoare wrote to the East India Company with updates on occurrences that included a boat with 21 of the company's servants arrived with tidings of pinnace *John* lost on Jambi bar, with 715 peculs pepper, weighed by William Flint, amounting to 4,300 Rs. (Pieces of 8), four iron minion and four brass falcons and falconets, and all her provisions." *CSP-C, EI&P, 1630-1634, p. 111.*

8 September 1631 "pinnace *John's* disposure that way and disastrous success through the master's improvidence." *CSP-C, EI&P, 1630-1634, p. 182.*

5 October 1631, "the pinnace *John* cast away on the bar of Jambi, whereof and the disastrous fire there Mr. Hope will advise." *CSP-C, EI&P, 1630-1634, p. 208.*

If a wreck has been located or hopefully will be discovered near Jambi that contains "four iron minion and four brass falcons and falconets" with additional cargo, then the *John* has been located and charts and maps can be updated.

Jambi is the capital and largest city of the Indonesian province of Jambi on the island of Sumatra. The city is a busy port on the Batang Hari River and the location of an isthmus that has most certainly changed since 1631 and is the logical location for the *John.*

The last letter mentioned a fire, so it may be safe to assume the John burned to the water line and then sank. There are no records of salvage or recovery of goods, but taking into consideration the width and depth of the Batang Hari River at Jambi, divers could recover some or all the contents of the John. The pepper, though a very valuable cargo, has long since spoiled, but the ordnance most likely remains and could be used to identify a wreck in the deep mud should the river change course again.

Bosheston wreck.

15 January 1631. "George Ellis to Sir Thomas Canon. A miserable wreck took place at Bosheston, in November last of a ship from Ireland. All the people and cattle perished. The wreck which came ashore was seized by Mr. Lort, alleging that he had title; but he has proved only a right within Combe Martin, where this did not occur. The dead bodies still lie stripped naked

upon the rocks and sand, unburied. A commission from the admiralty has been inquiring about this and other wrecks; but Mr. Lort is sick, and the chief actors keep out of the way. One of his sons is in London, to get, as is reported, a new patent for all wrecks between the two fresh waters." *CSP-D, Charles I, 1629-1631, #59, p. 482-483.*

20 January 1631. "Commissioners appointed to inquire concerning certain wreck lately found near Bosheston co. Pembroke, to Sir Henry Marten, judge of the admiralty. Certain persons necessary to be examined have willfully made default in appearance, or have so obscured themselves that the messenger could not summon them, by reason whereof the writers were forced to give over the further execution of the commission." *CSP-D, Charles I, 1629-1631, #82, p. 487.*

20 January 1631. "Schedule of the names of the witnesses above mentioned, the chief of them being Henry Lort, of Stackpoole Cowrt, co, Pembroke, with Judith his wife, Amma his daughter, and others of his family." *CSP-D, Charles I, 1629-1631, #82-1, p. 487.*

Bosherston (Welsh: Llanfihangel-clogwyn-gofan, translates to St. Michaels above the cliffs of St Gofan) is a village and parish in Pembrokeshire, Wales, within what is now the Pembrokeshire Coast National Park. It would be safe to speculate this ship sank off the coast and what floated, was either washed to the shore or with tides into the ocean. It is safe to speculate that small amounts of money, personal items of the crew, ordnance, tackle, and furniture sank with the ship.

The *Janakin* of Amsterdam.

17 March 1631. The court of the admiralty; "for delivering and restoring or causing to be delivered and restored to two merchants of Amsterdam a ship called the *Janakin*, which ship was cast away near Portland in the county of Dorset, having been driven by wind upon the rocks or sands and there bruised and broken, to be delivered and restored, or caused to be delivered and restored all the tackle and furniture and goods in the ship at the time of the wreck and recovered." *APC, 1630-1631. p. 402.*

That is the only record discovered in archives. If the *Janakin* was travelling from Amsterdam, then she could have been driven onto the rocky shoreline of the east side of Portland Island by a storm.

Isle of Wight wreck.

30 May 1631. "Richard Jolliff to Nicholas. Excuses his non-attendance before the council in consequence of the wreck of a ship of Anquusion (Enckhuysen, Netherlands) of 250 tons, on the coast of the Isle of Wight, and his consequent occupation in preserving the goods for the owners." *CSP-D, Charles I, 1631-1633, #75, p. 62.*

No further information was located. It would appear the Isle of Wight claimed another ship.

Isle of Wight wreck (2).

I am confident this wreck on the Isle of Wright is different from the previous wreck for several reasons to include the time difference and the mention of weather conditions.

10 November 1631. "Captain John Pennington to the lords of the admiralty. Extreme foul weather. Damage done to the St. Claude. Has kept the channel and ranged all our coast, and looked into every bay where any pirates might lurk. None have been on the coast for six weeks. Dunkirkers ride in our harbors under the names and colors of Hollanders until any Hollanders come in or out, and then they clap them aboard presently, or set sail with them and do it as soon as they are out. The French ships that were on our coast are in the Bay of Biscay, and six others of that king's ships under Mons. Rasille, who pillage all nations. The ships at Havre de Grace and St. Malo are unrigging for the winter. A great ship was cast away on Friday last (November 7, 1631) on the south side of the Isle of Wight. She was beaten all to pieces and all her men drowned. Conceives she was an English ship from Malaga laden with fruit. Has come to an anchor in the Downs, where there is a large fleet much tottered [sic] and torn with the foul weather." *CSP-D, Charles I, 1631-1633, #24, p. 180.*

I was unable to locate additional information in archives. Captain Pennington was not able to illuminate in greater detail about the wreck site location. There are no records of salvage attempts or cargo floating to shore. "A great ship" could reference the ship's size, or a name that was well-known at the time.

The English ship departed Malaga Spain with fruit and perhaps wool, wine, and or a quantity of reales, to wreck anywhere along about 13 miles of the southern coast of the Isle of Wight. Whatever went down with the ship will remain a secret until the ship is discovered.

1632

Plymouth wreck.

It was not until a final edit that a previously overlooked record emerged that provided valuable information.

8 June 1631. "Officers of the Navy to the Committee of the Council of War. Report upon a petition of Capt. Heigham referred to them. Capt. Heigham being provost marshal in the expedition to Rhé, at his coming from thence laded on his own account aboard the Joan and the Return of London, 21 tons of wine, which was afterwards by Sir John Watts, on order from the Lord Admiral, converted into beverage, but it was never used. Capt. Heigham should seek his remedy from Capts. Thomas and Buxton, the commanders of the two ships." *CSP-D, Charles I, 1631-1633, #43, p. 71*

14 March 1632. Captain Buxton informed the admiralty that he loaded 11 tons of wine from Captain George Heigham on the Return of London and "the ship was bulged at Plymouth, who had the wines." *CSP-D, Charles I, 1631-1633, #41, p. 288*

11 April 1632. "Mayor and others of Plymouth to Secretary Coke. Enclosed an answer to a letter from the council concerning wines belonging to Captain Heigham, which came to the hands of Caus and Hallett, merchants of their town, also examinations relating to a charge against John Bussereau, a Frenchman, who was charged with having informed other Frenchmen that the French king was preparing a great fleet to invade England, and with having advised them to return home and get employment in the said fleet, assuring them that if they came to England he would aid and assist them all he could. The writers conceive that the accusation comes of spleen and malice, but they have taken bail of Bussereau to be forthcoming." *CSP-D, Charles I, 1631-1633, #29, p. 305-306.*

Enclosed letter. "Mayor and others of Plymouth to the council. With respect to Captain George Heigham's wines, on return of the fleet from Rhé, Captain William Buxton's ship was cast away in the harbor of Plymouth, and after having lain under water two months was sold by Nicholas Warren, the owner to Caus and Hallett. By their pains the ship was recovered, and in the hold were found nine butts of French wine. Having taken the salt water they were all brackish, and in short time smelt so moisome that they were staved and cast away. Send examinations respecting the charge against Bussereaw above mentioned." *CSP-D, Charles I, 1631-1633, #29-1, p. 306.*

It is possible the ship that wrecked in Plymouth harbor was named Joan; Captain William Buxton's ship and the other ship mentioned in the "ship was bulged at Plymouth," in the 14 March 1631 letter. Archival search of the *Joan* in the *Calendars* series from 1633-1636 offered no results beyond the last record of 14 July 1631. From that record forward, the incident was tracked through the loss of the wine and names. The cargo of French wine was a valuable cargo, most of which was recovered. It is difficult to determine if the "ship was recovered" indicates the ship returned to service or the sea eventually claimed whatever could not be salvaged. There may be smaller personal items of value on the ship.

St. Genny's wreck.

16 April 1632. "Francis Bassett to the same. About two months since a ship from Barbados laden with fustick wood and tobacco was wrecked on the north of Cornwall and no man saved. The ordnance and merchandise were seized for the king as belonging to the manor of Tintagel. Wrote to Mr. attorney to inquire whether it did not belong to the king as admiral, but got no reply. In the meantime one Gewin and others have obtained a commission to dispose thereof. The writer is ready now to begin his journey, to struggle for an order for the ordnance, worth at least £400. Has written to Mr. attorney again. Longs to see Nicholas and his other friends, but dares not attempt it without valuable business, knowing Mr. attorney would rattle him for an idle journey. The dirty, smoky, stinking tobacco trade has so choked up all fair trade there that were he to hear of a pirate more he should leave that part of the country." *CSP-D, Charles I, 1631-1633, #46, p. 309.*

46. I. "Note of the wreck above mentioned and especially of the precise spot on which the ship came ashore." *CSP-D, Charles I, 1631-1633, #46-1, 309.* Note: the "note" was unavailable for review.

46. II. "John Benoke to Francis Bassett. Mr. Worthewale has procured a commission, joining with him auditor Gewin and Nicolas Opie, the Feodary of the duchy, to examine all persons who have saved any part of the wrecked ship or goods. They have precepted 200 people and more to be at Botreaua Castle on Thursday next. Botreaua Castle, 1632, April 9." *CSP-D, Charles I, 1631-1633, #46-2, p. 309.*

28 May 1632. "Francis Bassett to the same. Sends commissioners names for a commission respecting a wreck which happened at St. Genny's in January last. This commission peaceably obtained, and the general peace confirmed by the punishment of Michel and his accomplices, he begs of Nicholas to effect." *CSP-D, Charles I, 1631-1633, #91, p. 338.*

No additional records were located. St. Genny's is a coastal civil parish and small settlement in north Cornwall, England about seven miles south-west of Bude and northeast of the coastal village of Crackington Haven. The sea eventually claimed the ship after it was stripped of everything.

1633

The *Royal Merchant*.

The wreck of the *Royal Merchant* has recently attracted creative writers to produce fantastic stories of unrecovered "billions" of dollars. This shipwreck will be treated the same as any other treasure ship in this book. These are the known records of the *Royal Merchant*.

3 January 1633. In a letter to Secretary Coke, "there is William Stephens, who built the *Royal Merchant* of 600 tons, so able a shipwright as there is hardly such another to be found in this kingdom, and two or three others." *CSP-C, 1574-1660, 158.* This information establishes her size.

2 December 1637. "Lords of the admiralty to the officers of the navy. We are informed that the *Royal Merchant*; and the *Swan* are prepared for a voyage to the southwards, that the *Mercury* is laden with perishable goods, and that the owners of the *Peter and Andrew* have prepared £10,000 worth of commodities, and that the ship is ready for sea. You are to discharge these ships if these allegations are true." *CSP-D, Charles, 1637-1638, V12, p. 4.*

20 January 1640. Giovanni Giustinian, a Venetian ambassador in England wrote; "many ships from Spain have arrived in port with 400 chests of money, most of it destined for the expenses of Flanders... I regret that the bad weather, which has lasted three weeks and caused the loss of twenty large ships on these coasts, has prevented my own for all those weeks from reaching you."

A foot note is included, "on the night of the 6-7 January, there was a particularly violent storm which even wrecked ships in port." *CSP&M, V &I, V25, 1640-1641, p. 7-8.*

24 February 1640. The Venetian Ambassador wrote, "many ships have arrived here from Cadiz this week, bringing a large quantity of silver which will be transported to Flanders." *CSPM, V&NI, V25, p. 20.* This record may suggest the *Royal Merchant* departed Cadiz or St. Lucar, (Sanlocar de Barrameda).

20 April 1640. The Venetian ambassador in England wrote "to the great satisfaction of the Catholic ministers here five ships arrived in these ports from Cadiz last Monday, bringing 500 chests of money, destined for the campaign in Flanders." *CSPM, V&NI, V25, p. 37.*

1 June 1640. The Venetian ambassador indicated "two ships arrived from Cadiz this week with a considerable sum of money. This will be sent over to Flanders with the usual escort of his majesty's ships." *CSPM, V&NI, V25, p. 50.*

30 September 1641. "Thomas Wiseman to Sir John Pennington. Yours of the 27th instructions has satisfied those fears I had of your not being well in that hideous and violent storm this day se'nnight, (seven night?), of which I never yet heard the like. The king for certain now is resolved to bid Scotland adieu very shortly, and within 10 days the queen expects him at Theobalds. I believe, for all the fair show [that] is made of his contentment there, tis otherwise, or else his departure thence would not be so sudden, contrary to the apprehensions of most men, who by many probable conjectures did not believe he would have come towards London yet a good while. The sickness, I hope, will every week diminish, [the deaths] being less by 42 than the last [week], whereby both his majesty and the houses of parliament may meet again without that fear of danger, to compose the great distempers imminent to church and people as matters now stand. I suppose you have understood of the loss of the Royal Merchant coming into our road, which is the greatest that was ever sustained in one ship, being worth £400,000 at least. The merchants of Antwerp will be the greatest losers, for she had in her belonging to them £300,000 in bullion; if so be the infante cardinal lose not upon it Flanders for want of money to pay the soldiers. Mr. auditor Hill is still sick of his ague; and I hope, whether he live or die, your money may be well paid; yet if it were mine I should wish it in other hands unless you have somebody bound for it besides himself." *CSP-D, Charles I, 1641-1643, #53, p. 128.*

18 October 1641. At the conclusion of a long-multiple page letter wrote by the Venetian ambassador in England to the Dode and Senate and rather insignificantly mentioned and sparsely worded in comparison to the content of multiple pages of the letter, "The merchants of this mart are greatly perturbed by the wreck in English waters of a ship which was bringing from Spain to these shores a cargo of £300,000 sterling in silver, as well as spices and goods worth as much."

A valuable footnote preceded the letter, "the *Royal Merchant*, Captain Limberi (?) with 180 chests of reales, 500 bars of silver and gold and jewels worth over a 'million of gold.'" Sources mentioned are from *Additional Manuscript Collection, 27962-1,* and *CSP, D, 1641-3, p. 128.* This source is *CSP&M-V&NI, V25, 1640-142, p. 227.*

Within the general index of *volume 25, 1640-1642-Calendar of State Papers and Manuscripts, Relating to English Affairs...Venice...Northern Italy,* page 374, is this title; "*Spain and Spaniards 1641: silver from, for Flanders, page 216, rich cargo lost,*" (the *Royal Merchant*). The original compliers of the *Calendars* from the

Public Record Office of London published in 1924 placed the loss of Spanish silver from Spain to Flanders, Belgium.

No additional information was located in archives.

With the assistance of a wonderful archrivalist at the British Library, I reviewed the *Cotton, Harley, Sloane, Royal and Lansdowne* manuscript collections, producing no additional information. Furthermore, the Spanish, Vatican, and Dutch archives were searched producing no additional information. Please allow me to mention that this incident is merely a grain of sand, though perhaps slightly larger, on a vast beach of correspondence and a rather insignificant event at a time when events such as the Spanish Inquisition, the constant threat of war on the horizon and gossip about royal figures dominated the topics in correspondence.

An early historian believed the Royal Merchant developed a persistent leak. The shipwrights or carpenters aboard the Royal Merchant and other ships often placed their lives in jeopardy attempting to stop or slow a leak to save their ship and the lives of the crew. If the bilge pump(s) were unable to keep up with incoming water flow and she was unable to make port for repairs, then the captain or master would try to run the ship on shore, if possible, understanding the importance and value of their cargo.

Records indicate the Royal Merchant was a ship of 600 tons. Based on that, the average statistics for a ship that size include a crew of about 180-200 mariners, 30 gunners and 80 soldiers carrying about 36-40 pieces of ordnance of various types.

"The merchants of Antwerp will be the greatest losers, for she had in her belonging to them £300,000 in bullion," and "180 chests of reales, 500 bars of silver and gold and jewels worth over a million of gold," certainly stimulates the imagination, but it is unfortunate the records offer no better location where the Royal Merchant rests.

I believe the *Royal Merchant* was caught in an eastward blowing tempest at her stern after she entered the channel and had possibly passed the Isle of Guernsey and the tip of France during the recorded 6-7 January 1640 storm that "caused the loss of twenty large ships on these coasts." All a seasoned captain or master could do is battle the storm, but the storm over powered them and they sank off the English coast and no records of recovered goods are known. The wording in the 30 September 1641 letter is an indication that it was written post event. Working on that theory and an account that she sank in "English waters" and not French waters could possibly place her west of Hastings to Poole or Weymouth, or about 2,800 square miles.

If a wreck was located off shore with 36-40 pieces of ordnance, muskets, ball and other implements of war and most certainly the discovery of 180 chests of reales, 500 bars of silver and gold and jewels, would ensure nautical charts and maps would be updated as museums planned their display of lost Spanish treasure.

Contained within *The Voyages of Sir James Lancaster, of the East Indies* under a list of ships of the East India Company, p. 295, mentions that the *Merchant Royal's* name was altered to the *Bear* in 1619 and had sailed, then changed to the *White Bear* that was burnt by the Dutch in 1620.

The *Salmon.*

9 February 1633. "Draft, corrected and endorsed, by Nicholas, of the warrant of the lords of the admiralty to the commissioners in the Isle of Purbeck touching the *Salmon*, a Dutch ship cast away there." *CSP-D, Charles, Addenda, March 1625-January 1649, p. 448.*

I am unable to uncover additional information regarding the Dutch ship *Salmon*, or a more accurate location of where on the Isle of Purbeck she wrecked.

The Isle of Purbeck is a peninsula in Dorset, England that is bordered by water on three sides: the English Channel to the south and east and by the marshy lands of the River Frome and Poole Harbor to the north. It is safe to speculate the Salmon may have wrecked on the South side of the island.

Seaford wreck.

22 May 1633. "Examination of John Baker, taken before Dr. Thomas Rives. A ship was cast away at Seaford, in Sussex, on a Sunday in January last. Having heard thereof at almost sunset he put his sheep in fold and went down to the ship; he found the country already come in. It was dark. He had out of a room in the hinder part of the ship a scarlet cloak, a pair of knee tops of cloth, one silk garter, a piece of cloth lined with black taffeta, and one glove wrought with silver. When he heard the goods were inquired for he gave them up to a Frenchman and received 6s. for his pains." *CSP-D, 1633-1634, #25, p. 67.*

"Similar examination of John Chambers. He went up into the ship, found there 100 men, some of whom he names, and says they were taking the main sail from the yard. Took from a countryman, who had it under his arm, a black velvet doublet and a fine shirt. Gave the doublet up before any commission came down and the shirt afterwards. Had 3s. for his pains." This was written on the same sheet of paper as the preceding. *CSP-D, 1633-1634, #25, p. 67.*

This ship may have wrecked somewhere along 10 miles of the coastline of Seaford, East Sussex, England. During the Middle Ages, Seaford was one of the main ports serving Southern England. It is clear the local inhabitants pilfered anything of value prior to the two men arriving and was eventually stripped of everything to the hull that the sea would eventually claim.

The *St. Andrew.*

Within the examination of Thomas Sheppard is mention of several wrecks. Though all intriguing, only this one yielded enough information to include.

23 November 1633. "Petition of Francis Brooke to the lords of the admiralty. Charles Clarke, purser of the *St. Andrew*, now in harbor at Portsmouth, has, by the death of a kinsman, lands fallen to him in Kent, and is desirous to leave his purser's place." *CSP-D, Charles I, 1633-1634, #16, p. 295.*

12 January 1634. "Examination of Thomas Sheppard, porter of Southsea Castle being an information against Francis Brooke, deputy vice-admiral of Portsmouth, and John Brooke, his brother, for applying to their own use various wrecks occurring within the limits of the deputy vice-admiralty of Francis Brooke. The charges are;

1. That Francis took from three of the gunners of Southsea Castle a boat of one ton and a half burthen, which they had seized about a year before as wreck at that castle, and sold the same for £4.

2. That Francis took from two Frenchmen, survivors of the crew of a French bark cast ashore, their bark of 30 tons, that he repaired and employed her to sea, and that she was thenceforward known as 'Brookes's bark.'

3. That Francis seized another French vessel driven ashore between Southsea Castle and Portsmouth, and that she is now lying in the king's dock at Portsmouth, where Francis dwells, but what has become of her lading examinant cannot tell.

4. That a Flemish ship of 120 tons was wrecked to the south-east of Southsea Castle, all the crew being saved. John Brooke said that he bought the wrecked ship and goods of the Flemings for £20. He afterwards received £18 for some of the sails sold, and has sold linen cloth to Mr. Peters and other inhabitants of Portsmouth." *CSP-D, Charles I, 1633-1634, #58, p. 412.*

17 January 1634. "Lords of the admiralty to Sir Henry Marten. A Dutch ship, the St. Andrew, of Rotterdam, of 120 tons, Isaac Powelson, master, was about the beginning of December last wrecked on the south-east shore Southsea Castle, having in her four small pieces of ordnance, and the goods mentioned in a note enclosed. He is to issue a commission to the persons

under named to inquire for and seize all goods saved from the wreck and sold or embezzled." *CSP-D, Charles I, 1633-1634, p. 419.* I was unable to locate the note mentioned.

January 1634. "Particular of goods in the *St. Andrew* of Rotterdam, Isaac Powelson master, before her grounding on the south coast of England." *CSP-D, Charles I, 1633-1634, #92, p. 466.*

"Note of such goods as I had off the *St. Andrew* endorsed by Nicholas as Mr. Brooke's, that is, Francis Brooke's, note of goods in the Dutch ship wrecked near Southsea Castle." *CSP-D, Charles I, 1633-1634, #92-1, p. 466.*

No additional information was located in archives. Southsea Castle, also historically known as Chaderton Castle, South Castle, and Portsea Castle, is an artillery fort originally constructed by King Henry VIII on Portsea Island, Hampshire, in 1544. The *St. Andrew* wrecked on castle's south-east shore, presumably the channel side. Without the notes, it is impossible to determine if all the goods were recovered. I am unable to speculate about the 4 pieces of ordnance, tackle, cable, or furniture that possibly remained with the ship before the sea claimed her.

Little Holland wreck.

4 December 1633. The first mention of this incident. Written at Colchester. "Edward Nuttall to Nicholas. Lets him know how the current Colchester goes there about the wreck. She is held strong in the possession of Sergeant Darcy. Whether his grant bars the king that the writer leaves to Nicholas to consider. If it should be absolutely the king's, he suggests that some merchant should be found to buy the ship and all things in her. Now all the country comes down, and every man catch what they can, and stave and stroy more than they get. All goods that are taken out and come into their parts Nuttall has in possession, and his deputy at Ipswich does the same. Begs authority and direction." *CSP-D, Charles I, 1633-1634, #15, p. 315.*

13 December 1633. "Richard Pulley, deputy vice-admiral of Essex, to Richard Maldon Wyan. On Friday Mr. Spicer and the writer went to Colchester. The latter went to Mr. Nuttall, and acquainting him with the commission, he seemed much troubled, and produced a warrant from the lord treasurer, dated 3d inst., whereby he was solely authorized for seizing all the goods. The writer urged the execution of the commission, and in the meantime Spicer and he went to Little Holland where the ship lay, and there found Sergeant Darcy, a sergeant-at-law, whose answer was, that the ship lay upon his manor, and that he had all wrecks of the sea. The writer put an officer on board to keep possession for the king, and took order for boats

and men to save the goods. He then rode to Harwich and Nacton after goods claimed by the bailiffs of Ipswich, Sir Richard Brooke, lord of the manor, and Thomas Cleere, customer at Ipswich, which goods the writer seized, and went afterwards to Ipswich and Harwich for the like purpose, and thence to Colchester to open the commission. Many persons complained of Nuttall for taking goods from them. In his justification, he produced another warrant from the lord treasurer, dated the 9th inst. When the writer saw this he was much moved, but in the end resolved to get an inventory, and took the same as if he were Mr. Nuttall's man, and the lord treasurer's warrant of more force than the king's commission. If Sir Henry Marten be acquainted herewith the writer presumes he will move the lord's commissioners therein, that at least the court of admiralty may have a concurrency of jurisdiction." *CSP-D, Charles I, 1633-1634, #44, p. 321-322.*

16 December 1633. "Lords of the admiralty to Thomas Wyan, Richard Pulley, deputy Whitehall, vice-admiral of Essex, John How and Philip Allen, merchants, and David Spicer. A ship was lately wrecked, or left derelict, on the coast near Colchester or Harwich, and a commission is issued out of the court of admiralty directed to them, to take the ship and goods into their custody for his majesty's use. Being informed that goods belonging to the ship are embezzled and carried away into towns corporate, which pretend to be exempt from the admiralty, they are to seize the same for his majesty until further order, and if any persons hinder them they are to bind them over to answer the same before the lords. All mayors and other officers are to aid them in the execution of their commission." *CSP-D, Charles I 1633-1634, p. 323-324.*

24 February 1634. "Lords of the admiralty to all mayors, sheriffs, and others, Whitehall. A commission having been issued on the 4th inst. directed to Richard Pulley, deputy vice-admiral of Essex, John How, Philip Allen and others, to make sale of a ship wrecked or left derelict between Colchester and Harwich, the persons addressed are to aid the commissioners in the execution of their commission." *CSP-D, Charles I, 1633-1634, #98, p. 473.*

No additional information located in archives. It is safe to speculate that the wreck on the coast near Colchester or Harwich, was stripped of everything worth value.

Mismere wreck.

21 December 1633. I believe this letter is relevant. "Order of the lords of the admiralty on the petition of Baitain Whitehall. Semaes and his fellows, prisoners in the Marshalsea and in Faversham. Petitioners stated that having

come from Dunkirk with a lawful commission against the Hollanders, they happened to meet three Holland pinks about the mouth of the Thames, which having taken, petitioner and his fellows were put into them to be sent to Dunkirk, but the people of Faversham sending after them recovered two of the pinks, killing two or three of the petitioners' fellows and taking the rest, whom they keep still in prison. The third pink being set to sea for Dunkirk was forced by weather up to Gravesend where she was seized, and petitioner with six more sent to the Marshalsea and there kept twelve days, suffering extremity of hunger and cold. They prayed for their liberty. The judge of the admiralty was ordered to certify the true state of the business and to bring his certificate to the lords on Monday afternoon." *CSP, D, Charles I, 1633-1634, p.333.*

14 January 1634. "Henry Dade to Secretary Coke. A pink was wrecked on Friday seven at night about Mismere haven not far from Aldborough, which was seized to his majesty's use, when none could come to her but by boat, yet John Ingram of Theberton, bailiff to Mr. Miller, a mercer in Cheapside, who pretends to be lord of that soil where the pink was seized after certain goods were taken out of her, has so terrified Mr. Miller's tenants that they dare not suffer the marshal for the admiralty to look to the goods. Prays the secretary to send for Mr. Miller, and refer him to Sir Henry Marten to justify his claim and his bailiff's actions." *CSP, D, Charles I, 1633-1634, #63, p. 413.*

"Statement of Jeremy Nymans, of Dunwich, that on Friday 3rd January inst. Aslack Anderson and others found a Flemish pink lying in the water near Mismere haven so that none could go to her without a boat. [This statement is corroborated by the signatures of the actual finders]. Jan. 14. Ipswich." *CSP, D, Charles I, 1633-1634, #63-1, p. 413.*

No additional information was located about this ship in archives. It would appear that, though the ship was only accessible by boat, most if not everything of value may have been removed. Mismere is on the coast of Suffolk, south of Dunwich Heath, encompassing a single beach behind a vast area of marshes and broads. There may well be a ship submerged along this location with unknown items that survived.

1634

Red Sands wreck.

21 March 1634. "Sir Richard Plumleigh to Nicholas. Hoped this Nicholas should have received a letter of his from Portsmouth, but that expectation

is crossed by contrariety of winds. Has been completely manned and fitted these ten days, and has hitherto forborne to write because he is loath his letters should bear date from Tilbury Fort. The first breath of wind that blows he shall be ready to take, for never was man so weary of a jail as he of being wind bound there. The East Indian fleet are in the same predicament and lie fast at Gravesend. All our fishermen at Barking come drunk by them daily, with 'the wrack-sack' of a Malaga ship cast away on Saturday last about the buoy in the Red Sands." *CSP-D, Charles I, 1633-1634, #23, p. 519.*

"All our fishermen at Barking come drunk by them daily, with the wrack-sack (news?) of a Malaga ship wrecked on Saturday about the buoy in the Red Sands" suggests this ship wrecked off the east coast of the Isle of Sheppey and was from Malaga Spain. It is impossible to speculate what went down with the ship. There are no reports of debris washing on shore, or salvage attempts. This Spanish ship could have contained cloth goods, earthenware or even bullion.

The *Swan*.

6 January 1598. "The *Antelope* and Sir John Gilbert was responsible for capturing two ships: the *Poppingay* of Lubeck and the *Swan* of Rotterdam. The cargos were deemed as legal prize and to be sold." *APC-V.28, p. 224.* That entry fits with the following entry.

"During the year 1635 the Dunkirkers, with their hand against every man's, made a remarkable number of prizes; but in 1636 two of them, the Swan and the Nicodemus, were captured by the 'ship money' fleet under Northumberland, and were added to the navy as the fastest vessels afloat. Sir John Pennington, his vice admiral and one of the most experienced officers in the service, was so much struck with them that he advised the Swan being taken as a model in the English dock-yards, and the Nicodemus was said to run away from everything as a greyhound does from a little dog. The dimensions of the Swan are unknown, for before Pennington's advice could be acted on she was wrecked off Guernsey; but the Nicodemus we know to have been of 105 tons with a length of nearly 3 1/3 times her beam." *England in the Mediterranean, V.1, p. 182.*

September 1634. "The former for St. Lucar in the *Swan* of 300 tons and with 24 guns." *CSP-D, Charles I, 1634-1635, #66, p. 221.*

Searches beyond the base document in the wonderfully rich Calendars starting with volume 11 yielded no results of the Swan. Volume 12 contained many records of the Swan. No results in volumes 13, 14 or 15. Volume 16, 17 first references to an inn called the Swan. In volume 18 is a record of 8 July

1641, "The king is pleased that his new pinnace the Swan, now in Ireland, shall be employed this year for the guard of the Irish Seas; we therefore pray you to give order that it be forthwith prepared, victualed, and furnished for so long as you shall think requisite for guard of those seas." *CSP-D, V.18, Charles I, 1641-1643, p. 46.*

Additional record from Volume 18: 30 December 1642. Records of appointments of gunner and purser were recorded in Letters and Papers relating to the Navy. The new Swan is also described as a pinnace. *CSP-D, V.18, 1641-1643, Charles I, p. 434.*

"She was wrecked off Guernsey" is not decisive evidence that it sank. The new Swan may be a completely new ship, or resurrected. I was not able to close this incident. I look forward to a revision in the near future.

Isle of Wight wreck.

17 October 1634. "On Saturday last a ship was cast away on the Isle of Wight which came out of Ireland with soldiers, bound for Dunkirk, and had as the report goes, 200 men in her, whereof as they hear there is but forty saved, and a good part of them will not live, being very much bruised, and some of them had their legs and arms broken upon the rocks." *CSP-D, Charles I, 1634-1635, #68, p. 241.*

No additional information was located in the archives. This ship may have wrecked on 7 or 14 October 1634 with most of her cargo, ordnance, arms, and personal belongings. It is possible this ship carried pay for the soldiers.

Coleraine Ireland wreck.

8 October 1634. "Lord Viscount Chichester's account for the vice-admiralty of Ulster. I certify that I have no account to offer, and that no droits or casualties have come into the hands since two years ago last Michaelmas. A ship was wrecked in the river of Coleraine last May, and some of the crew who were examined confessed to piracy. After she had lain at sea a month, her cargo of cloth and wine was washed ashore and seized by the Lord of Kilkubery (Kircudbright] and his servants. They refused to give them up, and pleaded the Londoners' grant. An enquiry has been ordered by the lord chancellor, as judge of the admiralty." *CSP-I, 1633-1647, p. 80.*

20 December 1634. "Lords of the admiralty to the lord chancellor of Ireland. Understand from viscount Chichester, vice-admiral of Ulster, that

in May last a ship of about 80 tons was cast away near the bar of the river of Coleraine in his vice-admiralty, and diverse of her men confessed that they had robbed at sea such as they were too strong for, and that there was in the ship English cloth and merchandise. After the ship had lain about a month in the sea diverse of her goods were cast on shore, and were taken up by the Lord of Kilkuberie [Kirkcudbright], who pretends authority for detaining them in the right of the Londoners' grant, which claim is now depending before the lord chancellor as judge of the admiralty. Such pretenses are of late grown frequent, and for the most part without any color of truth or ground in law. For that this is a matter of value, importing his majesty's right and interest, they recommend the business to the lord chancellor's special care, so that his majesty's right may be vindicated from all intrusions." *CSP-D, Charles I, 1634-1635, p. 363.*

For all practical purposes, I believe the records indicate the Coleraine River in Ireland, and not the river of the same name in France. Early records mention that a persistent sand bar had prevented expansion of the river port at Coleraine since 1790 at the river mouth. The first record mentioned the ship was in the river and cargo washed ashore which could suggest the river had changed in width over the centuries. No additional information was located, nor any speculation as to cargo, and there are no records of salvage or cargo other than the items that washed on shore. If this ship was involved in piracy, then one may only speculate that very little remained when the ship sank. I believe that if additional items were removed from this ship, then it would have been mentioned in records.

1635

The *Santa Barbara.*

26 January 1635. The Venetian ambassador in England wrote: "At Havana three Dutch ships encountered two Spanish ones, which were on their way from the Indies in the company of six others, from which they were parted by the fortune of the sea. There was a gallant fight and one was taken by the Dutch, which in addition to other goods carried several chests of silver. But after the Dutch had changed the crews and removed the most precious part of the cargo, the Spanish ship was separated by a fresh accident and was brought by Dutch sailors into one of the ports here.* While they believed they might with security await an escort to proceed to Holland, the news quickly reached the merchants here, and the Spanish resident at once

obtained powers to have it seized. But the Dutch merchants were no less prompt and the Ambassador Joachimi not less active than he, and they forthwith sent to the ship to get away from the port. We do not yet know what has happened." *Calendar of State Papers and Manuscripts, Venice and Northern Italy, V. 23, 1632-1636 #418, p.326.*

> * A footnote reference in the letter noted, "The Ship was the Santa Barbara, captured in December and brought into Guavers Lake near Penzance by David Dinghemans and Cornelius Bergenaer Memorial of Joachimi."

9 February 1635. "The Spanish ship captured by the Dutch at Havana, which took refuge from a storm in the port of Monsbai, being warned by the Ambassador Joachimi of the arrest which the Spanish resident had obtained against it, to avoid the ill fortune of being seized in the port, put to sea, in the hope of continuing its voyage. But where it hoped to find the safer way of deliverance it encountered a worse fate in another furious tempest in which it perished miserably.* *Calendar of State Papers and Manuscripts, Venice and Northern Italy, V. 23, 1632-1636. #424, p. 332.*

> * A footnote in the letter noted, "The *Santa Barbara*; See No. 418 at page 326 above, and note. She was wrecked while riding at anchor in Mounts Bay."

Mount's Bay is a large, sweeping bay on the English Channel coast of Cornwall, United Kingdom, stretching from the Lizard Point to Gwennap Head and is resting place for the Santa Barbara. If the Santa Barbara perished as a result of a tempest, then she may contain some or all her cargo.

The *William and Anne*.

5 February 1635. "The William and Anne having arrived at Flushing from association, a person to be sent to take account of her goods." *CSP-C, 1574-1660, p. 196.*

5 March 1635. Minutes from a court meeting at Providence Island mention "Notice received that the William and Anne had been wrecked at Belle Isle upon the coast of Brittany, and a meeting fixed to advise what should be done. Wreck of the William and Anne at Belle Isle; 100 tons of braziletta and 40 tons of tobacco saved." *CSP-C, 1574-1660, p. 199.*

A 13 March 1635 meeting resolved to send an agent into France to take possession of the cargo. *CSP-C, 1574-1660, p. 200.*

20 June 1635. "Minutes of a meeting for association Island. Bartholomew Styles, late minister there, desires the company to approve his assignment of property in the William and Anne to Gabriel Barber." *CSP-C, 1574-1660, p. 210.*

That is the sum of information located in archives. If some or all the cargo was salvaged, it is possible some or all the tackle, cables and furniture or other valuables was recovered from the *William and Anne* that wrecked on Belle Isle off the coast of Brittany.

Isle of Wight wreck.

18 November 1635. "Richard Wyan to Nicholas. During the last storm there was a ship of Hamburg cast away near the Isle of Wight, but the men escaped alive, and since that time £4,000 or £5,000 and some goods have been saved out of the sea, and a good sum loose without marks or bags. He has sent down a messenger to seize all for his majesty's use. He may certify the lords as he sees occasion." *CSP-D, Charles I, 1635, #7, p. 487.*

1 December 1635. "Notes by Nicholas of business to be transacted by the lords of the admiralty. Officers of ordnance to bring in a better account touching powder sold by them. Consider Captain Rainsborough's paper against having galleries in the king's ships. Paper sent by the lord deputy of Ireland under the hand of Sir Beverley Newcomen concerning repairs of the *Ninth Whelp*. Order for calling in ships with Sir John Pennington that are not on the ordinary; their victuals will end on the 10th inst. Consider Thornhill's complaint of gentlemen in county of Dorset. Consider complaints against John Morrice, master and Lawrence, purser of the *Sampson*; [Margin. Discharged.] Richard Wyan advertises that he has taken order for seizing for the king's use goods cast away about the Isle of Wight; to the value of four or five thousand pounds. Consider account of saltpeter brought in last year. What shall be done concerning swearing officers of the navy and ordnance." *CSP-D, Charles I, 1635, p. 522.*

12 December 1635. "Lords of the admiralty to Richard Wyan, his majesty's Whitehall. Proctor in the admiralty. Out of a ship lately wrecked near the Isle of Wight, diverse sums of money and other goods have been brought on shore. He is with all possible speed to repair thither and take account of the same, and return the account to the lords. He is also to take such course for the preservation of the said money and other things that there be no embezzling or purloining." *CSP-D, Charles I, 1635, #131, p. 577.*

A letter was classified and placed in December 1635 of the *Calendar of State Papers*: "Relation of Richard Wyan touching the ship cast away near the Isle of Wight. On the 18th October last in Brixton Bay a ship of Hamburg, whereof Jurian Tome was shipper, was split in pieces. Her company escaped alive to the shore, and the same night by the means of one Newland, certain indigo, Spanish wool and silvester cochineal were saved, all which the shipper (having procured a bark) carried away. He also sold the wreck and left a letter of attorney with Newland, who built a watch-house on the shore, and kept laborers there and recovered several chests of Spanish money, and took other sums out of the sands and sea. Of the moneys recovered 16,000 pieces of eight, and a wedge of silver, weighing 73 lbs. are in the office of the admiralty, and 1,500 pieces with 600 India hides and other things are left in the Isle of Wight until adjudication, and the proportion of charges of salvage. Various other enumerated articles it is hoped will be recovered." *CSP-D, Charles I, 1635, #94, p. 611.*

16 March 1637. "Petition of William Newland to the lords of the admiralty. In October 1635, near the Isle of Wight, there was a Hamburger ship cast away, the captain whereof, called Jurian Tammes, sent for petitioner and acquainted him that there was treasure in his ship, and desired him to use means to save what might be. Thereupon petitioner built a watch house near the place, and caused the sea to be watched for a good time at his great charge, and by making engines, and employing men to wade into the sea, saved one wedge of silver and about 17,000 pieces of eight. The wedge and about 16,000 of the said pieces of eight were taken from petitioner by warrant of the lords by Mr. Richard Wyan, all which were claimed by Fleming's resident at Dover, but are now come to his majesty. Prays an allowance of salvage." *CSP-D, Charles I, 1636-1637, #7, p. 502*

No additional information was located in archives. It could be easy to assume that not all the Spanish pieces of eight or wedges of silver were salvaged based on the records. It is not known what the total sum of money was, or the full cargo without an inventory. The Isle of Wight claimed another ship, but this ship may contain valuables.

Isle of Selsey wreck.

15 December 1635. "Sir Thomas Bowyer to Nicholas. It occurred heretofore to acquaint him with a ship that was wrecked at the Isle of Selsey; there is now a very great ship wrecked, and goods swimming about the sea are taken up and embezzled. If any had authority, much would be found out and preserved. It was lost about Wednesday last." *CSP-D, Charles I, 1635, #21, p. 565.*

Several wrecks occurred about the same time on the Isle of Wight which made singling out this incident difficult. The information the singular letter contains is not similar to the other wrecks and the time frame is also different, so I felt that it could be treated as a separate incident. It would appear some items were recovered.

In the seventeenth century Selsey was very much more isolated than it is today, and the sand spit extended farther out to sea, thus sometimes creating a small island. There was only the causeway connected to the mainland and that was covered at high tide. This sounds like a large ship, 200 tons or larger.

1636

Isle of Wight wrecks.

4 January 1636. "Jerome earl of Portland to the lords of the admiralty. Last week two Hamburg ships with wines from Malego (Malaga), were cast away on the south of the Isle of Wight. One was split all to pieces and all the men drowned, save the steersman; the other lies on the rocks ready to perish, but all her men are saved. Officers being sent for preservation of goods, William Howard, servant to Mr. Cuttell, who has some land thereby, with many of Mr. Cuttell's tenants, with staves and bills set on them, and took from them much of the ship's goods, seven butts of wine, and two pieces of ordnance, notwithstanding they were commanded the contrary, Howard affirming that Mr. Cuttell would bear them out, though it cost him £1,000. If the lords think fit to make an exemplary punishment of this, it will be an advantage to his majesty's service, for there are many who pretend charters of wrecks upon their own ground, but have never produced any." *CSP-D, Charles I, 1635-1636, #20, p. 147.*

The first mentioned ship would have been destroyed by waves smashing it on the rocks leaving only what could have floated to shore as items salvaged. The second ship may have ultimately received the same fate after most of what could be salvaged was removed. Some ordnance may remain. There is no additional information discovered or recovery records.

Goodwin Sands wrecks.

2 February 1636. "They have had the sorest weather for these two or three months that ever he saw, and much shipwreck. Ever since Michaelmas the wind has hung between S.S.E. and W.N.W., with continual blowing and shifting. On Sunday last the wind came about to N.N.E., and a very great fleet of English and Dutch that had lain a long time there set sail, and amongst them the Swallow, which could never get a wind before to carry him to the

westward, but the same night the wind veered back and blew such a stress, that there are many of them cast away, some upon the Goodwin, and the rest are returned miserably tattered and torn, some having all their sails blown away, others cut their masts and yards by the board, and some all their upper works and quarters beaten away. The Swallow is come safe back though with some damage. Requests them to bestow a boatswain's place of one of the new pinnaces now building on William Parker, and that upon the picking of the captains for this year's employment they will be pleased to remember those that are there abroad with him; namely, Captains Stradling, Price, Lindsey, and the writer's lieutenant, Robert Fox. It will be requisite that he stands to the westward in the beginning of March, for in that month all the Newfoundland men go out, and if the Turk, who has a great invitation from the French, will come upon our coast, he will do it then. They have little hope of taking any of them, their ships are so foul, yet they will scare them from the coast and thereby prevent clamors. If they please he can fit up one or both of these small vessels to go with him." *CSP-D, Charles I, 1635-1636, #6, p. 205.*

The N.N.E. winds that finally allowed many of the ships to sail had changed sending several into the sands. There are no records mentioning recovery of cargo or ships, or any items blown on shore, or a more accurate number of ships, if any, that wrecked on the Goodwin Sands. If these ships did load, then they would have wrecked with cargo, and it is possible the local inhabitants enjoyed the prizes. This storm affected many other ships, but these are the only known wrecks.

Dover Castle wreck.

7 March 1636. "Sir John Pennington to the lords of the admiralty. Has the Vanguard, used all the means he could to meet with the shallops that pillaged in the Downs the packet boat, but as yet he cannot, but will continue his utmost endeavors, though it is a very hard thing for ships to take shallops, that can row away in the wind's eye, except it be in a fret of weather. They very much want small rowing vessels to meet with these shavers. Another unlucky accident happened yesterday at Dover. A Dunkirk sloop that had brought goods thither, and was discharged and returning back, had taken in some of the Dunkirkers that belonged to the ship which cast away under Dover Castle as passengers, and as they came out of the pier, there followed them a Hamburg hoy, laden with Holland goods and much money, and bound for the said place, which hoy they clapped aboard and carried her away for Dunkirk, which the wit of man could not prevent, except he had been by at the instant; neither will it be remedied till his majesty gives order,

either to beat them out of his seas or otherwise to apprehend the next man-of-war that belongs to that town that committed that fact, and make him give satisfaction. If this course were taken with them, it would quickly make them weary of these ways." *CSP-D, Charles I, 1635-1636, #64, p. 276.*

It is a shame that there is no additional information located in archives about this incident. A sloop is smaller and suited for carrying passengers. This ship could have sunk off the coast of Dover Castle intact, including the personal effects of some of the passengers and some of the mentioned "much money." "Wrecked below" Dover Castle could imply she wrecked west of the castle perhaps not as far as Folkstone. No records of recovery are located.

The *Anne Royal.*

It is described in the prefix of a letter of 2 May 1636; "some delay was caused by a mishap to the *Anne Royal*, the vice admiral, which bilged her own anchor when brought into the Thames, and became a total wreck through gross carelessness." *CSPM-V &NI, V.23, 1632-1636, preface, xlii.*

25 May 1636. "Yesterday the vice admiral's ship, foundered unexpectedly when proceeding to join the rest of the fleet, causing the death of more than twenty-four persons and the loss of all the munitions and goods on board. The disaster is attributed to the age of the ship. Some say the loss was designed. However that may be, his majesty is very sorry for it, not only for the loss of the ship, considerable in itself, but because the accident will delay for some days the sailing of the other ships, which are practically equipped with everything, because before they sail he wishes them all to be carefully inspected." *CSPM-V &NI, V.23, 1632-1636, #642, p. 550.*

The editor of the *Calendars* included a footnote to the preceding letter. "The Anne Royal, which was to carry the flag of Sir John Pennington. She was built is 1587, probably for Raleigh and named the Ark Royal and being bought for the royal navy, served as the admiral's flagship in 1588 against the Armada. She was rebuilt in 1608 and renamed Anne Royal in honor of James's queen. The loss was caused by her bilging her own anchor, when brought to in the Thames, when she came up from Chatham to be fitted. The third son of James Hamilton, first earl of Abercorn, a young man of 25 years of age."

Sir John Pennington transferred his flag to the *St. Andrew*, a ship of 670 tons built in 1622, because of the mishap to the *Anne Royal.*

20 April 1636. "Examination of William Gayney of Sandwich, late master's mate of the Anne Royal, taken as the preceding. Agrees with Merrick till their coming to an anchor in Tilbury Hope, but denies that there was eight fathom

water, for they came to anchor at full sea about one at noon, and rode all that ebb free of danger, without any water till nine at night, which was two hours flood; but at low water she lay on ground. But after two hours flood she sheered about to the southward, and upon a sudden the water came in as he thinks in [the] hold, and then the master commanded to loosen the foresail, and the ship being falling before was instantly overturned, which was about nine at night. If the ship had been anchored in deep water she could not have come to that mischance. He did not hear the pilot desire the master to come sooner to an anchor or to moor the ship. They anchored about "a falcon shot" from the shore. They discovered no imperfection in the ship before the mischance. She was a little tender-sided, but with more ballast would have been stiff enough." *CSP-D, Charles I, 1635-1636, V.9, p. 376.*

A second examination of 20 April 1636, of Thomas Rabenett, late boatswain of the Anne Royal. "They have cut holes in the sides of the ship to take out the goods of Sir John Pennington and of the master, which the master and lieutenant began first to do. The gunner cut a hole for his clothes, so did the carpenter, though forbidden to do so by examinant. Agrees that there was a difference between the pilot and master in Gillingham Reach. Conceives the anchor was let fall in not above five fathom and a half at high water, and at low 17 foot. The ship drew 17 foot 4 inches. They lay safe till two hours flood, which was at 9 at night, but at 7 they began to heave the capstan to come up nearer to the anchor intending to weigh, and then in the heaving, about 9 the ship suddenly fetched a sheer, and so struck upon a bank or wreck, and suddenly made a seal, and then presently the water came in "forcible" abash in the bread room or steward's room, which filled the ship. Then the master commanded the foresail and topsail to be set and cut her cable, thinking to run her near the shore, which cast her all upon her side, as she now lies. So they shot four pieces of ordnance for help which came and saved some of them. Examinant discovered no defect till this accident, only on a particular survey some rotten timber appeared. If they had anchored in deep water, and had moored, if it had been but there, in time, the ship had been safe." *CSP-D, Charles I, 1635-1636, V.9, p. 376-377.*

Contrary statements summarized that the Anne Royal anchored within a falcon (small cannon) shot of shore at Tilbury Hope. It may be possible she was low on ballast and rolled over when the tide ebbed followed by any attempt to salvage any personal possessions before the tide returned.

A list of the ships of the East India Company in The Voyages of Sir James Lancaster, Kt, to the East Indies, mentions an Anne Royal in 1617 at 900 tons with Andrew Shilling as master. A 1633 inventory of the king's ships indicated she had a 107' keel at 776 tons carrying 44 pieces of ordnance with a crew of 400.

A ship found there with 44 pieces of ordnance could help to identify the wreck as the Anne Royal. If some of the hull remained to present day, then the various holes cut would also aid in identification.

Land's End wrecks.

5 July 1636. "Anthony Gubbes, mayor of Penzance, and Roger Polkinhorne to John Thresher, captain of Pendennis Castle. This day there arrived at Penzance a bark of Tredarth (Tredagh), in Ireland, which came from Crossac, in Brittany, and the 3rd instructions met with a Turkish man-of-war of 100 tons, 5 pieces of ordnance, about 80 men, carvel build, with an English beck head, wearing English colors, which took the bark and captivated the merchant, his name being Christopher Fitzsimons, and carried him away. The master and the company, being Frenchmen, they set free with the bark and goods, and the captain of the Turks said they durst not carry Frenchmen into Sallee. In the same bark there sailed two Irishmen, who, having the French tongue perfect, escaped for Frenchmen. These two Irishmen report that there were eleven sail more that wear English colors, and that they intend to be about the Lizard Point and Land's End, against St. James's fair. Intended to wait in St. George's Channel to take passengers to Bristol fair. Desire Tresahar to give notice of this. 4th July 1636." *CSP-D, Domestic, Charles I, 1636-1637, #29-1, p. 52.*

10 July 1636. "Examination of John Daniel, of Salcombe, Devon, mariner, taken at Plymouth before the mayor and other justices of peace. On Tuesday last examinant came out of Tenby in the Swan of Salcombe, with two other barks of Salcombe, the Rose Mary and the Catherine, and a bark of Barnstaple, Christopher Browning master, all laden with coal. Coming off Padstow, examinant saw two big ships standing after him, which he believeth were two of his majesty's ships, and coming about the Land's End, off Mount's Bay, a Turkish man-of-war of one hundred tons burden gave chase to examinant and the other barks, and forced two of them to run on shore, where they were split, and the other two cast anchor as near the shore as they could, and got all on shore in their boats, except one man, who stayed behind and was carried away by the Turks, who carried off the said two barks, and after they had rifled them sunk them in examinant's sight. Examinant was informed at Falmouth that on Wednesday last was three weeks seven boats and two and forty fishermen in them were taken off the Manacles near the Lizard by the Turks." *CSP-D, Domestic, Charles I, 1636-1637, #54, p. 58.*

20 September 1636. "Sir Nicholas Slanning to Secretary Coke. On 19th instructions arrived a small bark of Jersey that had been to Newfoundland and Portugal, which was taken about 60 leagues off the Land's End by six Turkish men-of-war, which had aboard them certain French runagates who told the master of the bark that there were 20 sail of Turks more that had divided themselves into three squadrons, and came forth with design to wait the coming home of the Newfoundland English fleet, and the going out of the ships for the vintage. The master named himself a Frenchman of St. Malo, by which means he was released, for the Turks told him there was a league between them and the French. This news has much terrified the country, and it is feared that if the Turks be suffered long to continue, they will disable the English from any trade hereafter." *CSP-D, Domestic, Charles I, 1636-1637, #3, p. 134.*

It appears that two barks sank on the jagged rocky shore at Land's End within sight distance. Based upon the accounts shared in the correspondence, it would be safe to assume that anything worth salvaging was removed leaving just the basic ship behind.

The *Fourth Whelp.*

5 August 1636. "The ships in the Narrow Seas are the *Happy Entrance*, and the *Roebuck*, under Captains Carteret and Slingsby, to the westwards the *Adventure* and the *Fifth [Third ?] Whelp*; (as he takes it) commanded by Captains Price and Lindsey, the *Fourth Whelp*, whereof Sir Elias Hickes is captain was lately at Portsmouth, staying to transport somebody." *CSP-D, Domestic, Charles I, #13, p. 87.*

13 August 1636. "William Brissenden to Nicholas. Yesterday Sir Elias Hickes with all his company landed at Portsmouth, and certified that on the 4th instant the Fourth Whelp was cast away at Jersey, at noontide, a fair day, and before the wind. The pilot ran her against a small sunken rock, where she lies utterly wrecked, but not one man lost. The pilot is committed by the mayor of Portsmouth to the common gaol, and Sir Elias is this day bound for London. The writer is out of hope of the Third Whelp proceeding, since Mr. Surveyor has written down that no provisions of stores shall be laid on board her, or the Constant Reformation. Mr. Alcock likewise has desired Mr. Holt to forbear. The writer has exposed himself to a great deal of charge, which if she proceeds not, he is like to lose. The Black George is not yet gone her voyage, nor Sir John Harvey come from London. She proved very leaky of late, but is now much tighter than she was. Many of her passengers desire her speedy proceeding. The Dutch ship, the Black Bull, and the Dunkirk frigate,

yet continue there. It is reported that the Turks do much spoil on the coast, many barks being met with at sea with no people in them." *CSP-D, Domestic, Charles I, #37, p. 94.*

17 August 1636. "Sir Elias Hickes, captain of the *Fourth Whelp*; who transported Lord Danby, has landed at Portsmouth with 60 men that were saved out of his ship, which coming to Jersey, split herself upon a rock by the shore, in sight of all the people there standing." *CSP-D, Charles I, #44, p. 97.*

25 August 1636. Within the *Papers Relating to Appointment in the Navy*; "Kenrick Edisbury to Nicholas. Recommends John Browne, appointed to the *Fourth Whelp*, which had been cast away through boatswain Jackson's neglect. Will write to the lords for a remove on Hollyman's death." *CSP-D, Charles I, p. 326.*

15 April 1637. Within the *Papers Relating to Appointment in the Navy*; "officers of the ordnance to Nicholas, recommended Thomas Yates, late gunner of the *Fourth Whelp*, to succeed William Bishop, likely to be dismissed from the *St. George*. Yates is an able man, and lost the greatest part of his estate by the casting away of the *Fourth Whelp*." *CSP-D, Charles I, 1637. p. 265.*

Based on that information, the *Fourth Whelp* wrecked along any number of the jagged rock outcrops along 8 miles of the north Jersey coast. There are no known records of salvage attempts or recovery of goods floating to shore. The southeast side of the island toward France contains the greatest density of rocky outcrops and could be the primary search location of the possible wreck site.

I was unable to locate more information in archives. The *Fourth Whelp* appears in the 1633 inventory of the royal navy at 186 tons with a 62' keel and a crew of 70 and 14 guns. That ordnance, if the ship is found, would be key in helping to identify the wreck. There may well be likely other valuables contained in the remains of the ship based on the account of Mr. Yates that had not been recovered.

1637

The *Rose* of Amsterdam.

July 1637. "Petition of Cornelius Gisbets Vango and John le Gouch and company of Amsterdam, merchants, to the lords of the admiralty. In February 1633–34 the Rose, of Amsterdam, Outgar Martissen master, was cast away in Sussex, near Newhaven, yet eight of the mariners escaped to shore, whereby the ship and goods did not become wreck. Several commissions of inquiry were issued out of the court of admiralty, but Jonas Legg, of

Colchester, agent for the owners, not being able to produce the marks of the goods which were defaced, Richard Wyan, proctor of the admiralty, had, without the knowledge of Legg, sent a commission down to prize and sell the goods, to the prejudice of petitioners, the true owners. Pray an order to have their goods restored to them." *CSP-D, Charles I, 1637. #109, p. 344.*

26 September 1637. "Allegation exhibited in the same court of admiralty of the Cinque Ports on behalf of Emanuel Dias Henrickes and James Terrey, owners of the Rose of Amsterdam, respecting certain goods taken on board the said ship at Gallipoli to be conveyed to Amsterdam, and were brought to Dover or someplace there adjoining. The goods are particularly enumerated in three schedules to these articles annexed." *CSP-D, Charles I, 1637. #58, p. 443-444.*

The original letter of 20 pages would have included a detailed inventory of the cargo, but these records no longer exist due to space restrictions in archives.

15 October 1637. "Order of the king in council. Secretary Coke having acquainted the board with a letter of the agent of Holland, wherein he complains that the Rose of Amsterdam, was about Portland, met with by five ships of war of Dunkirk, and having most of her men slain, and the ship almost sunk, the residue of the men saved themselves in the skiff, and the ship came to land about Seaford, where she was pillaged by the inhabitants, and diverse of the goods coming to land were adjudged as wreck by the lord warden, and forth with sold, only 15 days being given to the proprietors, resident in Amsterdam, to reclaim their goods. It was ordered that the proprietors may appeal for the recovery of their goods if they be found not to be wreck, and that in the meantime the proceeds of the goods shall remain deposited in the admiral court of the Cinque Ports." *CSP-D, Charles I, 1637. #81, p. 476.*

The name *Rose* and some variants are common throughout this era, but this ship was easier to distinguish from others, and I believe I reviewed all available archives for this ship. There are no records of cargo or mention of cargo washed on the shore, salvage or attempts to salvage and if there had been, I am sure some mention would have been recorded.

Based on the accounts, she was travelling from about the Isle of Portland to encounter the war ships and she managed to travel as far as about Newhaven to wreck on the shore. It would be safe to assume that local inhabitants would have scavenged whatever was available.

The *Fifth Whelp.*

4 July 1637. "Captain Edward Popham to Algernon earl of Northumberland. According to your order directed to the captains of the Pleiades, riding at the industry, and myself, we wafted to the Brill three vessels with goods and servants of the prince elector, and on the 26th June we stood off again to sea. On the 27th there ensued a storm from the N.W., which continued all night. The next day my ship (the Fifth Whelp) took in much water and sprung a leak. I plied the pumps [as minutely described], but she sunk in the afternoon of the 28th June, 16 leagues from the coast of Holland. Seventeen men sunk with the ship; myself and forty men got into a small boat and rowed from four o'clock in the evening until eight the next morning, when we made an English ship riding before the Brill and bound for Rotterdam, where "he" landed me and the rest of my men that were saved. At Rotterdam I had news of some of his majesty's ships at Hellevoetsluis, where I found the St. George, the Vanguard, and the William, and aboard of these ships I have placed my men. As soon as wind and weather give me leave, I will wait on you with a more full relation, and receive commands for disposing of my men." *CSP-D, Charles I, #29, p. 283-284.*

30 July 1637. "Lords of the admiralty to officers of the navy. You cannot but hear of the loss of the *Fifth Whelp*, which foundered on the coast of Holland by reason of a leak. We much marvel how it happens that vessel, which came so lately out of the dock, should prove so defective, and pray you to send word which of the shipwrights had charge of repairing her last before she went to sea, and what you conceive to be the cause of so great a leak." *CSP-D, Charles I, p. 339.*

3 August 1637. "Officers of navy to lords of the admiralty. According to your warrant, we required the master shipwrights to certify which of them repaired the Fifth Whelp before she went last to sea, who returned answer that Mr. Apslin had charge of her (whose skill and fidelity we esteem to equal any of the masters), but the pinnace at first being built by great for a particular service of mean sappy timber, we conceive in that great storm by her working in the sea that unhappy disaster happened, for we have had sufficient experience of the weakness of all the Whelps, which occasioned extraordinary charge to maintain them this long. For the lords' better satisfaction, we enclose the masters' certificate, who have likewise estimated the charge in repairing the Nicodemus frigate at £130 10s. 0d., the earl of Northumberland having for her weakness and leakiness sent her into Chatham, desiring that if she could have been repaired in a few days to

return her to the fleet, otherwise to discharge her men, who were paid off the beginning of last week." [1 p.] Enclosed. *CSP-D, Charles I, #17, p. 350-351*

Enclosed letter. "Edward Boate, Nathaniel Apslin, and Augustine Boate, master shipwrights, to officers of the navy. Certify as above stated respecting the last repairs of the Fifth Whelp and the cause of her disaster."

2nd August 1637. "Endorsed as being the request of Robert Whetnall, on behalf of Sir William Russell, for Mr. surveyor, Kenrick Edisbury to draw a letter to the lords in conformity with the certificate of the master ship-wrights." *CSP-D, Charles I, #17-1, p. 350-351*

The *Fifth Whelp* was in the 1633 inventory of the royal navy with the same statistics as the *Fourth Whelp* with a 62' keel at 186 tons and a crew of 7 men and 14 guns.

There are just enough clues to make this wreck interesting. It was described as sinking about 16 leagues, or about 55 miles from the coast of Holland and the small boat rowed about 16 hours, or about 45 miles, to find an English ship close to Brielle Holland. The tidal currents in the English Channel that flow eastwards and ebb westwards would have affected the small row boat and to arrive near Brielle, the row boat could have travelled south or southeast suggesting the ship sank northwest of The Hague at about 55 miles.

There is no mention of the cargo, so had there been valuables on board it would be safe to assume it would have been mentioned in the correspondence. The quantity of ordnance would help to determine the identity of a ship found in that area.

Seaford wreck.

For the most part, this wreck distinguished itself from the *Rose* of Amsterdam even though they occurred within the close frame of time. Though I was unable to locate the inventories, it certainly commanded a great deal of the court's resources.

16 July 1637. "Charles Earl of Nottingham to the lords of the admiralty. My deputy vice-admiral of Sussex, being at London, received the enclosed letter concerning a ship cast away near Seaford, one of the Cinque Ports. It appears diverse of the goods were taken out of the ship at sea by small boats by the inhabitants of Seaford, and there landed, whereby I cannot execute any commission in that town, because the lord warden claims them to belong to him. The ship and goods are of good value. I desire you to send me such as you think fitting, to the end the king may receive the benefit thereof. Annexed." *CSP-D, Charles I, 1637, #3, p. 314.*

"Thomas Paynter to William Marlott, at the King's Head, Southwark, or at Richard Gould's house in Fenchurch Street. Last night I received news by a Dover man of a ship cast on shore at Seaford, and this morning I went thither, where I find a ship, by all likelihoods of Hamburg of about 300 tons, which came out of the Straits, and has met with some enemy, which after they had pillaged her of all the rich goods, cut two great holes in the side of the ship to sink her, but being laden with oils it bore the ship, and these winds put her ashore. She first grounded far off at low water, and Seaford boats went aboard and brought ashore various bales of silks. The next high water brought her to the gravel, and various other goods were saved by those of Seaford. There was a dead man found aboard with his head shot off; and by his state it appears that the ship has driven long at sea. I think the lord treasurer's warrant may be got to take the goods for the customs, and to pay salvage. Shoreham, 13th July 1637." *CSP-D, Charles I, 1637, #3-1, p. 314-315.*

16 July 1637 (?). "Petition of Sackville Porter and Thomas Elphick, on behalf of themselves and other inhabitants of Seaford, Sussex, to Sir John Manwood, lieutenant of Dover Castle, and Dr. Thomas Rives, king's advocate and judge of the admiralty of the Cinque Ports. A ship laden with goods of great value, having been in a sea fight, and having never a man left alive, was lately driven upon the rocks at Seaford, and there beaten to pieces. Petitioners, with great peril of their lives, saved goods to the value of £2,000. Pray that according to former usage you will allow them half the goods in kind so saved." *CSP-D, Charles I, 1637, #7, p. 315*

22 July 1637. "Examinations taken this day at Seaford, and on the 29th instructions at Hastings, before John Wilson, Ralph Beard, and William Wilson, commissioners appointed by the lord warden of the Cinque Ports, touching the wreck and saving part of the cargo of a ship which July 22 had been cast ashore and had gone to pieces at Seaford.

The witnesses examined were:
John Hide, tailor,
Richard Seaman, blacksmith,
John Swane, tailor,
John Ollwark, carpenter,
John Tayler, droit-gatherer,
Adam Mersh, laborer,
Richard Dunton, the like,
John Dunton, the like,
John Wycarsham, the like,
Henry Payne, the like,

Peter Glover, the like,
William Hollyboue,
Stephen Bene,
John Wiilet, laborer,
Mark Awood,
Nicholas Semons,
Lall of Seaford.
John Tester, shoemaker,
Thomas Stockttevell, laborer,
Edward Gates, laborer,
William Hide,
Richard Bevis,
William Longly,
William Budd, laborer,
John Swane, laborer,
John Hide, tailor [above mentioned],
Edward Goff,
Michael Beck, laborer,
John Jarvis, blacksmith,
William Izack, smith,
Repent Hastinge, husbandman,
John Browne, the like,
Robert Goff, gentleman, of Bletchington.
Henry Bene, husbandman, the same.
John Pullen.
William Parry, of Newhaven, clerk, and Margaret his wife.
Thomas Pamer, of Alciston.
Edmond Payne.
Richard Gates.
William Bellingham.
Richard Landaye.
Humphrey Row, of Bletchington.
John Hersali:
Adam Barnden.
John Sergant,
Thomas Harris,
William Furner,
Edward Parson,
William Lovill."

28 July 1637. "Notes by Mark Thomas respecting various quantities of oil probably obtained from the ship wrecked at Seaford. It commences with notice of a quantity found at sea by H. Musse, baker, and concludes with a memorandum as to what Joseph Browne found, which he sold in France." *CSP-D, Charles I, 1637, #81, p. 335.*

1 August 1637. "Theophilus, earl of Suffolk, constable of Dover Castle. Lord warden of the Cinque Ports, to the mayors of Hastings and Rye; the bailiff of Lydd; the bailiffs of Pevensey and Seaford; and also to John Barley, John Crump, and William Lovell, jurats of Hastings; Mark Thomas, John Nowdell, and Joseph Benbrigge, jurats of Rye; Thomas Stronghill the elder, William Godfrey, and John Couchman, jurats of Lydd; Abraham Kenchley, George Carleton, and Thomas Weller, jurats of Peveneey; Sackville Porter, Thomas Elphick the elder, and John Tayler, jurats of Seaford; and John Jacob, sergeant of the admiralty of the Cinque Ports. Recites that a wrecked ship, laden with oils and other goods, and furnished with ordnance, has lately been driven on ground near Seaford, within the jurisdiction of the admiralty of the Cinque Ports, and many of the said goods and other things had been driven on shore and been taken up. The persons addressed are to return an inventory and valuation of the same. Annexed. Inventory and appraisement taken at Seaford, 3rd August 1637. Total, £1,968." *CSP-D, Charles I, 1637, #9, p. 348-349.*

17 August 1637. "Information of William Stratford, one of the attorneys of the court of admiralty of the Cinque Ports, exhibited in the said court on behalf of the earl of Suffolk, lord warden and admiral of the Cinque Ports. States that on the 12th of July last a wrecked ship was driven on ground near Seaford, and that certain enumerated quantities of oil and yards of silk and grogram, and certain pieces of ordnance, anchors and cables, had been saved thereout at Seaford, Pevensey, and Hastings, all within the jurisdiction of the Cinque Ports, all which articles belonged to the lord warden." *CSP-D, Charles I, 1637, #93, p.376*

There are several additional records that for the most part only duplicate those above. This incident certainly commanded a great quantity of correspondence. Without the inventory of 3 August 1637, it would be safe to speculate that only the basic ship remained with masts, yards, possibly furniture, cables and some ordnance. The sea would have eventually claimed the ship in time regardless of the two holes cut into the hull to sink her.

Ness Wreck.

26 November 1637. "Sir John Pennington to secretary Windebank. I will carefully perform the order to send a ship for the Duchess of Chevreuse, and with as much secrecy as if I knew nothing of it. I shall get the Bonaventure ready with as much expedition as I can, Captain Henry Stradling being her captain. He is a stout able gentleman, but speaks little French. I doubt not he will perform the service both carefully and honorably. I received a verbal command by this bearer that lord Holland desired to have Sir Henry Mainwaring sent on this employment in the Unicorn, which I shall be glad of, if you give order for his revictualling and have patience till it can be got aboard. I desire your sudden resolution herein, and shall go on making ready the Bonaventure in the meantime. The French king has made stay of all our English shipping now there, for something that young Wheatstone has done against them in the Straits. A very great ship was cast away upon Thursday night last on the Ness, supposed to be a Hollander. All the people were drowned." *CSP-D, Charles I, 1637, #56, p. 568.*

27 November 1637. "Sir John Pennington to the lords of the admiralty. The 22nd I sent in the Expedition, and I purpose to send away the Unicorn, the 1st of next month, if I have no order to the contrary in the meantime. The 25th I was commanded, under the seal of the court of admiralty, to release the Talbot of London, which I performed. We had very ill weather last week, wherein a great ship was cast away upon the Ness. I cannot learn what she was, but it is supposed that she was a Hollander. Report of the stay of English ships in France, with the addition to what was previously stated (No. 56) that what young Wheatstone had done was in revenge of his father's death and loss. Those that come out of Spain report that the king of that country is raising a great army to send into Portugal to appease the late broils." *CSP-D, Charles I, 1637, #59, p. 569.*

Without additional information, I assume the location referred to is Orford Ness, a peninsula of and below the River Alde which seems more probable than Ness, a village on the Wirral Peninsula, in the part that remains in the ceremonial county of Cheshire, England near to the town of Neston.

Orford Ness is about 50 miles North East of the Thames. The letters do not mention the castle which is about 12 miles northeast of Ipswich built about 1170 by Henry II of England. That would have been a noteworthy landmark.

A great ship could be 100 tons or larger and sank with full compliments of ordnance, cargo and any possible valuables it may have been transporting.

It is difficult to speculate where the ship was from or where it was headed, but November in the Irish Sea is often plagued with storms.

1638

Thames River wreck.

29 January 1638. "Venetian ambassador in England reported that M. di Vosbergh, (Gaspar von Vosberghen, Dutch ambassador in France) who recently left Paris, embarked on a Zeeland frigate, to hasten back to his masters. He encountered a furious tempest, was nearly lost on the coast of Flanders, and was followed so closely by Dunkirkers that if the furious wind had not driven him to this kingdom he would have fallen into their hands. He went to kiss his majesty's hands the day before yesterday, and in a long interview communicated his negotiations in France urging the king strongly to support the Swedes. He leaves to-day for Holland." CSP&M, Venice &Northern Italy, 1636-1639, V.24, #388, p. 362

A Venetian secretary in England reported on 5 February 1638, "M. di Vosbergh being advised that fourteen Dunkirk ships are at sea to take him, proposed to stay here until a force of Dutch ships arrives to escort him to Holland; but being persuaded by M. de Bellievre on the ground that the decisions about war which he carries may suffer from delay, to consign to him his dispatches in cipher so that he might get a ship from the king to send them with all speed to the Hague, he decided to embark unexpectedly upon his own very swift frigate, escorted by only two Dutch warships, in the hope of crossing the sea in a single night, with a good wind. Monsieur dell' Estrade embarked with him, sent by the most Christian to the prince of Orange to communicate his military plans, as he does every year, as a mark of confidence." *CSP&M, Venice &Northern Italy, 1636-1639, V.24, #389, p.364-365.*

12 February 1638, "One of the war ships escorting M. di Vosbergh perished when entering the sea from this river, but the men escaped, with all else therein." CSP&M, Venice &Northern Italy, 1636-1639, V.24, #397, p. 371.

That is the extent of available information. A Dutch ship of war, perhaps 500 to 800 tons sank in the mouth of the Thames. There are no records of salved goods. There is a chance that this ship contained money that could have accompanied M. di Vosbergh and the ordnance of the ship. The men referred to were either picked up by another ship or managed to swim to shore.

Bantry, Ireland, wreck.

1 February 1638. "Dublin. Robert Smith to Secretary Nicholas. A Dutch and an English ship have lately been lost at the Bantry, the latter with all hands. When I went down I found that Daniel O'Sullivan Beare, the lord of the manor, claimed the goods saved from the wreck. He is a person of great power in those parts. He waived his rights when letters came from Dublin, but his servants brought in nothing except what I discovered and forced from them. They have rifled a great deal. The bishop of Derry has let the ferriage at Coleraine, and probably at Londonderry. I chiefly hoped for those places, the ferriage of Dublin being already given to the lord deputy. There have been many shipwrecks near Dublin, and Hatton, one of the admiralty officials, has been imprisoned for malversation. The corporation of Youghal are opposing my jurisdiction, pretending a grant from King Edward IV. I should like leave to come to England for six months. I hope the new patents will not grant admiralty jurisdiction to lords of manors." *CSP-I, 1633-1647, p. 179.*

Based upon the only letter regarding the Dutch and English ship, the only possible link is on 1 May 1638; "Robert Smith to Nicholas. May Day. I thank you for securing my continuance in the Irish admiralty's service. I am trying to recover the embezzled goods of the wrecked *Bonadventure*; at the Bantry. Upon my return thence I came by Kinsale, where I saw the *Swallow* upon the careen, her keel above a foot above the water, and a false keel put upon her to prevent her rolling." *CSP-I, 1633-1647, p. 188.*

The *Bonadventure* is mentioned in a 1633 inventory of the king's ships at 552 tons with a crew of 200 and 32 pieces of ordnance, but the *Bonadventure* is also mentioned in a 1 March 1652 inventory of vessels belonging to the state's navy as a third rate, 479 tons and a crew of 180 with 40 guns. The "wrecked" *Bonadventure* in the 1 May 1638 letter is the only mention of the *Bonadventure* as wrecked. I am not able to determine if the *Bonadventure* is one of the two ships wrecked at Bantry, or is an unnamed English ship. The first letter of 1 February 1638 does not mention a name, but that is not conclusive evidence that it was not the *Bonadventure*. No further information was located in archives about a wreck at Bantry.

Bantry is a town in the civil parish of Kilmocomoge in the barony of Bantry on the southwest coast of County Cork, Ireland. It lies in West Cork at the head of Bantry Bay, a deep-water gulf extending for 30 km to the west. These ships could lie off this coast and it would appear some, if not all the cargo was claimed. There is no additional information available.

1639

Carmarthen Wreck.

A memorandum was written on 3 February 1639 regarding issues of shipping which included a "bark wrecked at Llanethy, co., Carmarthen last year loaded with brown bastard wines and figs, alleged to be Dunkirkers foods and deemed to belong to the admiralty, but very little had been recovered and the wine and other goods wasted." *CSP-D, 1638-1639, p. 421.*

There was an attempt by the court to recover the goods, but no additional actions are recorded, and no additional information could be located in archives. No records were found of salvage or goods washed on shore. It is possible the bark sank in Baecartyrddin, in the mouth of the River Towy to Carmarthen. It is more probable she sank within a couple miles of the river opening with most of the cargo, furniture, cable, and tackle.

Battle of the Downs, 1639.

Old Naval Prints, Their Artists and Engravers. Commander Charles, N. Robinson, London.

This battle has also been called the Spanish Armada of 1639. I have encountered so much conflicting/contradictory information recorded at the time that I have come to understand the plethora of conflicting/contradictory versions in modern sources.

Of all the early sources of information reviewed for the Battle of the Downs, two accounts stand above the others.

First: *An Historical and Critical Account of the Life and Writings of Charles I, King of Great Britain. London, 1758.* The information contained in that edition are some of the same sources found in *The Calendars of State Papers* and that information has been verified in the many volumes of *Calendars* reviewed.

Second: *The Journal of Maarten Harpertszoon Tromp, Anno 1639*. Translated and Edited by C. R. Boxer, Cambridge, University Press, 1930. Providing an English translation of Tromp's log during the battle and well-rounded in-depth edition for the author's narratives, makes this a valuable reference.

English, Dutch and Spanish Fleets in the Downs, October 1639.

The Journal of Maarten Harpertszoon Tromp, Anno 1639, p. 182

This book is concerned with three battles of the Battle of the Downs: the battle in the Channel of 16 and 18 September 1639 and the Battle of the Downs on 21 October 1639.

14 October 1639. "Upon the rumor of the fight to be begun between the Hollander and the Spaniard, I returned to the Downs in company off another friend, where before our arrival, all was over. There saw we some relics of the ruined Spanish Fleet, viz., 7 ashore, whereof one burned, the rest bulged and utterly lost; the country people at work about some in breaking them up for the timber and iron work. One of the sunken ships is a great galleon (the Santa Teresa) with 2 galleys. About 14 more were yet riding at Anchor, but how they may get away is uncertain." *The Travels of Peter Mundy in Europe and Asia, 1608-1667. V4, London 1925. p. 41.*

Contained in the easily overlooked footnotes on page 148 of *An Historical and Critical Account of the Life and Writings of Charles I, King of Great Britain,* Mr. Harris shares his source information regarding the Battle of the Downs.

In 1639, says Mr. Burchet, the Spaniards fitted out a considerable fleet under the command of Antonio de Oquendo, supposed to be to dislodge the Dutch ships from before Dunkirk, and land the troops there for the relief of Flanders, and the rest of the Spanish provinces. The Dutch having two or three squadrons at sea, the Spanish fleet, coming up the Channel, was met near the straights of Dover by one of them, consisting of seventeen sail, under the command of Herbert Van Tromp; who, notwithstanding the enemies great superiority, ventured to attack them; but finding himself too weak, got to windward, sailing along towards Dunkirk, and continually firing guns as a signal to the Dutch vice-admiral, who lay off that place, to come to his assistance; who accordingly joined him the next morning between Dover and Calais, where engaging the Spaniards, a very sharp fight ensued between them, which lasted several hours, wherein the Dutch had greatly the advantage; and having taken one galleon, sunk another, and much shattered the rest, at length forced them upon the English coast near Dover. This done, Tromp, being in want of powder and ball, stood away for Calais, to borrow some of the governor of that place; who presently supplying him with what he demanded, he returned again to Dover; upon whose approach the Spaniards got within the South-foreland, and put themselves under the protection of the neighboring castles.

The two fleets continuing in this posture for many days observing each other, the ministers of both nations were not less employed in watching each other's motions at Whitehall, and encountering one another with memorials. The Spanish resident importuned the king, that he would keep the Hollanders in subjection two tides, that so in the interim, the others might have the opportunity of making away for Spain: but the king being in amity with them both, was resolved to stand neuter; and whereas the Spaniards had hired some English ships to transport their soldiers to Dunkirk, upon complaint made thereof by the Dutch ambassador. Strict orders were given that no ships or vessels belonging to his majesty's subjects should take any Spaniards on board, or pass below Gravesend, without license, however, after great plotting and counterplotting on both sides, the Spaniard at length somewhat outwitted his enemy, and found means, by a stratagem, in the night, to convey away through the Downs, round by the North-Sand-head and the back of the Goodwin, twelve large ships to Dunkirk, and in them four thousand men; in excuse of which gross neglect of the Dutch admirals, in leaving that avenue from the Downs unguarded, the Dutch accounts say they were assured by the English, that no ships of any considerable burden could venture by night to sail that way.

The two fleets had now continued in their station near three weeks, when king Charles sent the earl of Arundel to the admiral of Spain, to desire him to retreat upon the first fair wind; but by this time the Dutch feet was, by continual reinforcements from Zealand and Holland, & increased to a hundred sail, and seeming disposed to attack their enemies, Sir John Pennington, admiral of his majesty's fleet, who lay in the Downs with four and thirty men of war, acquainted the Dutch admiral, that he had received orders to act in defense of either of the two parties who should be first attacked. The Spaniards, however, growing too presumptuous on the protection they enjoyed, a day or two after fired some shot at Van Tromp's barge, when he was himself in her, and killed a man with a cannon-ball on board one of the Dutch ships, whose dead body was presently sent on board Sir John Pennington, as a proof that the Spaniards were the first aggressors, and had violated the neutrality of the king of England's harbor.

Soon after which the Dutch admiral came to a resolution of attacking the Spaniards; but before he put it in execution, he thought fit to write to admiral Pennington, telling him, that the Spaniards having, in the instances before mentioned, infringed the liberties of the king's harbor, and become the aggressors, he found himself obliged to retaliate force with force, and attack them; in which, pursuant to the declaration be had made to him, he not only hoped for, but depended on his assistance, which, however, if he should not be pleased to grant, he prayed the favor that he would at least give him leave to engage the enemy, otherwise he should have just cause of complaint to all the world of so manifest an injury. This letter being delivered to the English admiral, Van Tromp bore up to the Spaniards in six divisions, and charged them so furiously with his broadsides, and his fire ships, as forced them all to cut their cables; and being three and fifty in number, twenty-three ran ashore and stranded in the Downs, whereof three were burnt, two sunk, and two perished on the shore; one of which was a great galleon (the vice-admiral of Galicia), commanded by Antonio de Castro, and mounted with fifty-two brass guns: the remainder of the twenty-three stranded, and deserted by the Spaniards, were manned by the English, to save them from the Dutch.

The other thirty Spanish ships, with Don Antonio de Oquendo, the commander in chief, and Lopez, admiral of Portugal, got out to sea, and kept in good order, till a thick fog arising, the Dutch took advantage thereof, interposed between the admirals and their fleet, and fought them valiantly till the fog cleared up, when the admiral of Portugal began to flame, being fired by two Dutch ships fitted for that purpose, which de Oquendo perceiving, presently stood away for Dunkirk, with the admiral of that place, and some few ships more; for of these thirty, five were sunk in the fight, eleven taken and sent into Holland, three perished upon the coast of France, one near Dover, and only ten escaped. I have been the more particular in the account of this engagement, because of the relation it hath to our own affairs, and have reported it in all its circumstances the most material of which have been omitted, even in that said to be Sir John Pennington's own account of it, for that otherwise the English government would appear to have departed from the common rights of all nations, in suffering one friend to destroy another within its chambers, and not animadverting upon the Dutch for that proceeding, did it not appear that the Spaniards committed the first hostility, which was the plea the others made in their justification for though, by the law of nations, I am not to attack my enemy in the dominions of a friend common to that enemy and myself, yet no laws, natural, divine, or human, forbid me to repel force with force, and act in my defense, when or where so ever I am attacked. But, however it must be confessed the Dutch well knew their time; and had the like circumstances happened twelve or fourteen years after, when the usurper ruled, they would probably have waited for further hostilities from their enemy (one or two random shot only being liable to exception, and to be excused as accidental), before they had ventured upon such an action.

But whether the Spaniards had committed the first hostility or no, the Dutch admiral would certainly have attacked them, as appears from the following passages in a letter from count D'estrades to cardinal Richlieu, dated Aug. 26, 1639. The prince [of Orange] desired that I should write to you, that the orders you had sent to the sea ports of France to assist the fleet of the States, had determined him to fight the Spanish feet in the Downs, whether he had certain advice they would repair, and give orders to admiral Tromp not to engage so soon; but to detach a squadron, in order to harass such as he found separate from the main body of the fleet, and to follow them close until they should get into the Downs, and then to draw up his fleet in a line of battle in the entry to the Downs, there to wait till such time the admiral of Zealand, John Evressens, should join him; after which he should send a flag-officer to the admiral of England, to acquaint him, that he had orders from the States to fight their enemy wherever he should find them, and to desire him to withdraw the king of England's ships, as he had orders from the States not to engage with them, unless they should join themselves to the enemy; but in case they would not remain neuter, his orders were to fight both one and the other.

His orders we see were well executed, and an action performed in the opinion of D'estrades the most illustrious which could be thought of, that of defeating the fleet of Spain in an English port, though assisted by English ships It will be proper to compare this with what follows, contained in a letter from Algernon earl of Northumberland, to Robert earl of Leicester, dated Windsor, Oct. 10, 1639. His majesty's deigns are a little to be wondered at, that he should endanger the receiving an affront, and expose his ships to much hazard, rather than command both the Spanish and Holland fleets out of the Downs. He sayeth now, that at his return to London on Saturday next, he will appoint a time for them to depart out of his road, which is all the Hollanders desire.

They have at this instant above one hundred sail of men of war, besides fire-ships: this great force of theirs, makes them begin to talk more boldly than hitherto they have done; for their admiral hath lately sent Pennington word, that they have already had patience enough, and that they will no longer forbear; for his instructions are to destroy his enemies where so ever he can find them, without exceptions of any place; and it is hourly expected that they should assault the Downs. What will become of our six ships that are there, I know not; for their direction is to assist those that are assaulted. The other ships that were made ready on this occasion, have lain wind bound in the river these ten days, and cannot yet possibly get out, by reason of the easterly winds that have blown constantly near three weeks.

The Spaniards pretended that they want of powder was a principal cause of their long stay: whereupon the Holland admiral sent to offer them 500 barrels, paying for it the usual rates; but the Spaniards would not accept of it. In a letter written to the same, Nov. 28, 1639, Sidney's from London, he says, On Sunday last Arssens the Dutch ambassador had a private audience from the king. It was expected that he should have made an apology to have given his majesty satisfaction for the late violation offered by them in the Downs; but I do not hear that he mentioned that particular. And in a third letter, written by him to lord Leicester, from London, Dec. 19, 1639, he says, 'The express sent from hence to Spain with the news of the defeat of their fleet, returned to this court some days since; and upon Sunday last the dispatches brought by him from Sir Arthur Hopton, were communicated to the foreign committee'. Those letters say, that this messenger brought to Madrid the first news of that overthrow, which much troubled them; but the conde of Olivares told our ambassador, that if our king would I be sensible of the affront done unto him, in this action by those base people, the king of Spain would rest well satisfied, and not at all regard the loss of those ships; for the next year they intended to have five times as many in there seas as were in that fleet.

Arssens hath, since my last writing to your lordship, excused, with the best reasons he could bring, the carriage of their admiral in the Downs. Tis, I think, plain, from comparing these relations, that the behavior of the Dutch in this affair arose chiefly from the consideration of the weakness of Charles, the English court considered it as an insult: they expected an apology for it; and the Dutch ambassador made the best excuse he was able, which, probably, was but a very a poor one. A spirited prince would have had a satisfaction as public as the injury itself, and thereby have shown the world that he was worthy of the sovereignty of those seas which he claimed.

May it never again be the fate of the British nation to be thus treated; but may it always assert its rights, and avenge itself on those who shall presume to set its power at defiance! Wise and honest, counsels, public economy, vigorous measures, and a regard to the subjects liberty, will enable a British king to render himself respectable to his fellow sovereigns, and effectually hinder them from treating him with contempt, either by words or actions. Heaven grant such a prince may be the lot of this island at all times!" *An Historical and Critical Account of the Life and Writings of Charles I, King of Great Britain, p. 148-154.*

According to that account, there were twenty-three ships that ran ashore, two sunk and two perished on shore with one a 'great galleon' (the vice-admiral of Galicia) commanded by Antonio de Castro. These numbers seem to correspond with other early accounts, so, that is what I will present.

Surprisingly, the greatest frequency of entries regarding the Battle of the Downs is found in the *Calendar of State Papers and Manuscripts, Relating to English Affairs...Venice, ...Northern Italy, Volume 24, 1636-1639,* and not in the *Domestic* or *Colonial series of Calendars* or *Acts of the Privy Council.*

English, Dutch and Spanish Fleets in the Downs, October 1639.

The Journal of Maarten Harpertszoon Tromp, Anno 1639, p. 182

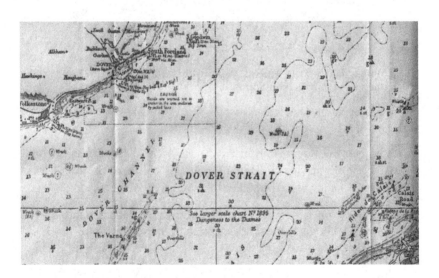

Chart of the Channel from Dover to Dunkerque

The Journal of Maarten Harpertszoon Tromp, Anno 1639, p 47.

NOTE: Admiralty chart #1406 used in the journal does not include wrecks from 1639. Admiralty charts were produced by the United Kingdom Hydrographic Office which did not begin publishing until after 1800.

Tromp's flagship the Amelia. Built at Rotterdam about 1637 and named after Amalia von Solms.

The Journal of Maarten Harpertszoon Tromp, Anno 1639, p. 94

In the *Journal of Maarten Harpertszoon Tromp, Anno 1639*, Mr. Boxer not only translated the original log of Maarten Tromp but enhanced the information learned from that log with the following account:

> The looker-on, it is said, see most of the game. In a belief that this is so, we cannot give a better description of the action of October 21 than that of Peter White.

> In the morning at 4 of the clock the wind at N.N.W. Foggy weather, we did hear a piece of ordnance to the N.N. eastwards of us, the which we took to be a warning piece from the Holland's admiral, for all his fleet to prepare themselves for the fight, which proved according to our expectation, for at daylight most of the Hollanders had their topsails out, and their sheets hauled home, whereupon our admiral called a council, and we with all our fleet made preparation, and tore down all our boarded cabins between decks, and heaved them overboard. At the council we all agreed to turn up to the

northwards, to get the wind of them, the Holland's admiral and all his fleet standing in under the flood to get the wind of the Spaniards, but the wind was so little that they could hardly stem the flood. We set sail and stood off to the northwards with all our fleet, being but 9 in number. The *Unicorn* admiral, the *Henrietta Maria* vice-admiral, these two of the second rank, the *Bonadventure*, the *Antelope*, the *Dreadnought* of the third rank, the *Providence* of the 4th rank, and the *Greyhound* pinnace of the 6th rank, and two merchant men.

The *Unicorn* captain Popham, and the *Exchange* captain Brown; we all set sail and stood off, and the Holland's vice admiral with 30 ships of war, and the 3 fire ships without us did the like, who it seems were ordered to attend upon us. By that time that we were under sail, Holland's admiral was very near the Spanish admiral, the weather being somewhat misty and thick; we heard a piece of ordnance, and some of our men said that it went from the Spaniards, presently after that we heard another, after which whole broad sides without number, and instantly after this, came a Holland's captain aboard to our admiral, with a very large letter written in Dutch, which captain did protest that they broke not the peace, for the Spaniards shot the first shot, Sir John answered that might very well be so, but it was because they came so near him with their fire ships, by which they broke not the peace, the ordnance went off wonderful fast, for the space of almost half an hour, in which time there came such thick fog that they could not see one ship from another, neither could we see any of them, whereupon the fight ceased, for they could not tell when they shot, whether it would hurt their foes of their friends, we being now by guess (for we could neither see ship nor land) and far enough to the northwards to weather them, we cast about and stood in towards the shore. And all the Hollanders that waited upon us did the like, and kept close to windward of us, the weather not being so thick where we were, as it was nearer the shore where the great fleet was.

We stood in thus half an hour in all which time we heard not one piece of ordnance, which caused our admiral to doubt that they might all chopped an anchor, until it cleared up, and demanded of me what I thought of it; I answered that I doubted that they were all come to an anchor until they could see one another, and likewise I said to him, that if they were anchored, the tide of ebb being come we stood in, we should fall to leeward's of them, and bring ourselves in danger of both their shot, and be unable to help either party, upon which he demanded of me, what course I thought best fitting to be taken; to the which I answered, that if he pleased, it being very little wind, we might let drop our anchor for a very small time, and to have it ready to heave up again upon a sudden and not to take in ourselves, only to strike our topsails upon the caps and to haul up our foresails in the Brayles; and if so be the Hollanders that waited upon us did the like, if he thought fitting he might either send to them by message, or being to fight with them; this council being approved of by him, we brailed up our foresails, and the Hollanders did the like, then we stroke our topsails, they likewise stroke theirs, then we let drop our anchor, and all our fleet did the like, but the Hollanders did not let fall their anchors.

Our admiral sent presently to all our fleet to be very ready to weigh, for he did intend to weigh as soon as the Hollanders should be fallen a little to leeward's off us; within half an hour after we anchored, the Hollanders were fallen a little leeward's of us; we all weighed our anchor and stood in after them, upon the weather gage of them, and presently after when it cleared up, we did see Admiral Tromp and his fleet all in a huddle together, right thwart of Deal Castle, and all the Strand full of ships, at which ships the Hollanders let fly their ordnance as fast as they could. And we with our fleet, and also the Castle of Deal shot as fast at them, upon wish they bore room and made all the haste they could after the rest of the Spaniards, which were run away as far as the S. foreland, being in number 25 sail of the better sort of their ships, and there was upon the shore 25 sail of Spanish fleet.

One of them being the vice-admiral of Spain, Don Andrews de Castro commander, who run aground and 6 or 7 more all in a huddle together between Warmer Castle and the village of Kingsdown, and a fire ship amongst them, which burnt two of them and had fired the bow-sprit and foremast of another, but they quenched it; also there was a 2 Hollanders ashore between Deal and Sandown Castle, the two castles shot at them, but they shot again, (to begin where I left) the Hollanders bore away to the southwards, shooting at them ashore as they passed by, and some of them ashore shot at them, and we following them our fleet plied our ordnance upon them, as fast as we could charge and discharge, but they never shot one shot at any of us, so we chased them out of the road, but the more we chased, the farther they were from us, and our admiral perceiving some more Hollanders coming from northwards through the Guls, fearing that they might if we did run out of the road, haul in and take their ships from the shore, for the better securing of them anchored against Kingsdown.

The wind heartened on and was with the Hollanders long before it came to the Spaniards, which caused them to fetch up the Spaniards before they were as far as Dover, (note this, that the Hollanders displayed no colors till he was past the foreland) and the Hollanders having the advantage of them, but the means that their ships did sail better than the most of the Spaniards they battered them exceedingly, but the Spaniards neglected not to answer them. For the Spanish admiral Don Anthony de Oquendo, his ship going better than the rest of his felt, kept close to the Portugal admiral Don Lopus de Ossa, which were two hot ships, and behaved themselves so bravely, that as I was informed from sufficient (reliable) men of Dover, not one of the Hollanders did come up along their broadside, until one desperate spoke in one of the Holland's pinnaces clapped the Portugal admiral aboard, upon the weather bow, amongst his anchors, which entangles him and hindered his way, and presently five of their fire ships boarded him on both sides, and fired all on a sodaine and burnt all 7 together.

Don Anthony de Oquendo upon this fearing the like, made all sail that he could to the westwards, diverse of the rest of the Spaniards they took. But of that here after. *The Journal of Maarten Harpertszoon Tromp.* Page 60-63, "Order of Battle of the Spanish Armada, 27 August 1639"

Several sources were used in the composition of the following list, but the primary source is *The Journal of Maarten Harpertszoon Tromp, Anno 1639, p. 223-226.*

	Ship Name	Squadron	Guns	Comments
1	Santiago	Castile	60	Royal flagship escaped into Dunkirk. 1639
2	San Antonio	Masibradi		Driven ashore. 1639
3	San Agustin	Martin Ladron de Guevara		Driven ashore. 1639
4	Sant Tereza	Portugal	60	Destroyed in action. 1639
5	San Jeronimo			
6	San Agustin	Naples		Driven ashore. Sank 3-4 days later. 1639.

7	El Gran Alejandro	Martin Ladron de Guevara		Taken by the Dutch. 1639
8	Santa Ana	Portugal		
9	San Sebastian			
10	Santa Catalina	Guipuzcoa		Driven ashore. 1639
11	San Lazaro			
12	San Blas	Masibradi		Driven ashore. 1639
13	San Jeronimo	Masibradi		Burnt in the Downs. 1639.
14	San Nicolas			
15	Santiago	Castile		Burnt off Dover, on night of 23. 1639.
16	San Juan Bautista	Guipuzcoa		Sunk. 1639
17	Esquevel	A hired Dane	16	Taken by Dutch, 18. 1639.
18	San Jose	Dunkirk		
19	Los Angeles	Castile		Driven ashore. 1639
20	Santiago	Portugal		Driven ashore. 1639.
21	Delfin Dorado	Naples		Driven ashore. 1639.
22	SanAntonio	Naples		Driven ashore. 1639.
23	San Juan Evangelista	Dunkirk		
24	El Pingue	Hired ship		Sunk in the Downs, 21. 1639.
25	San Carlos	Masibradi		
26	San Nicolas	Masibradi		
27	San Miguel			
28	Orfeo	Naples	44	Lost on Goodwin Sands, 21. 1639.
29	San Vicente Ferrer	Dunkirk		
30	San Martin	Dunkirk		
31	Nuestra Senore de Monteagudo	Dunkirk		Escaped into Dunkirk, 22, 1639.

32	Santigo	Galicia	60	Captured by Dutch, 21. 1639.
33	?	Flagship of Masibradi		Taken by Dutch, 18. The retaken same day. Escaped to Dunkirk, 22. Wrecked 4 days later. 1639
34	Santo Tombs	Martin Ladron de Guevara		Driven Ashore, 21. 1639
35	Nuestra Senora de Luz			
36	Santa Clara			
37	San Gedeon	Dunkirk		
38	San Jacinto			
39	San Carlos	Dunkirk		Sunk, 21. 1639
40	Santo Cristo de Burgos	San Josef		Lost off French coast, 21. 1639.
41	San Pablo	Masibradi		
42	San Miguel			
43	La Corona	Hired ship		
44	La Presa or San Pablo la Presa	Castile		
45	San Esteban	Martin Ladron de Guevara		Taken by Dutch, 21. 1639.
46	San Pedro de la Fortuna	A hired ship.		Driven on shore but got off, 21. 1639
47	Los Angeles	Hired ship		
48	Aguila Imperial			
49	La Mujer			
50	Santo Domingo de Polonia	A hired Polish ship		Driven ashore, 21. 1639.
51	San Jose	Flagship of Vizcaya		Taken by Dutch, 21. 1639
52	San Salvador	Flagship of Dunkirk		Escaped into Dunkirk, 22, 1639

53	Sao Balthazar	Vice-admiral of Portugul		800 tons. Back at Lisbon in 1640
54	San Francisco	Rear-admiral of Dunkirk	50	Escaped into Dunkirk, 22. 1639
55	San Pedro el Grande	Flagship of Ladron de Guevara		
56	Santiago	Martin Ladron de Guevara		
57	Jesus Maria (pinnace)			
58	San Pedro Martir (Urca)	A hired ship		Driven ashore, 21. 1639
59	Fama (Urca)	A hired ship		Driven ashore, 21. 1639
60	Santa Cruz	Masibradi		
61	San Daniel	Guipuzcoa		Driven ashore, 21. 1639
62	San Juan Evangelista	A hired ship of Hamburg		Driven ashore, 21. 1639
63	Santa Agnes (frigate)	Naples		Stranded but got off, 24. 1639
64	Grune (?)	Castile		Driven ashore, 21. 1639
65	Santa Tereza (Saetia)	Castile		Taken by a French privateer. 1639
66	Exchange	Hired English transport		Put into Plymouth, 3-13, 1639, reached Downs, 12-22 1639 where they were detained.
67	Peregrine	Hired English transport		Put into Plymouth, 3-13, 1639, reached Downs, 12-22 1639 where they were detained.
68	Assurance	Hired English transport		Put into Plymouth, 3-13, 1639, reached Downs, 12-22 1639 where they were detained.

Mr. Boxer included his research on the preparation of the armada and at the conclusion of his description of the ships in the Spanish armada; he indicated; "According to the books of the fleet paymaster, 25,000 rations were distributed daily. It carried 97 infantry and 53 naval captains, three generals, six colonels, six vice admirals, four councilors of war, munitions in abundance, and money for the payment of troops till the following summer to the tune of 800,000," or about $11,520,000 in present monetary values.

These funds were carried only within a few of the Spanish ships of this armada. How much of those funds are still on those wrecks will only be known when the sites are explored and I look forward to a revised edition in the event of a new discovery.

Downs Wreck

This incident is not related to the battle of the Downs.

30 April 1639. "Two Scotch ships came into the west country last week of 12 and 14 pieces of ordnance, one with wines from Bordeaux, the other from the Straits; they are both seized, and one Scotch ship with near 200 pipes of Canary wine was cast away in the Downs last week, and all this good wine lost, but all the men saved. The covenanters complain they will want wine this year, but they have enough of Scotch ale, which is much too good for them, unless they were better." *CSP-D, Charles I, 1639, #99, p. 99.*

No other information could be located regarding this wreck. The Downs claimed another ship.

Berwick wreck

28 May 1639. "The king declares that if the Scots in hostile manner come within 10 miles of the English border, it shall be interpreted as an invasion. This day it is most certainly reported that Lesley has sent a most insolent message to my lord of Holland, by a gentleman who came with six horse [men]; their errand was that if the king would withdraw his army and send home his navy, then they would parley. If not, let him come on and do his worst. To make this good, I heard one Captain Burley, who is come into this harbor with one of the king's pinnaces, protest that he came from before Edinburgh yesterday; that in the way he chased a Scotch ship and ran her ashore about 12 miles hence; that in the rescue there instantly came forth about 1,000 men well armed and 100 horse; that he saw about 10 colors flying, which all were in readiness in less than a quarter of an hour, and that in a

rage they came within pistol shot of his ship; so that had he leave he could have slain 500 of them with a broadside. He landed or made show to land in several places to try them, and in all found the like readiness and forces, and thinks that between this and Edinburgh there cannot be so few as 30,000 or 40,000 well-armed men. This the captain spoke aloud in the presence [of the king] this afternoon, vowing to make it good with his life. I fear my letters are as full of faults, nonsense, and impertinences, not having leisure to read what I write, as these country oats are of dust and straws. I pray sift it for me, and let the haste and good meaning excuse the rudeness and ill writing." *CSP-D, Charles I, 1639, #78, p. 251.*

The letter was written at Berwick by Edward Norgate.

Considering the length of the letter and the possible links that could have been associated with them, there was no other information located in archives regarding this Scottish ship that was ran aground off Berwick. This appears to be a war ship and was perhaps loaded with ordnance and other implements of war and there may be pay on board for the soldiers.

1640

The *Henry and John.*

31 January 1640. "The council to Sir Francis Popham. We send you enclosed the copy of a petition presented to the lord high admiral by Gerlach Moma and James Staneire, who in 1636 freighted the Henry and John, of Weymouth, with butter and tallow at Cork, in Ireland. In her passage to Dartmouth the ship was cast away, but the crew saved, and great part of the butter and tallow taken up at sea, and detained from petitioners till they obtained a commission of inquiry and restitution, the execution of which they entrusted to Mark Hawkins. From the petition it appears that you now question Hawkins in the court of common pleas for delivering the said goods to petitioners, pretending admiralty jurisdiction at or near the place. You are to return to this board your particular answer to the same by the last of February that the lords may take such further order as shall be fit." *CSP-D, Charles I, 1639-1640, #42, p. 404-405.*

A foot note preceding a letter from Gieronimo Giustinian, Venetian ambassador at the Hague wrote from London; "on the night of the 6-7 January 1640, there was a particularly violent storm which even wrecked ships in port." *CSP&M, V &I, V25, 1640-1641, #13, p. 7-8.*

31 January 1640. "The council to the attorney employed by Sir Francis Popham. You are to make stay of all proceedings in the suit commenced by Sir Francis Popham in the court of common pleas against Mark Hawkins, for having gathered and received the salvage of the Henry and John, of Weymouth, until Sir Francis shall have returned answer to the letter of this board, and further directions be given by the board in that behalf." *CSP-D, Charles I, 1639-1640, #43, p. 405.*

A search of archives for relevant information during the year 1636 when the first letter indicated the ship was loaded with butter and tallow, yielded no results. It seems odd that this wreck was addressed almost 4 years after, even taking in consideration the time these matters take at the time. It appears that the butter and tallow were recovered, and the crew made it to shore safely, but based on the limited supply of information, it is very difficult to determine where the ship sank. The ship left Cork, Ireland to Dartmouth. That is a lot of coastline to explore.

1641

London Bridge wreck.

8 July 1641. "You will have heard of the disastrous misfortune of Mrs. Kirke, who, shooting the bridge, was drowned, the barge over tossing. The Queen has taken very heavily the news, and, they say, shed tears for her." *CSP-D, 1641-1643, #23, p. 47.*

8 July 1641. "The court is very sad by reason of a great mishap happened to a barge coming through London Bridge, wherein were diverse ladies, and amongst the rest Mrs. Kirke, drowned. The barge fell upon a piece of timber across the lock, and so was cast away. Lady Cornwallis, it is thought, will not live." *CSP-D, 1641-1643, #24, p. 48.*

15 July 1641. "I am sure you have heard by what a sad accident Mrs. Kirke, who was of the queen's bedchamber, was the last week drowned." *CSP-D, 1641-1643, #50, p. 53.*

Mrs. Kirke served Queen Henrietta Maria (wife of King Charles I of England) in her private bedchamber and would have known each other intimately through the queen's private life and their children, so it is understandable the sad news of her drowning would have been tragic.

This being a barge, it would have been a small, shallow draft ship that when it sank, should not have presented a hazard in the Thames River. Though the depth of the Thames varies with tidal flow, there are no records that the barge caused problems with shipping. Perhaps the tide had changed and a torrent of water around the footings pushed the barge into the beams. The barge may have contained personal belongings of the ladies.

1644

West Wales wreck.

Thought the first letter does not mention the supply ship had wrecked, it is helpful to set the stage of what occurred near Red Castle and Montgomery Castle over looking the town of Montgomery in Powys, mid Wales.

8 December 1644. "Sir Thomas Middleton to the committee of both kingdoms. I assume the boldness to acquaint you with my present state and the condition of these remote parts. Having received intelligence from my foot forces commanded by Colonel Beale and Lieutenant Colonel Carter, which landed in Pembrokeshire four months since from London, that they were on their march by land towards me through Cardigan and other cos. (counties?) in the possession of the enemy, I drew out the remainder of my horse and dragoons, about 200, and with those few forces after a long and tedious march of four days met with my foot at Lampeter-Pont-Stephen, under the personal command of Sergeant-Major-General Langhorne. The enemy, having got intelligence that they numbered only 140 foot, besides my horse and dragoons, and of the way they intended to return, did set upon them at a bridge near Machynlleth. The enemy numbered about 1,000 men under Rowland Pugh, Esq., a commissioner of Array, and Major Hookes. In the skirmish which took place on the 27th November we killed 20, took 60 prisoners, most of them forced men, and the rest fled, the town, bridge, and Mr. Pugh's house falling into our hands; in all which march and flight we lost not a man. Within the week after, upon intelligence that about 200 of the enemy were garrisoning a very strong house, anciently an abbey, called Abbey-cwm-hîr, in South Wales, distant not above 11 miles from Montgomery Castle, wherein there is a garrison for the parliament, we marched thither on Wednesday night last, and on Thursday morning about 8 o'clock we stormed it and entered the house. We took as prisoners Colonel Barnard, the governor, two foot captains, one horse captain, several officers, and 80 soldiers, with their arms, besides about 40 horse, 3 barrels of gunpowder, 60 firelocks, and a little ammunition."

"In the house we also took Hugh Lloyd, Esq., the prime commissioner of the array, and late high sheriff of that county. He was the most active and bitterest man of all others in those parts against the parliament. We were forced to burn the house; otherwise we could not render it unserviceable for the future, so we returned without the loss of one man, either in the storming or taking of the house. I have likewise made an entrance into Flintshire, and placed a small garrison in Mr. Dymock's house, which I hope to maintain against the enemy's forces, who since my coming thither have burned Bangor, where formerly they had a garrison. They are now grown desperate, and care not what spoil they make. I purpose to oppose them with the weak strength which I have here, hoping that God will prosper our endeavors as he has hitherto done. I crave pardon for my tediousness." *CSP-D, Charles I, 1644-1645, p. 181-182.*

9 December 1644. "Sir Thomas Middleton to the committee of both kingdoms. It is now two months since I importuned your board for a supply of gunpowder, arms, and ammunition, but could never yet receive answer. I am now enforced to renew my request, because the ship which carried my arms out of Pembrokeshire is cast away with all my arms and 50 barrels of gunpowder, as it was going to Liverpool which has exceedingly disappointed me. I must truly inform you that our supply is so reduced by supplying the several garrisons and our daily employments, that if an enemy were now to fall upon us we should not able to hold out any considerable time in any of our garrisons for want of powder and match, wherefore I beseech you to consider our condition and to give speedy order for the safe sending to us of 50 or 100 barrels of gunpowder, with match and arms." *CSP-D, Charles I, 1644-1645, p. 182-183.*

Though the letter was written at Red Castle, slightly south of Liverpool, this is not enough information to narrow the 180 miles of coast this ship loaded with gunpowder and small arms is located. Relevant letters following the 9 December 1644 letter only address the need for powder and no additional information on the loss of the ship. No additional information was located in archives.

1645

Duncannon frigate wreck.

4 January 1645. Within the *Letters and Papers Relating to the Navy*. First mention of the Duncannon frigate with a crew of 50. *CSP-D, Charles I, 1644-1645, p. 629.*

20 November 1645. "That it be recommended to the committee of the admiralty to appoint a convoy for the provisions going to Youghal, and to represent to them the danger of that place." *CSP-D, Charles I, 1645-1647, #4, p. 231.*

10 September 1645. Within the *Letters and Papers Relating to the Navy.* "It is not unknown to you how this frigate was, upon 17 July last, blown up during her service before Youghal, then besieged by the rebels, in which misfortune 18 of her company lost lives, and 8 or 9 more dangerously hurt. Petitioners, being 25, were since employed in the service, and lately sent up to this port with two prizes, arriving on 4th of September. Petitioners pray you to give order that their pay may be continued to the time of their arrival with the prizes at this port, and forth-with to be paid accordingly." *CSP-D, Charles I, 1645-1647, p. 293.*

10 September 1645-II. "Certificate of the commissioners of the navy. That in regard of the loss of their clothes in the Duncannon frigate, their employment ever since, and the bringing up of the two prizes, the *Mighell* of Crostwick, and the *Blessing* of Amsterdam, petitioners ought to have 1 1/2 months pay, which we leave to your decision." *CSP-D, Charles I, 1645-1647, p. 293.*

31 January 1646. "Petition of captain Samuel Howett to Robert earl of Warwick. That he was commander of the Duncannon frigate when she was cast away in the river of Youghal in July last by a shot from the enemy falling into the powder room, since which time he has been unemployed. Prays that your lordship would further his application for a command as formerly in the fleet now preparing for the seas." *CSP-D, Charles I, 1645-1647, #29, p. 330.*

5 October 1647. Within the *Letters and Papers Relating to the Navy.* "The like to enter Henry Elliott, late gunner in the Duncannon frigate, which was blown up before Duncannon, to be gunner of the *Fellowship*, vice Richard Loane, transferred to the *Sternmost* frigate, building at Deptford." *CSP-D, Charles I, 1645-1647, p. 609.*

It appears this ship was involved in the siege of Duncannon during the Irish confederate wars and lays perhaps within the first mile of the River Blackwater and could be a historical wreck site for the country of Ireland. This frigate could be recognized or differentiated by the ordnance she carried. Even if the powder magazine did explode, her cannons would be close to the ship when she sank off Youghai Ireland. Being as though she suffered a violent end, there is a very good chance nothing was recovered.

This ship or any recovered artifacts could be an interesting addition or augmentation to the facts about the siege of Duncannon. If this ship is located, please honor the men that lost their lives on this ship for their country and treat it as a war memorial.

1647

The *Falcon*.

Contained within a collection of letters and papers relating to the navy and admiralty of 1647 are two entries.

29 April 1647. "The commissioners of the navy. The admiral and vice-admiral of the Irish seas have often intimated to this committee the necessity of having two small vessels there as ketches and for landing men in Ireland, also to ascend rivers where the great ships under their command cannot come near. The Katherine, True Love and the Falcon frigates, two prizes taken by the Irish squadron, and now at Bristol, being very fit vessels for that purpose, and the admiral and vice-admiral offering to man and victual them out of their great ships, so that their charge will be very small to the state, in respect of the extraordinary good service they will in all likelihood do, these are to pray you to give order for their fitting forth to sea." *CSP-D, Charles I, 1645-1647, p. 604.*

13 May 1647. "We are informed that the *Falcon* ketch, assigned to captain Crowther, vice-admiral of the Irish fleet, is cast away on the coast of Cornwall. These are to require you to take order, that any prize vessel which captain Crowther may nominate to you as fit to perform the service intended by the *Falcon* may be fitted with the necessary stores for this summer's expedition. Provided that she be manned and victualed out of the ship *Bonaventure*, under captain Crowther's command." *CSP-D, Charles I, 1645-1647, p. 604.*

The *Falcon* was included in a 1625-1629 East India ship inventory described as a frigate: a three-mast ship about 300-400 tons. There are no known records of salvaged goods, but that does not mean recovery did not occur from the *Falcon*. As it was described as a prize, it perhaps once belonged to the Dutch. No additional information was located in archives.

Unknown

Dover wreck.

This was placed in a general collection of unknown dates during the reign of Charles I.

"Petition of George Pounsett and John Eustace, his majesty's native subjects, to the Privy Council. Coming over from France they were wrecked at Dover and committed by the lieutenant of that castle to prison for not taking the oath of allegiance, and so do remain prisoners at the mercy of his majesty and this honorable board. Having been nurtured in the Roman Catholic faith they refused the oath, not out of any willful disobedience or disloyalty to his majesty, but only out of the tenderness of their conscience, as being ignorant how far the same may be contrary to their religion. Having suffered wreck of all they had, and being ready to give security for their loyalty and their forthcoming at any time when required, they pray you to pity their distress and give them liberty to endeavor their own relief and suppuration, being now like to perish." *CSP-D, Charles I, 1648-1649, #53, p. 389.*

There is enough information in this singular record to differentiate this incident from the others in this volume and place it as a separate incident. Unfortunately, neither date nor enough information to narrow the wreck location to within a few miles was located in archives.

Part 4. The Storms.

This part, though perhaps more of a novelty, shares records of storms around the United Kingdom. The gaps in time can be attributed to the lack of reporting and not the lack of storms, or those that were worth recording. Each event was extracted from longer letters.

3 September 1601. "...in the morning there came on the fiercest storm; that ever man saw and it lasted 3 or 4 days, with south and south-west wind..."

9 October 1601. "...I very nearly lost my masts in this storm; owing to the giving way of shrouds, and lost my long boat..."

14 October 1601. "...I then went towards Kinsale but when off Dungarvan was caught in a violent storm; and driven into Waterford..."

21 February 1602. "...a Scotch and French ship were driven in by storm; to Ilfracombe..."

27 September 1602. "...they are all cast away, for the storm; was such that Thursday night, as they had much ado to live themselves..."

11 February 1603. "...seen by an English ship to sink in a small storm; not far from our coast..."

18 November 1606. "...was the rage of a storm, which put him upon that coast, beyond all expectation of safety..."

30 November 1606. "...after 12 hours' fair sailing with a flattering wind and a succeeding storm; of 48 hours, arrived safely on the 29th of October..."

5 April 1608. "...when, through a most terrible storm; he had been tossed for six weeks together upon the coast of Spain..."

9 January 1610. "...King of Sweden, driven by storm; into the Thames..."

22 October 1612. "...terrible storm; in which fifty vessels were cast away near Yarmouth..."

7 February 1615. "...Captain Button no sooner laid forth his anchors than he was encountered with a long and mighty storm; in two days and a half-no way able to come on shore..."

24 January 1616. "...the recent storm; has Deal Castle, carried away the beach and part of the outer wall of Deal Castle..."

5 July 1617. "...Sir Walter Raleigh's fleet scattered by a storm..."

27 November 1620. "...driven to sea by a storm, ran on shore near Calais..."

28 January 1621. "...much injured by a storm on Jan. 28, 1621..."

18 September 1623. "...restoration of his anchor, lost during a storm in the Downs..."

3 October 1624. "...a terrible storm has done great damage to ships in the Downs; 20 sail out of 120 are missing..." This storm was mentioned for another month in records.

8 June 1625. "...describes great damage done by a recent thunder storm, the like of which had never been heard of in any age..."

20 June 1625. "...he purposed to have gone in himself, but a storm from the north-east forced him out to sea..."

17 October 1625. "...21 of the Holland ships lying before Dunkirk were almost destroyed by a storm; five driven into Dover dismasted..." There are many records of the damages this storm caused within a month.

3 November 1625. "...loss of the King's horses in the great storm from the sea ..." This storm has several records of mention.

12 January 1626. Ireland. "...we lost all our masts and sails there and were nearly wrecked and drowned in a great storm..."

19 January 1626. "...sending report of shipwrights as to the damage done to the *Adventure* in the storm..."

22 October 1626. "...and especially of the damage done to the *Triumph*, the Admiral's ship, in a storm on the 12th and 13th inst., which compelled him to return to England..."

10 November 1626. "...reported loss of several ships, and other damage done in a great storm..."

10 April 1627. Ireland. "...separated from her by storm off West Coast of Ireland, about the 16th of April..."

25 April 1627. "...his ships, the *St. Peter* and the *Blessing*, having been driven by storm, one into Ilfracombe, the   other into Dartmouth..."

14 May 1627. "...Stephen Hilariet, Master of the *Unicorn*, of St. Savenien, driven by storm into Plymouth..."

18 July 1627. "...unsuccessful chase of 13 Dunkirkers, and great storm, in which, for three hours, they expected nothing else but to be cast away..."

3 October 1627. "...crossed over to the Texel in a great storm. Entered the river on the 29th..."

18 October 1627. "...the Earl of Holland has been put back by an extreme storm, but will not lose an hour in setting sail..."

30 October 1627. "...but at night they were driven back by a storm, the violence of which he describes, and in which the ships were in great danger, and sustained some damage..."

14 November 1627. Ireland. "...they sailed for the English Channel, but was driven by a storm to Bungarvan..."

26 November 1627. "...sickness of the seamen. Great storm, in which the *St. George*, Sir Henry Mervyn, was saved, with the loss of her mainmast..." There are several separate records of the damage this storm caused to ships.

21 April 1628. "...the palisado, and ships sunk before the entrance to the harbor, had been broken by storm..."

2 July 1628. "...on board the French coast until Saturday night, when, by a violent storm..."

5 November 1628. "...on 28th a great storm, which did considerable damage to the fleet..."

9 January 1629. "...a Hamburgher bound for Calais with tar, tallow, and bides, but parted from her in the storm..."

28 October 1629. "...in the great storm on Tuesday night a new ship came on ground on the Long Sand..."

December 26 1629. "...in going from Yarmouth towards Lynn had suffered damage from storm; and been driven back to Yarmouth..."

January 1630. "...the said ship being much broken down by a great storm..."

9 February 1631. "...met Lord Denbigh on Wednesday last. He had a great escape in the storm on Friday before..."

12 September 1631. "...great storm last night, in which three small ships were forced to cut their masts by the board..."

23 October 1631. "...was forced in here yesterday by a storm..."

22 November 1631. "...furious storm, in which many ships in the Downs have received much damage. Nov. 22..."

14 April 1633. "...could not send his boat ashore with information by reason of the great storm..."

19 October 1633. "...came over in the Oct. 29. nick of time between a storm; and a contrary wind..."

6 June 1634. "...then 7 June followed a storm, when a ship bound for Bristol was lost..."

29 July 1634. "...No sooner had John Griffith set his foot on land there but there arose such a storm as though heaven and earth would have come together, which continued for about twelve hours. The like was never heard nor seen at that time of the year..."

8 April 1635. "...ships employed on the Irish coast in the late storm lost the long-boat of the *Bonaventure*..."

19 June 1635. "...the 19th January last, by reason of a storm at Stornaway in the Isle of Lewis, one of the ships of petitioners laden with herrings, as also one of their busses riding at anchor in the harbor there, were forced ashore..."

10 October 1635. "...being forced the day before into Plymouth by a storm; he understands that it is not yet passed by this place..."

18 November 1635. "...during the last storm; there was a ship of Hamburg cast away near the Isle of Wight..."

24 January 1636. "...it was chased in there by a Flushing man-of-war-, it being a storm..."

2 March 1637. "...in that hideous storm; when the *Rainbow* and the *Bonaventure* and many other ships were lost at Portsmouth..."

17 March 1637. "...agreed that petitioner should build up the spire of the said church (taken off by a sudden storm)..."

3 May 1637. "...the *Garland* that suffered much harm by an extraordinary storm; in January last..."

4 July 1637. "...on the 27th there ensued a storm from the N.W., which continued all night..."

3 August 1637. "...in that great storm; by her working in the sea that unhappy disaster happened..."

20 March 1637. "...the Sallee man-of-war was lost in a storm at Rochelle..."

28 March 1638. "...but for the greatness of a mighty storm of frost and snow, which lay long in this county..."

14 November 1638. "...Tassell [Texel ?] during the last great storm, amongst which there were two ships that had 2,000 chests of sugar..."

24 May 1639. "...swore he saw all our ships sunk in a storm; another came the next morning and swore he saw them all under water..."

16 June 1639. "...and by a great storm was driven into Birlington (Bridlington) bay..."

31 July 1639. "...the *Friendship* was, by reason of a storm on the 24th June last, run into by the ship *Long Robert*..."

5 December 1639. "...by reason of the foul weather, a shallop came to fetch us off, and the storm increased so fast, that our boat was continually half full of water..."

30 January 1640. "...on having escaped the storm and returned into the Downs..."

5 May 1640. "...Norway the ship was caught in a storm, but was relieved by one of the king's ships..."

17 July 1640. "...on Wednesday last, there being a great storm..."

22 July 1640. "...here was such a storm; yesterday that it was like to have sent all the Scotch ships we have here to sea again..."

30 September 1641. "...in that hideous and violent storm; this day se'nnight, of which I never yet heard the like..."

21 September 1641. "...moreover it appears it was in a storm, and in that storm, the flyboat had spent all her anchors and cables..."

7 February 1642. "...I hope, now the storm is ceased, that the wind will be fair..."

27 February 1644. "...or the danger of an eastern storm, they having now no place left them on our whole eastern shore..."

21 December 1646. "...many of our ships being scattered by a storm..."

11 January 1649. "...his vessel being much disabled in the then late storm..."

THE AUTHOR

Mr. Taylor is a well-decorated expeditionary veteran of the Unites States Navy who served honorably from 1977 to 1983. He was assigned to the U.S.S. Wichita AOR-1; homeport at Naval Air Station, Alameda California. In 1980, the ship was assigned to a WESTPAC (Western Pacific) cruise that included numerous ports while traversing the North Pacific, Sea of Japan, East China Sea, and the Philippine Sea where they encountered a persistent typhoon. The ship rocked so much that the following day the author had to wash his footprints off the bulkhead (wall) of a hallway outside the fireroom (boiler room). He had to use the seatbelt in his rack that night so he would not be thrown out.

This voyage continued through the Gulf of Thailand, the Bay of Bengal and last, but certainly not least, with a considerable amount of time in the Indian Ocean supporting the operation into Iran to rescue United States hostages which began with the loss of the U.S. Embassy in Tehran. Military and civilian lives were lost in the failed first attempt by US forces to rescue the hostages.

On the return trip to Naval Air Station Alameda, while transiting the Gulf of Thailand, the ship encountered a boat full of Vietnamese refugees being robbed by Thai pirates. The Wichita rescued the refugees and took them to Pattaya Beach Thailand and taken to a refugee camp. One of the refugees recently contacted those who served on the ship at that time to thank everyone for saving the lives of his family and he eventually through hard work and dedication became a high-ranking individual in the aerospace industry, though now retired.

During his time at sea, the author participated in what is called the Line Crossing Ceremony as a "pollywog," a ritual that marked a sailor's first crossing of the Equator. The ceremony is sometimes explained as being an initiation into the court of King Neptune. After completing a grueling and exhaustive two-day ceremony, the sore and stiff author was admitted to the honored ranks of King Neptune himself. The origins of the Line Crossing Ceremony, "Order of Neptune," are lost in time but historians believe the ritual dates back at least 400 years in Western seafaring. In the 19th century and earlier, the line-crossing ceremony was quite a brutal event, often involving beating pollywogs with boards and wet ropes and sometimes throwing the victims over the side of the ship, dragging the pollywog in its wake. In more than one instance, sailors were reported to have been killed while participating in a line-crossing ceremony. Certainly, many of the men on the ships in this volume underwent this ceremony.

This is a copy of the author's Shellback certificate from his first line crossing on 17 July 1980.

The navy has toned down the ceremony since the author's time in service. Imagine what barbaric forms such "hazing" early mariners endured centuries ago! At the time of this writing, we have a much 'kinder and gentler navy.'

"I have seen very rare, spectacular, and awe-inspiring sights in the deep blue ocean under the millions of stars that illuminate the sky. I fully understand the tales mariners have shared for centuries about their experiences at sea. Unless you have seen and experienced them, you could not fully and appreciate those extraordinary experiences. At least for me, they are truly humbling."

James D. Taylor Jr., AF, RHS-UCL

Bibliography

Abbreviations used in references throughout the book

APC-D. Acts of the Privy Council of England.

BN. Biographia Nautica, or Memoirs of Those Illustrious Seamen. Volume 4 was consulted.

CM-Constable's Miscellany, or Original and Selected Publications.

CSP-C. Calendar of State Papers Colonial.

CSP-C, EI, C&P. Calendar of State Papers Colonial, East Indies, China and Persia.

CSP-C, EI, C&J. Calendar of State Papers Colonial, East Indies, China and Japan.

CSPM, V&NI. Calendar of State Papers and Manuscripts, Venice and Northern Italy.

CSP-D. Calendar of State Papers, Domestic, James I.

CSP-D. Calendar of State Papers, Domestic, Charles I.

CSP-I. Calendar of State Papers, Ireland.

CHC. Catalogue of the Harleian Collection of Manuscripts.

HCEV-Hakluyt's Collection of the Early Voyages, Travels, and Discoveries.

LEIC. Letters Received by the East India Company.

MRP-Memoirs of the Rise and Progress of the Royal Navy.

NGCV- New General Collection of Voyages and Travels.

NHGB-The Naval History of Great Britain.

SFLB-Sea Fights and Land Battles from Alfred to Victoria.

Primary Sources

Acts of the Privy Council of England. V.32, 1601-1604, London. Various Printings.

Boxer, C. R. *The Journal of Maarten Harpertszoon Tromp, Anno 1639.* Cambridge, University Press, 1930.

Butter, Nataniel. *Famous and Wonderful Recovery of a Ship f Bristoll, called the Exchange, from the Turkish Pirates of Argier.* London, 1622.

Campbell, J. Dr. *Biographia Nautica, or Memoirs of Those illustrious Seamen, to Whose Intrepidity and Conduct the English are Indebted.* Five Volumes, Dublin, 1785. Volume four was used.

Calendar of State Papers Colonial Series, East Indies, China and Japan. London. 4 Volumes. Various Printings.

Calendar of State Papers Colonial Series, East Indies, China and Persia. London. Various Printings.

Calendar of State Papers Colonial Series, East Indies and Persia. London. Various Printings.

Calendar of State Papers, Domestic, of the Reign of James I. London. 4 volumes. Various Printings.

Calendar of State Papers, Domestic, of the Reign of Charles I. London. 23 Volumes. Various Printings.

Calendar of State Papers, Relating to Ireland. Charles I. London. 7 Volumes. Various Printings.

Calendar of State Papers and Manuscripts, Relating to English Affairs, Venice and Northern Italy. London. V.10-25.

Catalogue of the Harleian Collection of Manuscripts in the British Museum. London, 1808.

Constable's Miscellany, or Original and Selected Publications. Edinburgh, 1827.

Corbett, Julian S. *England in the Mediterranean.* London, 1904. Volume 1.

Derrick, Charles. *Memoirs of the Rise and Progress of the Royal Navy.* London, 1806.

Famous and Wonderful Recovery of a Ship f Bristoll, called the Exchange, from the Turkish Pirates of Argier. London, 1622.

Foster, William. *Letters Received by the East India Company, From its Servants in the East.* London, 1902. Two volumes reviewed.

Harris, William. *An Historical Account of the Life and Writings of Charles I King of Great Britain.* London, 1758.

History of Shipwrecks and Disasters at Sea, From the Most Authentic Sources. London, 1833. Two Volumes.

Markham, Clements. *The Voyages of Sir James Lancaster, Kt., to the East Indies.* New York. 1877.

Temple, Sir Richard Carnac. *The Travels of Peter Mundy in Europe and Asia, 1608-1667.* V4, London 1925.

Secondary Sources

Articles of Peace, Entercourse, and Commerce. London, 1630.

Bruce, John. *Annals of the Honorable East-India Company, from their establishment by the charter of Queen Elizabeth, 1600, to the union of the London and English East-India Companies, 1707-8.* Three volumes. London, 1810.

The Continuation of our Weekly News from the 4 of October to the 10 of the Same. London, 1627.

Clowes, William Laird. *The Royal Navy, A History from the Earliest Times to Present.* Five Volumes. London, 1898.

Colliber, Samuel. *Columma Rostrata, or a Critical History of the English Sea Affairs.* London, 1727.

*Constable's Miscellany, or Original and Selected Publications...*London, 1833.

Crane, Ralph. *A Brief Abstract, Exposition and Demonstration of all Terms, Parts and Things Belonging to a Ship; and the Practice of Navigation. 1626.* This handwritten manuscript is a valuable asset for ships of the period.

Daniel, Samuel. *The Collection of the History of England.* London, 1650.

East-India-Trade, a Most Profitable Trade to the Kingdom. London, 1680. Many of the valuable volumes were later destroyed by the company.

Foster, William. *A Guide to the India office Records, 1600-1858.* 6 Volumes. London, 1919.

Husband, Edward, Printed for. *An Act Declaring the Grounds and Causes of Making Prize the Ships and Goods...*London, April 20, 1649.

> *An Act for Preventing Injuries and Wrongs Done to Merchants at Sea, In Their Persons, Ships, Goods...*London, 1650.

Kerr, Robert. *General History and Collection of Voyages and Travels.* Multiple Volumes. Edinburgh, 1812.

Lecky, Halton Stirling. *The King's Ships*. 6 Volumes. London, 1913.

Maluezzi, Virgilio. *The Chief Events of the Maonarchie of Spain*. London, 1647.

Oppenheim, M. *The Naval Tracts of Sir William Monson-Six volumes. Printed for the Naval Records Society,1913.*

Pennant, Thomas. *A Journey from London to The Isle of Wight*. London, 1801.

Reports on Manuscripts in Various Collections. Volume 1-6. London. 1901-1914. Note: A same titled volume has different contents from other same titled volume.

Skrine, Henry Duncan. *The Manuscripts of Henry Duncan Skrine. Salvetti Correspondence*. London, 1887.

Smith, John. *A description of New England, or, The observations and discoueries of Captain Iohn Smith (admirall of that country) in the north of America, in the year of our Lord 1614*. London, 1616.

Smith, Captain John. *The General History of Virginia, New England, and the Summer Isles*. London, 1632. (Original Edition)

Speeches and Passages of This Great and Happy Parliament. London, 1641.

Wright, John. *An Ordinance and Declaration of the Lords and Commons Assembled in Parliament*. London, 1642.

Print and Art

Old Naval Prints, Their Artists and Engravers. Commander Charles, N. Robinson, London, 1924.

Nautical map of Java prepared and published by the Defense Mapping Agency, copyrighted in 1996.

INDEX